The Debian Linux Handbook

A Practical Guide for Users and Administrators

Robert Johnson

Published by HiTeX Press

For permissions and other inquiries, write to:
P.O. Box 3132, Framingham, MA 01701, USA

Contents

Introduction

Debian Linux stands as one of the most influential and enduring distributions within the Linux ecosystem. Celebrated for its robustness, security, and extensive community support, Debian forms the foundation for numerous derivative distributions, including well-known projects like Ubuntu. As an operating system developed and maintained by a highly diverse and dedicated group of contributors, it embodies the principles of free software, offering users unparalleled freedom to modify and distribute its code.

This book, **The Debian Linux Handbook: A Practical Guide for Users and Administrators**, aims to provide a comprehensive resource that caters to both new users seeking guidance and experienced administrators striving to harness the full potential of Debian. Each chapter is crafted to focus on specific aspects crucial to understanding, utilizing, and managing a Debian system effectively.

In this introduction chapter, we will lay the groundwork by briefly touching upon the fundamental concepts surrounding Debian. We begin with a view of its historical development and the philosophical tenets that guide the Debian Project. Understanding these elements reveals the core values embedded in Debian's structure: stability, reliability, and a commitment to open-source ideals.

As we delve deeper, we explore the features and advantages that make Debian a preferred choice for various applications, from personal computing to enterprise environments. These include the rigorous testing processes that ensure stability, the comprehensive software repository that provides access to thousands of packages, and the robust security mechanisms inherent in the system.

The discussion extends to Debian's organizational framework and its unique approach to governance. The Debian Project is an exemplary model of a community-led endeavor with a democratically elected Project Leader. This collective effort results in a highly cooperative environment, permitting users from all over the world to contribute, influence, and benefit from the project.

A critical understanding of Debian's release cycle is essential, allowing users to choose the right version for their specific needs. We clarify the distinctions between the stable, testing, and unstable branches, offering guidance on selecting suitable releases based on required stability, features, and latest updates.

Moreover, this book guides readers through the initial steps of preparing for Debian installation, understanding the various installation methods available, and configuring essential system settings post-installation. We address both graphical interfaces and command line options, ensuring readers can comfortably navigate and operate within the Debian environment.

The ensuing chapters will explore these themes in detail, systematically building upon foundational knowledge to cover advanced topics, including software management with APT, system administration, networking, security, automation, and troubleshooting. Each section is meticulously designed to facilitate a deep comprehension of Debian's capabilities and applications, empowering users and administrators to confidently manage their systems.

10

By integrating practical insights with technical rigor, **The Debian Linux Handbook** aspires to serve as an invaluable companion for anyone embarking on their journey with Debian, equipping them with the knowledge required to leverage this powerful platform to its fullest potential.

Chapter 1

Introduction to Debian Linux

Debian Linux, grounded in principles of open-source and community collaboration, offers stability, security, and extensive software support. Tracing its evolution underscores its role in the Linux ecosystem. With a structured release cycle and a vibrant community, Debian caters to varied computing needs. This section outlines its philosophy, benefits, and organizational framework, preparing users to engage effectively with one of the most trusted Linux distributions.

1.1. History and Philosophy of Debian

Debian Linux originated in 1993, initiated by Ian Murdock who envisioned a distribution that was developed openly and collaboratively. At its inception, the goal was to create a system where the collective intelligence of its developers and users could be harnessed to build a robust and reliable operating system. The Debian project quickly evolved beyond a simple distribution to become an influential force in the Linux ecosystem, championing open-source principles and pioneering practices that have since become standard across many projects.

The early history of Debian is characterized by a commitment to community-driven development. Unlike proprietary software models, the Debian project was founded on a philosophy that emphasized transparency, inclusivity, and collective decision-making. This approach was central to the creation of the Debian Social Contract, a document that articulates the ethical and operational framework of the project. The Social Contract outlines commitments to free software and the rights of all users, ensuring that Debian remains a distribution that anyone can inspect, modify, and distribute. The Free Software Guidelines, which have further influenced numerous other distributions, are a direct outcome of this commitment. These guidelines have placed Debian at the forefront of the free software movement, setting benchmarks for software freedom that extend well beyond any individual project.

Debian's philosophy is deeply intertwined with the principles of the broader free and open-source software (FOSS) community. The project's development model emphasizes peer review, extensive discussion, and consensus-based decision making. Such practices ensure that every release of Debian undergoes rigorous scrutiny before being made available to users. This methodical approach underpins its reputation for stability and reliability. Furthermore, the community's dedication to open knowledge and collaboration has fostered a culture where developers, users, and contributors work together to solve problems, share insights, and push technical boundaries.

The foundational elements of trust and collaboration have strongly influenced Debian's technological and organizational strategies. One of

14

the early decisions in the Debian project was to adopt a package management system that would simplify software installation and updates. This decision was driven by the practical needs of users and the desire to create an ecosystem in which software could be managed efficiently. As a tangible example reflecting this philosophy of accessibility and reliability, consider the familiar usage of the APT package management system. Users interact with Debian through a series of commands that abstract away the complexities of software dependency resolution, thereby reinforcing Debian's commitment to usability and robustness. The following code snippet demonstrates a typical command used in Debian systems to update the repository information:

```
sudo apt update
```

This command encapsulates the Debian philosophy of providing simple, effective tools that empower users while adhering to the principles of transparency and open collaboration.

The organizational structure of Debian is built on a decentralized model that mirrors its philosophical foundations. Rather than a strict hierarchical organization, Debian comprises a wide array of teams and working groups that operate with considerable autonomy. This structure not only encourages innovation but also ensures that decision-making is distributed across the community. The Debian Project Leader (DPL), elected annually by the contributors, symbolizes this open governance model. The role of the DPL is not to enforce a top-down strategy but to represent the collective interests of the community and to facilitate coordination among diverse groups working on different aspects of the project.

Debian's approach to software licensing further exemplifies its adherence to ethical principles. The project has consistently supported licenses that promote freedom to use, modify, and distribute software. This commitment ensures that Debian remains a reliable repository for software that respects the users' rights. Developers and users alike benefit from the assurance that the software they work with adheres to a set of ethical principles, which in turn cultivates an environment of mutual trust and respect. This licensing framework has wide-reaching implications within the Linux ecosystem, influencing other distributions and becoming a cornerstone of discussions around software ethics and digital rights.

The community's values are also evident in efforts to ensure that Debian remains accessible and adaptable to various use cases. Its broad range of supported hardware architectures and comprehensive software repositories are a testament to the project's inclusive ethos. Debian has consistently incorporated support for emerging technologies and hardware platforms over the decades, a decision driven by both user demand and the community's foresight regarding technological evolution. By maintaining flexibility and broad compatibility, Debian has secured its place as a foundation upon which countless other derivative distributions and systems have been built.

A notable aspect of Debian's influence in the Linux ecosystem is its role as a base for many other distributions. Its stability, extensive package repository, and robust support for different environments have made it a prime candidate for adaptations tailored to a wide range of applications, from personal desktops to servers and embedded systems. This multiplicative effect has further entrenched Debian's technological and philosophical ideals in many areas of the computing landscape. The project's insistence on rigorous quality control and adherence to free software principles has helped mold the standards by which Linux distributions are judged today.

The evolution of Debian's development practices reflects an increasing sophistication in how distributed projects are managed in a digital age. Early challenges, including issues related to package conflicts and dependency resolution, spurred innovations that went on to affect soft-

16

ware management practices more broadly. The architectural decisions and systematic improvements made over the years have turned Debian into a mature and widely respected platform. Its development lifecycle is marked by iterative improvements that balance the need for new features with the equally important requirements of system stability and security. Voluntary contributions, both in code and in community support, have been integral to this evolution.

The philosophical tenets that guided the inception of Debian have provided a blueprint for addressing both technical and social challenges that naturally arise in open-source projects. As the community navigates the complexities of modern software development, these principles remain a source of inspiration and guidance. For instance, the emphasis on transparency has led to the adoption of open development practices, which include publicly accessible mailing lists, code repositories, and discussion forums. Such practices not only build community trust but also invite scrutiny and contributions that drive continuous improvement.

The interplay between technical evolution and community-driven philosophy is further illustrated by Debian's response to emerging security challenges. The community's commitment to free software mandates that vulnerabilities are disclosed openly and addressed collaboratively. This open policy has contributed to a proactive culture in which security is managed not only by dedicated teams but also by a network of conscientious users and developers. An example of this commitment is evident in the way Debian handles security updates. The process involves rigorous testing and clear documentation of each update, ensuring that systems remain secure without compromising on performance or stability.

Practical examples of Debian's transparent development model can be found in the way the project tracks and resolves issues. Users and developers can access detailed bug reports, feature requests, and development logs, all managed through open databases. This open access has fostered a problem-solving environment where collective input leads to effective and often innovative solutions. Consider the following snippet that demonstrates a typical debugging command used to monitor system logs for issues on a Debian system:

```
tail -f /var/log/syslog
```

This command is illustrative of the Debian approach: providing users with the tools to directly engage with their systems, enabling a hands-on understanding of both operational mechanics and inherent challenges. Such practices demonstrate the practical implications of Debian's philosophical commitments, where users are both empowered and encouraged to contribute to the security and enhancement of the distribution.

The historical narrative of Debian is one of continual adaptation, measured growth, and unwavering commitment to a set of principles that prioritize freedom, collaboration, and technical excellence. The evolution of the project from its modest beginnings to a widely respected and influential Linux distribution serves as a concrete example of how community-driven efforts can yield systems that meet the highest standards of technical quality and ethical integrity. The shared belief in open collaboration has been instrumental in shaping a project that is both resilient in the face of change and responsive to the dynamic needs of its diverse user base.

The legacy of Debian is evident not just in the technical innovations it has introduced, but also in how it has influenced the broader discourse on free software and open development. Its approach to governance, community engagement, and ethical software distribution remains a benchmark for many subsequent initiatives in the open-source community. The enduring relevance of Debian's guiding documents, such as the Social Contract and the Free Software Guidelines, serves as an ongoing reminder of the foundational ideals that continue to drive innovation and cooperation in the technology domain. These historical and cultural underpinnings secure Debian's place as a pivotal contributor to the evolution of Linux, ensuring that its impact will be felt across multiple generations of software development and reuse.

The intertwined narrative of historical development and philosophical ethos within Debian continues to inspire both current practitioners and future contributors. Its commitment to creating a transparent, inclusive, and technically robust platform has left an indelible mark on the Linux ecosystem and has fundamentally shaped the way decentralized, community-oriented software projects operate.

1.2. Features and Benefits of Using Debian

Debian has established a strong reputation based on several defining features that appeal to a wide spectrum of users, from desktop enthusiasts to system administrators in large-scale enterprise environments. Among these features, stability, security, extensive package support, and a well-integrated package management system stand prominently. These components not only foster a reliable computing experience but also encapsulate the core benefits of adopting a distribution that is meticulously crafted and community-driven.

One of the most significant advantages of Debian is its renowned stability. The Debian project employs a rigorous release cycle designed to ensure that each version undergoes comprehensive testing and validation. This process involves multiple stages, traditionally classified as unstable, testing, and stable. By gradually filtering the software through these stages, Debian minimizes the risk of system failures and unexpected behavior. This careful curation makes Debian especially suitable for critical systems where reliability is paramount. The underlying quality assurance processes ensure that both hardware and

19

software function predictably, which is an essential consideration for users who require robust performance in mission-critical applications.

Security is another critical benefit that has long been a central focus of the Debian project. Regular security updates and proactive vulnerability management are embedded into the philosophy and operational structure of the distribution. The Debian Security Team continuously monitors and addresses potential vulnerabilities, ensuring that users receive timely patches to mitigate possible threats. This established security framework is further reinforced by built-in tools that facilitate system monitoring and hardening. An illustrative example of these practices is reflected in the way administrators manage package updates. The command below allows users to secure their system by updating the package information and applying the latest security patches:

```
sudo apt update && sudo apt upgrade
```

This concise command sequence not only streamlines system maintenance but also exemplifies Debian's commitment to secure operations through simplicity and transparency.

The comprehensive repository of software available in Debian is another standout feature that significantly benefits users. With tens of thousands of packages maintained and continually updated by an active community, Debian offers unmatched software diversity. This extensive repository covers a wide range of applications, including development tools, multimedia software, server utilities, and desktop applications. The inclusion of a vast selection of software ensures that users can find packages that precisely meet their needs without resorting to external sources. Furthermore, Debian's adherence to the Free Software Guidelines guarantees that the software available is not only reliable but also respects the principles of open access and reproducibility.

The package management system in Debian, centered around Advanced Package Tool (APT), further enhances the user experience. APT provides a robust, user-friendly interface for installing, upgrading, and removing software packages. It abstracts away the complexity of dependency resolution and offers a streamlined approach to system management. Users can search, install, and remove software with simple commands. Consider the following example, where a developer installs a commonly used text editor:

```
sudo apt install vim
```

This command demonstrates how Debian simplifies the process of software management by automating dependency resolution and version control, thereby reducing the manual overhead typically associated with package installations.

In addition to its technical capabilities, Debian's design philosophy has led to a system that is highly customizable. The modular architecture of Debian allows users to tailor their experience to their specific needs. This flexibility is particularly valuable in diverse computing environments where different configurations or custom setups may be necessary. Whether deployed in a server environment or used as a desktop operating system, Debian's modularity ensures that users have the freedom to modify and enhance their systems without being constrained by rigid design parameters. Users frequently leverage scripts and automated tools to manage configurations and system states. An example of configuring a periodic security update via a cron job is shown below:

```
#!/bin/bash
apt update && apt upgrade -y
```

This script, when integrated into the system's scheduled tasks, reinforces the practical benefits of Debian's flexible infrastructure by automating routine maintenance tasks.

Debian also excels in providing a diverse and consistent user environment through its support for multiple hardware architectures and desk-

21

top environments. With support ranging from traditional x86 systems to ARM-based devices, Debian is adaptable to various hardware specifications. This broad compatibility makes it an attractive option for users with different computing devices, ensuring a uniform experience across platforms. The availability of multiple desktop environments such as GNOME, KDE, and Xfce ensures that users can choose the graphical interface that best aligns with their workflow and aesthetic preferences. These choices are supported by standardized configuration procedures that maintain consistency regardless of the chosen interface, thereby reducing the learning curve and migration challenges between different systems.

The long-term support (LTS) provided by Debian further enhances its appeal, especially for organizations that require sustained reliability over extended periods. LTS ensures that security updates and critical bug fixes are provided even after the official release cycle has ended. This extended maintenance window grants organizations the confidence that their systems will remain secure and operational without the necessity of frequent upgrades, which might introduce instability or compatibility issues. The support model highlights Debian's commitment to offering a dependable platform in environments where stability and continuity are of utmost importance.

Debian's emphasis on community involvement and open development is another critical factor that contributes to its unique benefits. The project thrives on contributions from volunteers around the world, with development, documentation, and support conducted in a transparent and inclusive manner. This collaborative approach ensures that Debian adapts dynamically to user needs while maintaining the highest standards of quality and security. The transparency of the development process allows users to inspect all changes and contributes to a culture of peer review and active participation. Such an environment is essential for building trust and ensuring that the distribution evolves in a manner that is both user-centric and resilient to external pressures.

For those interested in customizing their environments further, Debian provides user-friendly configuration management tools. The availability of configuration files and clear documentation empowers users to automate tasks and develop custom solutions tailored to specific system requirements. For instance, the configuration file for APT, located at `/etc/apt/sources.list`, is structured in a format that is both straightforward and highly configurable. Users can add or remove repositories based on their specific needs, thereby enabling a tailored selection of software sources while maintaining the security and integrity of the system.

The integration of these features into a cohesive ecosystem sets Debian apart from other distributions. Its structured approach to software management, coupled with a rigorous focus on security and the freedom to customize, provides users with a reliable and versatile system environment. The consistency in operational procedures, across both desktop and server configurations, exemplifies the generalized applicability of Debian's design principles. The predictability afforded by its careful release management and comprehensive support systems ensures that users are not only equipped with state-of-the-art technology but also with a framework that is conducive to efficient system management.

Debian's extensive package repository is supported by robust dependency management mechanisms that resolve software interrelations automatically, significantly reducing the risk of conflicts or breakages during system updates. This effectiveness is a direct result of the project's longstanding commitment to quality control and best practices in software packaging. Each package passes through a rigorous validation process before it is included in the repository, ensuring a level of quality that is rarely matched by alternatives. Through systematic tracking of package versions and automated conflict resolution,

Debian maximizes compatibility and performance, attributes that are particularly appreciated in environments where system uptime is critical.

Furthermore, Debian's comprehensive documentation and active community forums provide a solid support infrastructure for both novices and experienced users. Detailed manuals, FAQs, and troubleshooting guides are readily accessible, facilitating rapid resolution of issues and promoting the effective use of the system. This dedication to documentation further reinforces the distribution's commitment to transparency and education, making it a valuable resource for learning and professional growth. Clear documentation ensures that users are not only able to resolve immediate challenges but also to gain a deeper understanding of system internals, which is pivotal in troubleshooting and system optimization.

The ecosystem of Debian is designed to be self-sustaining, with an ongoing cycle of contributions that continuously enhance the distribution's capabilities. From kernel updates to user-space applications, every update is meticulously reviewed and tested. This ensures that new features are introduced without compromising the long-term reliability of the system. The strategic approach to system upgrades and the balance between new functionality and system stability are key reasons why Debian remains the preferred choice for many long-term users.

The benefits of adopting Debian extend into areas beyond traditional computing roles. Developers find its vast repository of development tools and libraries conducive to a productive environment that supports a variety of programming languages and frameworks. Whether one is engaged in web development, scientific research, or system programming, Debian provides the necessary tools and libraries to support development workflows with minimal friction. The ease of installing and configuring development environments directly contributes to higher productivity and reduced setup times.

Debian stands out by combining technical excellence with a robust ethical framework. Its unparalleled stability, extensive software support, strong security initiatives, and adaptable package management system collectively provide a computing experience that is both secure and highly efficient. The thoughtful integration of these features ensures that users across different scenarios—from personal computing to enterprise deployments—benefit from a system infrastructure that is both powerful and reliable.

1.3. Debian Versions and Release Cycle

Debian distributes its software in several distinct branches, each catering to different user requirements and stability expectations. At the core of these branches are *stable*, *testing*, and *unstable*. Understanding the differences among these versions and their respective release cycles is crucial for selecting the branch that best fits a particular use case, whether it is for production environments, development, or experimental testing.

The *stable* branch is the most widely used version of Debian. It has earned its reputation for robustness and reliability due to an extensive testing process and strict quality assurance. This branch is the product of a long validation cycle and focuses on delivering software that is tried and tested. Once a new stable version is released, it becomes the reference for deployments in mission-critical systems and environments where consistency and security are paramount. Users benefit from its long-term support (LTS), which ensures that security patches and critical bug fixes are maintained throughout its lifetime without introducing disruptive changes. The predictable release cycle of the stable branch allows organizations to plan upgrades and allocate resources efficiently. The transition from one stable release to another is deliberately paced, ensuring that system administrators have sufficient time to evaluate new features and perform comprehensive testing before implementing changes in a production setting.

In contrast, the *testing* branch serves as an intermediary between stable and experimental software. It is a dynamic repository where packages migrate after meeting basic integration standards but before they are deemed stable enough for general release. The testing branch offers access to more recent software versions than the stable branch while maintaining a reasonable level of system integrity. This branch is particularly attractive to users who require newer functionality but still need an acceptable degree of reliability. It offers a balance, allowing individuals or organizations to experiment with recent package versions while mitigating the risks associated with the most cutting-edge, untested updates. For developers and enthusiasts, testing represents an opportunity to influence the upcoming stable release by identifying bugs, proposing improvements, and contributing to the overall stabilization process.

The *unstable* branch, often referred to as sid, is the development frontier where active changes occur on a daily basis. In this branch, new packages and major updates are introduced with minimal delay, offering the latest software features and experimental innovations. Since it is intended for development and testing, the unstable branch can occasionally exhibit issues such as broken dependencies or misconfigurations. As a result, it is primarily used by developers, contributors, and advanced users who are comfortable troubleshooting issues and contributing fixes upstream. The inherently dynamic nature of the unstable branch ensures that it evolves rapidly, providing early access to software that will eventually promote the stability improvements found in the testing branch and, ultimately, the stable branch. This fast-paced environment is instrumental for the continuous improvement of Debian, as community feedback in the unstable branch informs the refinement process that takes place in subsequent branches.

A clear understanding of the Debian release cycle helps in deciding which branch to deploy. The *stable* branch is typically updated with a new release every two to three years, ensuring a balance between maintaining system stability and incorporating essential updates. This well-defined lifecycle allows system administrators to plan for long-term deployments with confidence, knowing that significant changes will not disrupt operational continuity. During its maintained period, stable receives security updates and critical fixes, while feature enhancements are deferred until the subsequent release cycle.

Conversely, the testing branch undergoes continuous integration, and its packages are periodically promoted to form the next stable release. As the testing branch matures, a freeze is imposed to halt the influx of new packages and focus on resolving outstanding issues, polishing documentation, and ensuring overall quality. This freezing process is critical for guaranteeing that the upcoming stable release inherits a level of reliability akin to the current stable branch. Users who adopt the testing branch benefit from access to newer features and improvements while preparing for the future release. System administrators may choose testing in setups where the slight risk of instability is acceptable in exchange for modern software capabilities.

Managing the different branches requires careful configuration of the system's package management settings. The Advanced Package Tool (APT) is instrumental in facilitating the management of software across these branches. The configuration file, /etc/apt/sources.list, is where users define the repositories that correspond to the desired branch. For instance, switching from stable to testing can be accomplished by modifying the repository entries as demonstrated in the code snippet below:

```
# Sources for stable release
deb http://deb.debian.org/debian stable main
deb http://deb.debian.org/debian stable-updates main
deb http://security.debian.org/debian-security stable-security main
```

```
# Sources for testing branch transition
# deb http://deb.debian.org/debian testing main
```

Users who wish to experiment with the unstable branch can similarly adjust their sources list. Adjusting repository settings should be undertaken with caution, as the branch selected directly impacts system behavior. Administrators managing large deployments often prefer the stability of the stable branch, while developers seeking the newest software improvements may deliberately choose testing or unstable.

The decision to adopt a specific branch is often dictated by the intended usage scenario. For instance, in a production server environment where downtime must be minimized, the stable branch is preferred. Its extended support and minimal introduction of new bugs translate into predictable performance and reliability. In contrast, test environments and development boxes may leverage the testing branch to familiarize themselves with upcoming features and to participate actively in the stabilization process. Advanced users who are capable of managing rapid changes and providing feedback often find the unstable branch to be the most engaging, as it offers a glimpse into the cutting-edge evolution of Debian software.

The release cycle of Debian is harmonized by both the need for innovation and the requirement for dependable performance. Developers herein must balance the introduction of new features against the potential for disruption. This careful calibration is reflected in the structured migration of packages from unstable to testing and eventually to stable. The process involves numerous checks, integration tests, and dependency verifications. By the time a package reaches the stable branch, it has been rigorously vetted and validated by both automated systems and community review. This meticulous process is vital for ensuring that the stable branch meets the high expectations of security, performance, and reliability demanded by critical applications.

From a technical perspective, package maintainers and system administrators utilize a set of diagnostic and monitoring tools to assess the health of the distribution across its branches. Commands such as `apt-cache policy` can be used to query the version and priority of installed packages, providing insights into branch-specific configurations. Consider the following example:

```
apt-cache policy firefox-esr
```

This command outputs detailed information about the firefox-esr package, including which version is installed, its available versions from different repositories, and the repository priorities. Such tools are essential for managing mixed environments where careful tracking of package versions is necessary to maintain compatibility and performance.

The structured release cycle of Debian provides a framework within which both community contributions and commercial deployments thrive. Developers are able to iteratively contribute to unstable and testing, knowing that the cumulative efforts will eventually be consolidated into a stable release. This iterative process fosters continued innovation while ensuring that the most critical operational environments benefit from an operating system characterized by high quality and minimal disruption.

The flexibility inherent in Debian's branching strategy has also led to its widespread adoption in derivative projects. Many derivatives of Debian select one branch as their foundation, tailoring the base system to meet specialized requirements. For example, distributions aimed at providing a cutting-edge user experience might adopt the testing branch as their baseline, while those requiring rock-solid performance lean on the stable branch. Such adaptability illustrates how Debian's release cycle not only supports diverse usage scenarios but also serves as an open framework for experimentation and innovation.

Understanding the nuances of Debian's release cycle enables users to make informed decisions regarding system upgrades, security management, and feature adoption. It underscores the importance of selecting the appropriate branch in accordance with specific operational demands. The deliberate and incremental nature of package migrations from unstable to testing and finally to stable embodies a model of progressive quality assurance that enhances user confidence in the distribution.

The defined release cycle coupled with Debian's open governance model contributes to a seamless and transparent process for managing change. This synergy between technological rigor and community oversight ensures that Debian continues to evolve in a manner that meets the diverse and dynamic needs of its global user base. Whether in high-stakes production environments requiring unwavering stability or in progressive development spaces where innovation is key, Debian offers a branch that aligns with the demands of the task at hand, thereby solidifying its role as a cornerstone of the Linux ecosystem.

1.4. The Debian Project and Community

The Debian Project is organized around a distinct governance model that emphasizes openness, collaboration, and decentralized decision-making. At the heart of this model lies the Debian Social Contract and the Debian Free Software Guidelines, which set forth the ethical framework and operational principles for the entire project. These documents not only define the relationship between the Debian developers and users but also serve as a guideline for contributions and decision-making. The project operates without a traditional hierarchical structure, instead opting for a meritocratic model where influence is derived from contribution quality and consistency rather than formal rank.

The organizational structure comprises various teams and groups that handle specific areas such as package maintenance, quality assurance, security, and documentation. Teams are often self-organized, with voluntary members coordinating their efforts through mailing lists, version control systems, and issue tracking databases. An example of community communication is the usage of the Debian mailing lists where developers openly discuss problems, review patches, and deliberate on future features. The mailing list ecosystem is crucial for maintaining transparency and ensuring that discussions are documented for future reference.

A central figure in the project is the Debian Project Leader (DPL), who is elected annually by active contributors. The DPL's role is to coordinate the overall direction of the project rather than to exercise centralized control. This leader acts as a facilitator, ensuring that the many teams work cohesively without imposing authoritarian decisions. The annual election process underscores the community's commitment to democratic processes and shared ownership, reinforcing the idea that Debian is built and maintained by its contributors.

The development model of Debian is heavily community-driven. The contribution process is open to anyone, which has resulted in a diverse community that includes software developers, quality assurance testers, translators, and documentation writers. This diversity of skills contributes to the robustness of the distribution. Every contribution is subject to peer review, and this system of checks and balances is fundamental to the project's high standards. For instance, when a developer submits a new package or an update, the changes are scrutinized by experienced maintainers who validate the integration with existing systems. In this regard, tools like the Debian Bug Tracking System (BTS) play a critical role, enabling contributors to follow up on bugs, suggest enhancements, and verify fixes.

One common workflow adopted by developers involves using version control systems such as Git to manage changes. The collaborative nature of Debian is evident in how maintainers encourage contributions via patches and commits. An example workflow may involve a developer forking a repository, making contributions, and then submitting a patch. The following code snippet illustrates a typical Git workflow for contributing to Debian packages:

```
# Clone the package repository
git clone https://salsa.debian.org/<team>/<package>.git

# Create a new branch for your changes
cd <package>
git checkout -b fix-issue-123

# Make modifications and commit your changes
git commit -am "Fix for issue #123: Corrected dependency resolution"

# Push the changes to your repository
git push origin fix-issue-123
```

This workflow not only fosters transparency in the development process but also encourages collaborative problem-solving. Contributions are continuously merged and refined through a rigorous review process, ensuring that each change adheres to Debian's overall quality standards and aligns with its long-term vision.

Another important portal for community engagement is the Debian Wiki and Bug Tracking System. The Debian Wiki serves as a centralized repository of documentation, best practices, and guidelines for developers and system administrators alike. It is frequently updated by volunteers and serves as a first point of reference for both new and experienced contributors seeking to understand project policies and technical details. Coupled with issue trackers and public repositories, this arrangement ensures that the entire community remains informed and actively involved in the maintenance and development of Debian.

The Debian community welcomes contributions in a multitude of forms, not limited to source code modifications. Translators, for instance, play a vital role by localizing user interfaces and documentation into multiple languages, thereby extending Debian's reach and usability in non-English speaking regions. Specialized teams focus on accessibility, ensuring that the software meets the needs of users with diverse requirements. Similarly, community members contribute by answering questions on forums, participating in discussion groups, and writing detailed guides on system configuration and troubleshooting. These contributions are collectively vital for maintaining the breadth and depth of Debian's support network.

Emphasis is placed on the principle of "release early, release often," which has evolved within the context of Debian's stable, testing, and unstable branches. This philosophy is active in the way the community engages with the development process, where continuous improvement is encouraged and feedback from a broad user base is instrumental in shaping the evolution of the distribution. The iterative development cycle ensures that any critical issues are identified and rectified through communal collaboration before they affect a stable release. Consequently, community members are encouraged to test new features on unstable and testing branches and report their findings through designated channels.

Securing contributions is streamlined by a robust infrastructure that includes continuous integration systems and automated testing frameworks. When a package is modified, the system generates build logs and test results that are accessible to anyone in the community. Tools such as lintian, a package checker specifically designed for Debian, help detect common issues in software packages before they are incorporated into the repository. An example command to run lintian on a Debian package is shown below:

```
lintian mypackage_1.0-1_amd64.deb
```

This automated tool not only simplifies quality assurance processes but also promotes standardization across contributions. The feedback provided by these tools informs maintainers and contributors about potential areas of improvement, reinforcing a continuous cycle of quality enhancement.

Community governance extends to regular meetings, virtual conferences, and events organized by local Debian groups. These gatherings are essential for networking, sharing expertise, and coordinating large-scale collaborative projects. Conferences like DebConf and local Debian Days not only serve as platforms for disseminating technical knowledge but also reinforce the sense of unity and shared purpose among contributors. The collaborative spirit in Debian ensures that even the most challenging technical tasks, such as system-wide migrations or comprehensive security audits, are tackled by a diverse group of individuals working towards a common goal.

The Debian project's inclusive model also supports mentorship programs aimed at integrating new contributors into the community. Mentors assist newcomers with navigating the contribution process, understanding the coding standards, and utilizing communication tools effectively. This system of mentorship has proven indispensable in lowering the barrier to entry, especially for individuals who are new to open-source development. The nurturing of new talent not only ensures the sustainability of the project but also brings fresh perspectives that continuously invigorate the Debian community.

The documentation accompanying the Debian project is comprehensive and is maintained by a dedicated group of volunteers. This documentation encompasses everything from system administration guides to detailed technical manuals covering package management, kernel configuration, and network setup. The decentralized nature of documentation updates ensures that information remains current and relevant. In addition to static documents, the Debian community utilizes version-controlled repositories for maintaining technical documents, which further reinforces the principles of transparency and collaboration.

34

The model of open governance that Debian exemplifies has broader implications for the Linux ecosystem. By adhering to a structure where contribution is independent of formal power hierarchies, Debian sets a precedent that many other projects have emulated. This operational model not only contributes to the resilience and robustness of Debian but also fosters an environment where innovation thrives through community oversight and collective responsibility. The decentralized decision-making process ensures that every contributor, regardless of their background, can influence the project's direction based on technical merit and community consensus.

Continual contributions, whether in the form of code, documentation, translation, or quality assurance, are facilitated by infrastructure that emphasizes accessibility and transparency. This has led to the evolution of sophisticated collaboration tools that enable seamless communication and coordination among geographically dispersed contributors. The adoption of platforms such as Salsa, Debian's GitLab instance, allows contributors to manage projects, review code changes, and track issues in a centralized, publicly accessible environment.

The Debian Community does not only focus on technical enhancements but also on social dimensions. Efforts to create an inclusive and welcoming environment are evident through the establishment of codes of conduct and community guidelines that address behavior, participation, and conflict resolution. These policies are designed to ensure that all contributors feel valued and supported, thereby boosting overall morale and productivity. The emphasis on inclusivity has proven effective in expanding the contributor base and ensuring that a wide range of perspectives and skills are represented in the project.

In practice, the degree of community involvement significantly affects the overall quality and evolution of Debian. Every new feature or critical update is a product of focused collaboration among dedicated teams that prioritize both technical excellence and communal integrity. The mechanisms established for conflict resolution, for example, ensure that any disputes are addressed in a timely and fair manner, thereby maintaining a stable development environment. Open negotiations on technical merits and potential policy implications are a regular occurrence, further highlighting the dynamic interaction between individual initiative and collective governance.

Ultimately, the strength of the Debian Project and Community lies in its ability to seamlessly integrate technical innovation with a robust, participatory governance model. The open, inclusive nature of the Debian community not only drives the ongoing refinement of the distribution but also serves as a model for collaborative development in the broader open-source landscape. The willingness to adopt diverse viewpoints, combined with strict adherence to quality standards and ethical guidelines, ensures that Debian remains a vibrant and evolving project, continuously setting benchmarks for open collaboration and technical excellence.

1.5. Debian Installation Overview

The process of installing Debian has been engineered to cater to a wide range of users, from those with extensive experience in Linux system administration to individuals attempting their first installation. The installation overview covers key aspects including hardware requirements, available installation methods, and the various configuration options provided during the process. Understanding these elements is critical to choosing a method that best aligns with the system environment and user requirements.

Hardware requirements for Debian installation are designed to be resource-efficient while supporting both legacy and modern systems. At a minimum, a typical installation requires 128 MB of RAM and approximately 2 GB of disk space for a basic command-line system, while a graphical desktop environment generally demands a minimum of 512 MB of RAM and 10 GB of disk space. It is advisable to review the latest hardware recommendations published by the Debian Project for optimal performance. Compatibility with multiple architectures such as x86 (i386 and amd64), ARM variants, and others reinforces Debian's flexibility and its commitment to supporting diverse computing environments.

Among the various installation methods available, several stand out based on user needs and system configurations. The primary installation methods include:

- **Graphical Installer**: Designed for users who prefer an intuitive installation process with a user-friendly interface, the graphical installer guides the user through hardware detection, network configuration, disk partitioning, and package selection.

- **Text-based Installer**: This method caters to environments where graphical system resources might be limited, such as servers or older hardware. It provides a text-based menu system while still covering all the essential configuration options.

- **Netinst (Network Installation)**: The netinst image is a compact installer that downloads the majority of packages from Debian mirrors during installation. This method reduces the image size and ensures that the most up-to-date software is installed.

- **CD/DVD/USB Installation**: Users can opt for installation media in the form of CDs, DVDs, or bootable USB drives. The method chosen depends largely on the available hardware interfaces and the desired installer type.

The initial phase of the installation involves booting from the chosen installation medium. Whether using a live USB or CD/DVD, the system must be configured to boot from the respective device in the BIOS or UEFI settings. Once the installer is launched, the system automatically detects available hardware and prompts the user to set language, location, and keyboard preferences. These initial steps are critical as they set the foundation for correct system configuration during and after installation.

Network configuration is an important step during installation that ensures the system is able to interact with remote repositories and receive updates. In many instances, the installer attempts to configure network settings automatically via DHCP. For users with specialized network environments requiring static IPs or manual DNS configuration, the installer offers the necessary options. Network connectivity is particularly essential for installations using the netinst image, which relies on downloading packages during the installation process.

Disk partitioning is one of the most customizable parts of the Debian installation process. Users are presented with several choices ranging from guided partitioning with the entire disk to manual partitioning for those who prefer full control over disk layout. Typical partitioning schemes include separate partitions for the root (/), home (/home), and swap areas. Advanced users may also choose to use Logical Volume Management (LVM) or encrypted partitions to enhance system stability and security. For example, during guided partitioning, a user might select partitioning a disk using LVM. In such cases, the installer automatically configures volume groups and logical volumes according to recommended practices, ensuring flexibility in managing disk space post-installation.

The installer then progresses to selecting software packages. Debian's package selection framework allows users to choose between predefined sets, such as "Desktop Environment" or "Web Server". In addition to standard configurations, users have the option to install specific software by selecting individual packages. During this stage, the installer may download packages using APT. A common post-installation

38

activity is to run:

```
sudo apt update && sudo apt upgrade
```

This command sequence ensures that all installed packages are updated to their latest versions. The installation process further includes the configuration of a bootloader—typically GRUB—which is critical for system startup and management of multiple operating systems on a single machine.

Different installation methods offer varying levels of customization and complexity. The graphical installer is well-suited for users looking for a more visually guided approach with minimal command-line interaction. Conversely, the text-based installer offers a lightweight alternative that is particularly beneficial in environments with limited system resources. Both methods ultimately provide access to the same underlying configuration options, ensuring that regardless of the chosen method, the resulting system configuration adheres to Debian's high standards for stability and performance.

Users employing the netinst image can take advantage of an installation that is expedited by a smaller initial download size. This method is optimal for environments with reliable and fast network connections, as it ensures that the most recent versions of packages are downloaded during installation. Infrastructure administrators often prefer netinst for deploying multiple systems, as it minimizes the need to distribute large images and allows for centralized control over package versions by utilizing local mirrors. A sample command to create a bootable USB from a netinst image on a Linux system is:

```
sudo dd if=debian-netinst.iso of=/dev/sdX bs=4M status=progress &&
    sync
```

In this command, /dev/sdX represents the target USB device. This process illustrates how system administrators can leverage standard Linux tools to efficiently prepare installation media for deployment.

The installation process also emphasizes security and system integrity. For example, users have the option to utilize full disk encryption during installation, which encrypts the root partition and adds a layer of protection against unauthorized access. Configuring encryption involves selecting encryption methods during partitioning, and the installer typically prompts for a passphrase. Although this process can slightly increase installation time, it significantly enhances data security, a factor that is especially critical in multi-user environments or systems exposed to potential physical security risks.

During installation, users might also configure additional system settings such as time zone adjustments, locale settings, and the establishment of non-root user accounts. Creating a non-root user account is strongly recommended as it provides an extra layer of security by reducing the risk of unintended system-wide changes. Users are typically asked to provide a username and a secure password, and the installer may offer insights into best practices for account security based on current standards.

The final stage of the installation process includes the installation of the bootloader, which is integral for managing the operating system boot sequence. GRUB is the default bootloader for Debian and is installed with default configurations suitable for the majority of systems. However, advanced users can access GRUB configuration options during the installation to tailor boot parameters or to integrate multiple operating systems in a dual-boot setup.

Post-installation configuration is equally important. Once the installation is completed, the first boot sequence leads to an environment where final adjustments can be made. Users may execute the following command to inspect the installation logs:

```
less /var/log/installer/syslog
```

Reviewing these logs provides insight into the installation process and can aid in troubleshooting should any issues arise. System administrators may also choose to run additional scripts or manual configurations based on their specific needs, such as setting up remote management tools or window managers for desktop environments.

The flexibility extended by the Debian installation process ensures that the distribution can be tailored to diverse environments, from single-user desktop systems to complex multi-node server architectures. The process is supported by thorough documentation available in the Debian Installation Guide, which offers step-by-step instructions and troubleshooting advice. This guide helps new users navigate potential complexities, while experienced administrators can leverage its comprehensive details to fine-tune their installations.

In environments where automated installations are preferred, Debian supports preseed files. A preseed file allows administrators to automate interactive prompts by providing responses in advance. This method is particularly advantageous when deploying Debian on a large scale. A simplified example of a preseed configuration might appear as follows:

```
d-i debian-installer/locale string en_US
d-i keyboard-configuration/layoutcode string us
d-i netcfg/choose_interface select auto
d-i mirror/http/hostname string deb.debian.org
d-i mirror/http/directory string /debian
```

By predefining responses, system administrators can streamline installations and ensure uniformity across multiple systems; a crucial factor when managing enterprise environments or educational institutions.

Furthermore, Debian's installation framework supports a dual-boot configuration, which is especially useful for users operating in multi-boot environments. In such cases, the partitioner allows users to designate spaces for Debian alongside other operating systems. The installer carefully detects existing operating system signatures, providing a safe

41

path to resize partitions and prevent data loss.

Each of these installation methods highlights Debian's commitment to flexibility, security, and ease of use. Whether through a graphical interface for beginners or automated scripts for seasoned administrators, Debian's installer has evolved to meet the dynamic requirements of modern computing environments. The process not only ensures a robust and secure base installation but also lays the foundation for an operating system that can be continuously adapted and optimized over its lifecycle.

The Debian installation overview offers insight into both the simplicity and complexity of deploying a system that is as versatile and reliable as Debian.

1.6. Debian Software and Package Management

Debian's approach to software packaging and package management is a cornerstone of its reputation for reliability and ease of maintenance. At the heart of this system lies the Advanced Package Tool (APT), a set of utilities that streamline the installation, removal, and updating of software on Debian systems. This section examines the structure of Debian packages, the mechanisms behind APT, and the processes that ensure system integrity and dependency resolution.

Software in Debian is distributed in packages that encapsulate executable binaries, documentation, configuration files, and metadata. Each package is built to conform to standardized formats and guidelines, ensuring compatibility across the system. The primary dimensions of a package include its version, dependencies, and conflicts with other software. This metadata is stored in a database that APT utilizes to make informed decisions during installation and updates. Packages are signed cryptographically to secure the integrity of the software being distributed. This process guarantees that users are installing software that has not been tampered with, reinforcing Debian's commitment to security and trustworthiness.

APT operates as an abstraction layer, simplifying package management by masking the underlying complexity associated with manual dependency management. Instead of handling individual packages, administrators and users interact with APT to perform higher-level operations. Common operations include updating the package index, installing new software, upgrading existing packages, and removing unwanted software. One of the most frequently used commands is the update command, which synchronizes the local package database with the repositories:

```
sudo apt update
```

This command retrieves package lists from repositories defined in the /etc/apt/sources.list file, ensuring that the system is aware of the latest available versions and dependencies.

Installation of new software is equally straightforward. APT automatically resolves dependencies, fetching and installing any required libraries or modules that are necessary for the target package to function properly. For example, installing a text editor such as vim is as simple as executing:

```
sudo apt install vim
```

In this process, APT checks for the existence of all required dependencies, downloads them if they are not already present, and installs them in the correct order. This automated dependency resolution is a major improvement over manual package installations and is one of the key benefits that distinguish Debian's package management system.

APT also efficiently manages system upgrades. When a new version of Debian is released or when security updates are available, users can

43

upgrade their entire system with minimal effort. The command to upgrade all installed packages is:

```
sudo apt upgrade
```

This command compares the current versions of installed packages with those available in the repositories, and updates any that have newer versions. For more extensive upgrades, such as moving from one release to another, the dist-upgrade command is used. This command not only upgrades packages but also handles changing dependencies, potentially removing obsolete packages to satisfy new requirements:

```
sudo apt dist-upgrade
```

APT's capabilities extend beyond basic installation and upgrading. It provides utilities to search for packages, inspect the details of available packages, and even analyze the dependency tree of a given package. For instance, to search for a package related to web servers, one can use:

```
apt search apache
```

The resulting output includes package names, summaries, and sometimes version information, enabling users to make an informed decision about the software they wish to install. For detailed insights into how a specific package is configured, the apt-cache show command reveals metadata such as version numbers, dependencies, and a detailed description:

```
apt-cache show apache2
```

This level of transparency in package information is a testament to Debian's emphasis on openness and reproducibility, allowing both novice and experienced users to delve into the specifics of system software.

In addition to the front-end tools, APT works closely with the Debian packaging system known as *dpkg*. While APT manages the retrieval, dependency resolution, and repository interactions, *dpkg* is the low-level tool responsible for the actual installation and removal of packages on the system. Commands like:

```
sudo dpkg -i package_name.deb
```

allow users to manually install packages, which can be useful in environments where packages are obtained outside of the standard repositories. This modular interaction between APT and *dpkg* provides both flexibility and control, enabling administrators to troubleshoot installation issues or perform custom configurations when necessary.

The integration of APT into the broader ecosystem of Debian software management is enhanced by several supporting tools. For instance, *aptitude* is a text-based user interface for APT that offers a more interactive experience for managing packages. It provides functionalities such as resolving complex dependency conflicts through an interactive interface, which can be particularly useful in advanced scenarios where package removal or installation might trigger cascading changes in the system.

APT's configuration files, primarily located in /etc/apt/, allow users to customize its behavior. These files determine the set of repositories from which packages can be downloaded and establish preferences for package versions and priorities. Advanced users may also configure APT to handle proxy settings or caching behaviors to optimize performance in large-scale deployments. By modifying files like /etc/apt/apt.conf and /etc/apt/sources.list, system administrators can tailor the package management environment to suit their operational needs.

Another critical aspect of Debian's package management is the maintenance of package repositories. Debian repositories are organized into components such as main, contrib, and non-free. These clas-

45

sifications reflect the licensing and freedom of the included software, aligning with the Debian Social Contract and the Free Software Guidelines. The `main` repository contains software that fully complies with the Debian Free Software Guidelines, ensuring that users benefit from legally unencumbered and freely distributed software. The separation of repositories based on licensing not only aids in compliance but also provides users with the option to include or exclude software based on their personal or organizational policies.

Apt-listeners and automated update tools further enhance the management of software in Debian. For example, tools like `apticron` notify administrators of available security updates and significant package changes, allowing for proactive system maintenance. This continuous monitoring of package repositories ensures that systems remain secure and up-to-date without requiring constant manual intervention. Using cron jobs to automate updates can improve system reliability and security. An example of configuring a cron job to update package lists is:

```
# Update package list daily at 2 A.M.
0 2 * * * /usr/bin/apt update >> /var/log/apt-update.log 2>&1
```

This automation exemplifies the integration of Debian's package management into system administration workflows, reducing administrative overhead while ensuring that systems adhere to the latest security standards.

Debian's package management system is also designed to support advanced customization through meta-packages. A meta-package serves as an aggregator, listing a set of packages that together provide a complete set of functionalities. For example, the meta-package for the standard Debian desktop environment will install all necessary components such as window managers, desktop utilities, and essential libraries. This abstraction allows users to install complex environments with a single command, streamlining the process and reducing the chance of omitting critical components.

The reliance on incremental updates through tools like APT has also contributed to the stability and longevity of Debian systems. By isolating package changes and adhering to strict release cycles, Debian manages to maintain a consistent environment where dependencies are carefully tracked and validated. This approach minimizes the risk of system breakage during updates and fosters a stable user environment where new features are introduced in a controlled manner.

Debian's transparent package management is complemented by a robust community infrastructure that supports continuous improvement and feedback. Issue tracking systems, community-maintained repositories, and collaborative development platforms ensure that any bugs or inconsistencies in package management are quickly identified and resolved. Developers and users alike contribute patches and improvements, driving the evolution of both individual packages and the APT system as a whole. The collaborative nature of these efforts reinforces the principles of open development, where every change is subject to peer review and community discussion.

The effectiveness of Debian's package management system is further underscored by its adaptability to various usage scenarios. Whether deployed on a personal desktop, a mission-critical server, or even embedded systems, the modular architecture of package management ensures that users experience a consistent, reliable interface for software maintenance. The ability to switch repositories, define custom installation options, and automate updates seamlessly integrates with the diverse needs of its global user base.

In summary, Debian's software packaging and package management system, spearheaded by APT, epitomizes the project's focus on stability, security, and ease of use. The intricate interplay between package metadata, dependency resolution, and system upgrades creates an environment where both novice and expert users can manage complex systems with relative simplicity. This streamlined approach, supported by a rich suite of tools and community-driven enhancements, continues to be a defining feature of Debian, ensuring that it remains a trusted and effective platform for diverse computing needs.

Chapter 2

Installation and Basic Configuration

This chapter guides users through the Debian installation process, from preparation and hardware considerations to step-by-step system setup and post-installation configuration. It distinguishes between graphical and command-line interfaces, ensuring users can navigate both. Essential tasks such as configuring software repositories and optimizing system settings are covered, equipping users with fundamental knowledge for efficient operation and management of a Debian environment.

2.1. Preparing for Installation

Before initiating the Debian installation process, it is essential to ensure that the target system is optimally configured and compatible with the Debian operating system. Adequate preparation involves two primary components: assessing and verifying hardware capabilities and obtaining the correct installation media. Each of these elements plays a critical role in determining the success of the installation and ensuring that the system meets the operational requirements of Debian.

The initial step is to evaluate the hardware. Debian is designed to run on a wide range of systems, yet certain hardware configurations may require additional preparation or verification. Central processing units (CPUs), system memory (RAM), storage devices, and networking components must be reviewed to confirm their compatibility with the latest Debian release. Prior to installation, it is advisable to document the existing hardware configuration. System administrators and users can utilize built-in Linux utilities to retrieve detailed hardware information. One common utility is lshw, which provides a comprehensive summary of system hardware. For example, executing the following command in a terminal yields insights into the system's processor, memory, and peripheral devices:

```
sudo lshw -short
```

This command generates a summarized inventory that includes critical internal components and peripheral devices. Furthermore, inspecting storage devices with commands such as:

```
lsblk
```

can help identify disk partitions, sizes, and existing file systems. Verifying that the disk layout is suitable for Debian installation is essential, especially if a dual-boot setup or partition resizing is expected. Additional commands, such as dmidecode, provide further insights by displaying hardware attributes stored in the system BIOS or UEFI firmware:

```
sudo dmidecode | less
```

These diagnostic tools allow users to ascertain details about the motherboard, BIOS version, and memory configuration, all of which are valuable during the installation process.

Hardware compatibility extends to peripheral devices, such as network interfaces and graphics adapters. In many environments, network connectivity is a prerequisite for obtaining software updates and additional packages during and after installation. Users are advised to check network interface configurations using tools like `ifconfig` or `ip a`:

```
ip a
```

This ensures that network adapters are recognized and operating correctly. If hardware drivers pose potential challenges, it is beneficial to review the Debian hardware compatibility list available on the official website to preempt issues that may arise from proprietary drivers or unsupported devices.

Obtaining the installation media is the subsequent aspect of preparedness. The Debian installation image is available in multiple formats, each catering to different installation scenarios. The DVD, CD, and USB installation images are tailored for desktop and server installations, with distinctions in file size and included packages. It is imperative to download the image corresponding to the target architecture (e.g., amd64 for 64-bit systems, armhf for ARM systems) from official Debian mirrors to ensure authenticity and integrity.

The procedure involves navigating to Debian's download page, selecting the appropriate media type, and subsequently verifying the digital signatures provided. Digital verification is a crucial practice to safeguard against corrupted downloads or malicious modifications. The Debian project provides checksums (e.g., SHA256) and GPG signatures; verifying these ensures that the downloaded file is genuine. For example, after acquiring an ISO file, one can verify its SHA256 checksum using the command:

```
sha256sum debian-install.iso
```

Comparing the resulting hash to the officially published value confirms the image's integrity. Additionally, the GPG signature of the ISO image can be validated with a series of commands. First, import the Debian signing key:

```
gpg --keyserver keyring.debian.org --recv-keys [Debian_Signing_Key_ID
    ]
```

Subsequently, check the ISO image's signature:

```
gpg --verify debian-install.iso.asc debian-install.iso
```

These verification steps are crucial for ensuring that the installation media has not been tampered with and that it originates from a reputable source.

In some installations, users opt to create a bootable USB stick rather than burning the image to a DVD or CD. This approach typically involves the use of dedicated utilities such as dd on Unix-like systems. Prior to executing this command, it is important to ensure that the target USB drive is properly identified to avoid accidental overwriting of other storage devices. A suitably cautious method involves first identifying the device using:

```
sudo fdisk -l
```

Once the device is identified (for example, /dev/sdx), the ISO can be written to the USB device using dd with a command such as:

```
sudo dd if=debian-install.iso of=/dev/sdx bs=4M status=progress oflag
    =sync
```

It is essential to exercise caution and verify the correctness of the target device path to prevent data loss. Alternative tools with graphical interfaces or specialized utilities, such as Rufus on Windows, provide additional safety features and monitoring capabilities during the process.

Another important aspect of preparing for installation is ensuring that the system's firmware settings are configured to support the chosen installation mode. Modern systems often feature UEFI firmware, which may require settings adjustments such as enabling legacy boot options or disabling secure boot. Users should access the system's firmware configuration menu and verify that the boot mode aligns with the preparation for Debian installation. Documentation provided by both the hardware manufacturer and Debian can offer guidance on these configurations.

In scenarios where systems involve RAID arrangements, advanced partitioning schemes, or logical volume management (LVM), pre-installation adjustments may be necessary. For systems employing RAID configurations, ensure that the RAID controller is recognized by Debian. Users may need to reconfigure firmware RAID settings or even opt for software RAID depending on system capabilities. Similarly, if the system utilizes UEFI with GPT partitioning, it is crucial to confirm that an EFI System Partition (ESP) is present and adequately sized. These considerations help avoid installation complications related to boot loader configurations and disk partitioning.

It is beneficial to plan the partitioning scheme prior to installation. Debian supports a variety of partitioning tools during its installation process, but a pre-determined layout can streamline the post-installation configuration. Whether separate partitions for /, /home, /var, or dedicated swap areas are required, drawing up a clear partition layout beforehand minimizes disruptions. This planning is particularly important in environments where disk encryption or dual-boot configurations are implemented. Utilizing partition editors from a live environment gives users the opportunity to resize or reformat partitions in a controlled manner before initiating the installation.

Furthermore, preparing a separate working environment using a live Debian session can provide an opportunity to perform test installations or hardware diagnostics without affecting the existing system configuration. Booting into a live session allows users to interact with Debian, verify peripheral functionality, and experiment with system settings in a safe environment. This approach is especially useful for administrators aiming to deploy installations on multiple systems or in complex network configurations.

User documentation and community resources play a significant role in addressing hardware-specific considerations. Debian's extensive documentation, community forums, and technical guides offer detailed instructions for troubleshooting hardware incompatibilities, driver issues, and firmware settings. Engaging with these resources prior to installation ensures that potential obstacles are identified and addressed beforehand. This level of preparation is valuable in both enterprise settings and academic environments, where minimizing downtime is critical.

Preparation also encompasses ensuring that necessary backups of existing data have been performed when working on systems that require a dual-boot arrangement or that contain critical information. Although the installation process can be performed in a non-destructive manner, misconfigurations, accidental disk formatting, or unforeseen errors can lead to irreversible data loss. Therefore, identifying and securing important data protects against system failures and enhances recovery procedures post-installation.

The entirety of the preparation phase should be documented to maintain an audit trail and facilitate troubleshooting. Detailed logs of hardware configurations, partition schemes, firmware settings, and verified installation media assist in tracking changes and provide reference points in case issues occur later in the installation or configuration process. Such documentation is particularly beneficial in collaborative environments where multiple administrators are involved.

Ensuring that all preliminary steps are methodically executed is fundamental to achieving a stable and reliable Debian installation. System requirements are matched with the appropriate variant of Debian, whether it is a minimal installation for a headless server or a full installation with a graphical desktop environment. Thereby, thorough hardware verification and careful procurement of authentic installation media lay the groundwork for a seamless transition to the subsequent phases of installation and configuration.

2.2. Step-by-Step Installation Process

This section provides a detailed walkthrough of the Debian installation process, focusing on partitioning the target system and configuring boot options. Following the preparation of the system and acquisition of the proper installation media, users are guided through a methodical sequence of steps to guarantee a successful installation.

When booting from the installation media, the system first displays a boot menu that allows the user to select the installation mode. The primary choices typically include a graphical installer and a text-based installer. The text-based installer is noted for its simplicity and lower resource requirements. Regardless of the chosen interface, the installer initiates a series of checks for hardware compatibility, ensuring that essential components such as storage and network interfaces are detected correctly.

The installer then proceeds to initialize the system, during which a series of pre-installation scripts run in the background. This phase confirms that all required drivers are available and that any connected peripherals do not interfere with the installation. When running in UEFI mode, additional firmware-specific support is loaded, and the user is often prompted to confirm boot settings that affect the secure boot features of the system.

A significant phase of the installation process is disk partitioning. Debian provides several partitioning methods that suit different deployment environments. The guided partitioning option is suitable for most cases; however, expert users may opt for manual partitioning to enforce a custom layout. For example, a common setup includes separate partitions for the root filesystem (/), the home directories (/home), and a dedicated swap region. This separation supports system stability and simplifies backup procedures. When partitioning manually, the installer displays the current disk layout, and users can create, modify, or delete partitions.

Disk partitioning decisions are critical to the system's performance and maintenance. If the installer detects pre-existing data partitions, it provides options to resize these partitions non-destructively. Partition management tools, such as fdisk or parted, play a central role during this step. For instance, when a user enters the manual partitioning mode, the interface may allow selection of the target disk followed by choices to format a partition with a specific filesystem (e.g., ext4, xfs, or btrfs). A typical command-line operation during partitioning using parted from a live session would be:

```
sudo parted /dev/sda --script mklabel gpt
sudo parted /dev/sda --script mkpart primary ext4 1MiB 50GiB
sudo parted /dev/sda --script mkpart primary linux-swap 50GiB 60GiB
sudo parted /dev/sda --script mkpart primary ext4 60GiB 100%
```

After creating the partitions, the installer prompts for mount point assignments and filesystem selections. The boot partition, often referring to the EFI System Partition (ESP) in UEFI systems, should be created with adequate space (typically around 512 MB) and formatted with a FAT variant. The installer automatically detects these configurations and guides the user through specifying the proper mount points.

For BIOS systems, ensuring that the boot flag is set on the active partition becomes the final preparatory step before writing the filesystem table to disk.

During partition selection and formatting, careful consideration is given to the layout and location of the swap partition. Swap acts as an extension of the physical memory, and its size is determined by the installed system's hardware. The installer presents recommendations based on memory size, but users can adjust the swap size to meet performance or energy conservation requirements as needed.

Once partitioning is complete, the installer transitions to package selection. Here, the system base and additional packages are installed according to the chosen profile. For installations that require a minimal environment, only essential packages are installed. More comprehensive profiles include a graphical desktop environment, software development tools, and network utilities. The package selection interface is organized to allow users to select groups of packages, meaning that choosing one option can trigger the inclusion of several related packages in the installation process.

Following the installation of the base system and selected packages, the configuration of bootloader settings commences. On most Debian installations, GRUB (GRand Unified Bootloader) is the default installer for boot options. GRUB must be properly installed on the primary boot device to manage the boot process reliably. During this phase, the installer identifies available disks and partitions, recommending the primary disk as the location for GRUB installation. For instance, on a system with multiple storage devices, the user might face an option to choose between /dev/sda and /dev/sdb, with the installer typically suggesting the first disk as the default.

The bootloader installation sequence includes updating configuration files that detail the available boot options and kernel parameters. Configuration entries indicate the location of the root filesystem and any necessary parameters such as system rescue options or kernel recovery modes. A simplified view of a GRUB configuration file entry is as follows:

```
menuentry "Debian GNU/Linux" {
    set root=(hd0,1)
    linux /boot/vmlinuz-5.10.0-8-amd64 root=/dev/sda1 ro quiet
    initrd /boot/initrd.img-5.10.0-8-amd64
}
```

In this configuration, hd0,1 denotes the first partition of the first disk, and the specified parameters ensure that the kernel mounts the appropriate root filesystem. The use of parameters such as ro (read-only during the boot process) and quiet (to minimize verbose output) aids in reducing the time to boot and simplifies initial troubleshooting in case of boot failures.

For systems configured with UEFI firmware, GRUB installation involves additional steps. The installer writes the bootloader's EFI files into the EFI System Partition and creates a corresponding boot entry within the firmware settings. Automated tools within Debian assist in updating the UEFI boot manager. Nonetheless, it is recommended that users verify the presence of the boot entry by examining the EFI variables. For example, the command below helps list current boot entries:

```
sudo efibootmgr -v
```

This command confirms that Debian appears in the boot menu and that the path to the EFI file is correct. If discrepancies are detected, administrators may need to manually adjust the settings within the UEFI firmware interface or reinvoke efibootmgr with corrective flags.

After the installation of GRUB, the remaining task involves finalizing system configurations. The installer initiates the creation of system user accounts, prompts the user to set passwords, and configures locale settings. A series of dialogs request confirmation of time zone, regional settings, and network configuration. These steps are critical in aligning the Debian system with the regional and organizational policies that may apply in enterprise or academic environments.

Advanced installation scenarios may require the utilization of preseed files. Preseed files allow fully automated installations by supplying predefined responses to installer prompts. This method is highly beneficial in deploying multiple systems with minimal interactive input. A sample snippet from a preseed configuration file may look as follows:

```
d-i debian-installer/locale string en_US
d-i keyboard-configuration/layoutcode string us
d-i netcfg/get_hostname string debian-host
d-i netcfg/get_domain string example.com
```

The above configuration demonstrates how to set fundamental parameters, ensuring that installations across multiple systems are consistent and aligned with organizational standards.

The installer concludes by writing all configurations, installing the bootloader, and generating the final system image. This phase typically involves repetitive logging of process details on the screen, allowing for real-time monitoring of progress. Should errors occur, diagnostic messages are displayed with corresponding error codes and log file locations. In cases where manual intervention is required, users are provided the option to access an expert mode shell, wherein commands can be executed to troubleshoot disk mounting issues, file system integrity, or network problems.

The step-by-step procedure is designed to minimize risk during installation by prompting for confirmation before any destructive operations are executed. Consistency checks are run throughout each phase to ensure that the intended configurations are applied as planned. The reliability of the process is underpinned by Debian's openness, allowing users to review pre- and post-installation settings and to execute custom scripts if specialized configurations are needed.

Emphasizing precision during partitioning and bootloader configuration is imperative. Misconfiguration in these critical areas can lead to issues like the inability to boot the system or data loss from incorrectly formatted partitions. The installer's interactive environment, while automated to a degree, offers ample opportunities for the administrator to review each setting and confirm that all choices are congruent with the planned system architecture. This attention to detail ensures that following the installation process, the Debian system is both robust and prepared to meet the operational requirements specified during the system preparation phase.

Every step during this process builds a foundation for the subsequent configurations, from initial system updates and network establishment to user account creation and repository management. Completing the installation process with careful consideration of partition layouts and boot configuration parameters ensures that the Debian operating environment operates continuously and reliably.

2.3. Post-Installation Configuration

After the Debian installation process is completed, the system enters a state where initial configurations are essential for its operational stability and security. This phase focuses on tasks such as setting up users, fine-tuning network configurations, updating the system, and ensuring that essential services are correctly initialized.

In the immediate aftermath of installation, establishing user accounts and managing privileges is a critical task. While the installation process typically creates a primary administrative account, additional user accounts often must be configured to segregate duties and enhance security. The adduser and usermod utilities provide a straightforward way to manage users and groups. For example, adding a new user to the system is accomplished using:

60

```
sudo adduser newusername
```

Once the new user is created, enhancing the account's privileges by adding it to administrative groups, such as sudo, fosters secure delegation of tasks without directly sharing the root account. The following command accomplishes this:

```
sudo usermod -aG sudo newusername
```

Administrators are encouraged to verify that changes are effective by checking group memberships through commands like:

```
id newusername
```

This approach helps in maintaining a robust permission structure that minimizes security risks resulting from overly privileged accounts.

Configuring secure remote and local access is another essential consideration. If the system is configured for remote access, generating and configuring SSH keys for passwordless authentication enhances both security and convenience. The ssh-keygen utility is used to generate a key pair, as demonstrated below:

```
ssh-keygen -t rsa -b 4096 -C "user@example.com"
```

Once generated, the public key should be added to the target account's authorized keys file on remote systems. This process is automated by copying the key using:

```
ssh-copy-id newusername@remote_host
```

These steps enhance system security by reducing reliance on passwords and by using cryptographic authentication measures.

Network configuration plays a vital role, especially in environments where the system must connect to remote repositories and services. Debian systems by default support configuration methods through traditional files as well as more modern approaches such as systemd-networkd or NetworkManager. In many cases, editing the /etc/network/interfaces file is sufficient to configure wired network interfaces. A basic configuration for a static IP might be written as follows:

```
auto eth0
iface eth0 inet static
    address 192.168.1.100
    netmask 255.255.255.0
    gateway 192.168.1.1
    dns-nameservers 8.8.8.8 8.8.4.4
```

After editing network configuration files, applying the changes often requires restarting the networking service to ensure that the modifications take effect. This can be performed by:

```
sudo systemctl restart networking
```

In environments that use DHCP, the corresponding configuration in /etc/network/interfaces is simpler:

```
auto eth0
iface eth0 inet dhcp
```

Verification of network connectivity is accomplished using commands such as ifconfig or ip a to inspect the interface's assigned IP address. Further, testing connectivity to external servers using utilities like ping or curl confirms that the network paths are properly established. A sample command is:

```
ping -c 4 google.com
```

Ensuring the system is up-to-date forms another pillar of post-installation configuration. Debian employs the apt package management tool, which is used to fetch the latest packages and security patches from configured repositories. Prior to installing new software, updating the package index is necessary:

```
sudo apt update
```

Following a successful update, the system should install available upgrades to ensure that the installed packages are current and secure:

```
sudo apt upgrade -y
```

This process retrieves updated packages and applies security patches. In some instances, a distribution upgrade may be recommended to align all packages with the latest stable version:

```
sudo apt full-upgrade -y
```

Automated updates can be leveraged for systems that require continual security monitoring. Configuring unattended upgrades by installing the package unattended-upgrades and modifying its configuration file provides an extra layer of security. A sample configuration snippet in /etc/apt/apt.conf.d/50unattended-upgrades might specify which repositories are trusted:

```
Unattended-Upgrade::Allowed-Origins {
    "Debian stable";
    "Debian-security stable";
};
```

Adjusting this configuration allows for periodic checks without manual intervention, ensuring the system remains patched against vulnerabilities.

Post-installation tasks also involve establishing system-wide configurations for logging, time synchronization, and other services. For time synchronization, Debian utilizes utilities such as systemd-timesyncd or ntp. Configuring systemd-timesyncd involves verifying that the service is enabled and that the correct time servers are specified in the configuration file:

```
sudo systemctl enable systemd-timesyncd
sudo systemctl start systemd-timesyncd
```

Inspecting the status of the service confirms its proper functioning:

```
systemctl status systemd-timesyncd
```

Further customization of time servers may be performed by editing the /etc/systemd/timesyncd.conf file. Establishing correct time synchronization is crucial in environments where accurate logging and security protocols are time-dependent.

Logging configurations are generally set up to capture system events that help diagnose issues during system operation. By default, Debian employs rsyslog for log management. Essential configuration files and directories such as /etc/rsyslog.conf and /var/log provide insights into system behavior. Fine-tuning these configurations may be necessary in systems with higher performance or security demands, where logs need to be rotated or archived frequently. Tools such as logrotate automate the process of managing log files. The default /etc/logrotate.conf along with supplemental configurations in /etc/logrotate.d/ help regulate log file sizes and retention periods.

Network security is another post-installation area that warrants meticulous configuration, particularly when the system is exposed to external networks. Configuring a firewall using iptables or more modern tools like nftables helps control incoming and outgoing traffic. For example, a simple firewall configuration using iptables might appear as follows:

```
sudo iptables -A INPUT -m conntrack --ctstate ESTABLISHED,RELATED -j
    ACCEPT
sudo iptables -A INPUT -p icmp -j ACCEPT
sudo iptables -A INPUT -i lo -j ACCEPT
sudo iptables -P INPUT DROP
sudo iptables -P FORWARD DROP
sudo iptables -P OUTPUT ACCEPT
```

After setting up such rules, saving the configuration guarantees that the firewall persists after a reboot. Tools such as iptables-save and iptables-restore support the migration of current rules to a persistent state in configuration files.

Additional post-installation configuration involves installing and configuring essential applications and services that support the intended system use. For desktop environments, configuring a display manager and graphical session parameters is imperative. For servers, setting up applications such as web servers, databases, or container runtimes often follows immediately after the core system configuration.

For users who operate in command-line environments, applying shell customizations and installing terminal multiplexers may increase productivity. Configuration files, such as .bashrc or .zshrc, should be updated to introduce aliases, environment variables, and paths customized to specific workflows. An example configuration snippet in .bashrc that sets up a few aliases for convenience is:

```
alias ll='ls -alF'
alias la='ls -A'
alias l='ls -CF'
export PATH=$PATH:/usr/local/bin
```

These modifications enrich the user experience and streamline routine operations.

Investing time into validating the overall system health after initial configurations is prudent. Reviewing logs, verifying network connectivity, and confirming that scheduled services are running correctly helps detect any discrepancies early. For instance, checking the system journal via journalctl can reveal hidden issues:

```
sudo journalctl -p err -b
```

This command displays any errors flagged during the current boot cycle. Running such diagnostics periodically ensures that the system remains stable and responsive.

With the combination of establishing secure user management, precise network configuration, routine system updates, and the verification of key services, the post-installation configuration phase thoroughly readies the Debian system for production use.

2.4.   Graphical vs. Command Line Interfaces

Debian supports a wide range of user interfaces, enabling users to choose between graphical environments and command-line interfaces (CLI) based on their preferences and operational requirements. Both interfaces provide distinct advantages. The graphical interface, typically managed by a display manager, offers ease of use for daily tasks and multimedia applications, while the CLI offers efficiency, flexibility, and lower resource consumption, which are beneficial for server environments and advanced system management.

In Debian, the graphical user interface (GUI) is provided by several desktop environments such as GNOME, KDE, Xfce, and LXDE. These environments vary in complexity, resource usage, and customization options. For users requiring a visually appealing and fully integrated desktop, GNOME or KDE may be preferred. For less resource-intensive systems, lighter alternatives like Xfce or LXDE present a viable option. The display manager responsible for managing user sessions also varies; examples include GDM for GNOME, SDDM for KDE, LightDM for Xfce, and LXDM for LXDE. Each display manager is responsible for handling user logins, session selection, and graceful transitions to the desktop environment.

The CLI, by contrast, serves as the backbone for more technical tasks. Debian makes extensive use of terminal interfaces, which allow users to execute commands, run shell scripts, and perform system administration with minimal overhead. Shell environments such as bash and zsh provide text-based interactive access to the system. The command-line interface is particularly attractive in server environments, system recovery sessions, and automated scripts, where graphical overhead is unnecessary or even detrimental to performance.

Users can switch between interfaces relatively easily, taking advantage of the strengths of both environments at different times. For instance, if a user is operating within a graphical session but wishes to access a terminal, they can invoke a terminal emulator such as gnome-terminal, konsole, or xfce4-terminal depending on the desktop environment. Conversely, a system booted into a graphical session may be switched to console mode by utilizing key combinations like Ctrl+Alt+F1 through Ctrl+Alt+F6. These key combinations bring up different virtual consoles that provide a pure command-line experience. To return to the graphical environment in a typical Debian configuration using systemd, a user might press Ctrl+Alt+F7 or Ctrl+Alt+F1 depending on the configuration of the display manager.

Switching between the CLI and GUI also extends to session initiation. Some systems may be configured to boot directly into a text console, which is a common configuration for servers. Users can start the graphical environment manually from the CLI using the startx command. This command initializes the X server and loads the default desktop environment or window manager. An example execution is as follows:

```
startx
```

This method is particularly useful for troubleshooting environments where the graphical system experiences issues, or when resources must be conserved by avoiding unnecessary graphical sessions. In more controlled environments, users may prefer to disable the display manager and boot in text mode by default. This can be configured by adjusting the systemd target. Changing the default target to multi-user.target disables the graphical interface on system boot:

```
sudo systemctl set-default multi-user.target
```

Once operating in text mode, reverting to the graphical mode is possible by switching back the default target:

```
sudo systemctl set-default graphical.target
```

The presence of both interfaces within Debian allows administrators to tailor system performance and usability. Graphical environments involve a higher resource footprint due to processes related to compositing, window management, and background services. In contrast, the CLI operates with minimal overhead, rendering it optimal for operations where resource conservation is paramount.

Some users may choose to leverage remote graphical access while still utilizing the CLI locally. Remote Desktop Protocol (RDP) and Virtual Network Computing (VNC) are popular methods for attaining graphical access to a Debian system remotely. Debian supports server applications such as xrdp and tightvncserver that facilitate remote desktop sessions. An administrator can install xrdp using the following command:

```
sudo apt install xrdp
```

After installation, the system must be configured to ensure that the appropriate desktop environment is accessible through the remote session. This might involve creating or modifying configuration files specific to the remote desktop tool in use.

Alternatively, if interacting with a Debian system primarily via the CLI, users might find that tasks such as software installation, configuration file editing, and system monitoring are more efficiently executed with command-line tools. Text editors like vim, nano, or emacs are commonly used alongside terminal-based system monitoring tools like htop, iftop, and netstat. For example, monitoring system processes can be accomplished effectively using:

```
htop
```

More advanced users might also take advantage of tiling window managers (e.g., i3, awesome, or bspwm) in their graphical session. These window managers provide minimalistic environments that facilitate a keyboard-driven work style, bridging the gap between the graphical

68

and command-line sessions. Tiling window managers optimize screen real estate and, when combined with terminal emulators, present a productive environment for users handling multi-tasking operations.

Debian also supports remote CLI management through secure shell (SSH). Accessing a Debian system using SSH directly places the user in the command-line environment, bypassing the need for a graphical session entirely. The command to establish an SSH connection is straightforward:

```
ssh username@server_address
```

Once connected via SSH, users have full access to system tools and utilities that allow them to perform maintenance, manage services, and monitor logs. This remote CLI capability is essential in cloud-based systems and data centers where graphical tools are often impractical due to limited bandwidth and the need for automation.

Practical experience demonstrates that mastering both interfaces enhances the overall administrative capabilities. For instance, many automation scripts and system management tools require operation in the CLI. A robust understanding of terminal commands and scripting languages such as Bash or Python empowers administrators to automate repetitive tasks and manage complex system configurations. An example of generating a report of disk usage with a simple one-liner is:

```
df -h | tee disk_report.txt
```

In contrast, during interactive sessions, the GUI enables users to quickly navigate file systems, manage multimedia content, and interact with IDEs for software development. Graphical package managers, such as synaptic, provide a user-friendly alternative for package management while still leveraging the powerful Debian apt infrastructure running in the background.

Understanding how to switch between these interfaces can prove beneficial during troubleshooting and system recovery. When a display manager fails to load, for example, the user can press the appropriate function keys to access the underlying virtual console. Once in CLI mode, inspecting system logs and reconfiguring the display manager may remedy the issue. A common troubleshooting step involves examining log files for display manager errors:

```
sudo journalctl -u gdm
```

The dual-interface design of Debian reinforces its versatility as an operating system capable of meeting the needs of diverse user groups. Beginners may start their learning experience within a fully featured graphical desktop, while advanced users and administrators often develop a preference for the efficiency of the CLI. Both interfaces coexist harmoniously, allowing seamless transitions and the utilization of each environment's respective advantages under various circumstances.

The methodology for switching interfaces also reflects Debian's adherence to the UNIX philosophy of modularity and clarity. By decoupling the graphical subsystem from core system operations, Debian ensures that even when the graphical environment is compromised, fundamental functionalities remain accessible through the CLI. This separation is crucial for system recovery and maintenance, as it preserves the ability to execute administrative tasks without dependency on graphical components.

Each interface mode is supported by extensive documentation available through Debian's man pages, online resources, and community forums. The man command can be used to access detailed information about a wide range of commands and configuration files, exemplified by:

```
man systemctl
```

By understanding the options available for graphical and command-line interfaces and knowing how to transition between them, users can optimize their interactions with the Debian system. This duality enhances productivity, simplifies troubleshooting, and ultimately creates a more resilient and adaptable operating environment.

2.5. Configuring Software Repositories

Debian relies on a robust package management system to provide users with access to a broad range of software and timely security updates. Configuring software repositories correctly is essential, as it determines where packages are sourced and how updates are delivered. A well-configured repository setup not only ensures access to the latest software versions but also maintains the system's stability and security.

The core system utilizes a repository configuration file, commonly located at `/etc/apt/sources.list`. This file contains references to package repositories, including main, contrib, and non-free sections. The structure of the entries in this file is simple: each line begins with the type of protocol (typically `deb` or `deb-src`), followed by the URL of the repository, the distribution (or suite), and the repository components. A typical entry might resemble the following example:

```
deb http://deb.debian.org/debian/ stable main contrib non-free
deb-src http://deb.debian.org/debian/ stable main contrib non-free
```

This configuration directs `apt` to use the official Debian mirrors for both binary and source packages. The separation of binary (`deb`) and source (`deb-src`) repositories allows administrators to retrieve source code if needed for debugging or compilation purposes.

In addition to the main repository entries, security updates are crucial for maintaining a secure environment. Debian provides a dedicated security repository that is often included as a separate entry in the sources list. For example:

```
deb http://security.debian.org/debian-security stable-security main
```

```
      contrib non-free
deb-src http://security.debian.org/debian-security stable-security
      main contrib non-free
```

Incorporating these entries ensures that the system can retrieve prompt security updates and patches, which are vital for mitigating vulnerabilities.

Debian also provides access to backports, which are newer versions of packages built for older stable releases. Configuring backports requires adding a dedicated entry that typically looks like this:

```
deb http://deb.debian.org/debian stable-backports main contrib non-
      free
```

Backports enable users to install updated versions of software without compromising the stability of the entire system. However, caution should be exercised as packages from backports might introduce dependencies that conflict with the stable base.

Configuration of repositories is not limited to the /etc/apt/sources.list file. The /etc/apt/sources.list.d/ directory provides additional flexibility by allowing administrators to create separate files for third-party repositories or custom package sources. This modular approach simplifies management and troubleshooting. For instance, adding a repository for a specialized software suite might involve creating a file named custom-repo.list with the following content:

```
deb http://example.com/debian stable main
```

This method helps segregate external repositories from the main configuration, reducing the risk of inadvertently disrupting the native package sources.

Ensuring the integrity and authenticity of packages from repositories is another critical consideration. Debian uses cryptographic signatures to verify that downloaded packages have not been tampered with. The package management system checks each package against a set of trusted keys. When a new repository is added, it is essential to import the corresponding GPG key into the system's keyring. This is typically accomplished using the apt-key utility or, in newer systems, by placing the key file in the /etc/apt/trusted.gpg.d/ directory. An example command to add a repository key might be:

```
wget -qO - http://example.com/repo.gpg | sudo apt-key add -
```

Verifying the successful addition of the key is essential. This process serves to ensure that packages originate from trusted sources and that their integrity remains intact during the download process.

Once repository configurations are adjusted, the subsequent step requires refreshing the package index. This is achieved with the apt update command, which retrieves the latest package lists from all configured repositories. Running the following command confirms that the system is synchronized with the available package repositories:

```
sudo apt update
```

This command not only updates the list of available packages but also verifies the validity of the repository signatures. Any discrepancies or errors during this process indicate potential issues with repository configuration or network connectivity. In case errors occur, administrators should inspect the repository URLs and GPG keys to ensure they are correct and up-to-date.

Managing repository configurations also provides an opportunity to prioritize certain repositories over others. Debian's package management system supports the concept of pinning, where administrators can assign priorities to different package sources. This mechanism is achieved by creating a pinning configuration file, typically located at /etc/apt/preferences or within the /etc/apt/preferences.d/ directory. Pinning allows the system to favor packages from a particular

73

repository, even if newer versions are available elsewhere. A sample configuration for pinning might be:

```
Package: *
Pin: origin "deb.debian.org"
Pin-Priority: 900

Package: *
Pin: origin "example.com"
Pin-Priority: 400
```

In this configuration, the official Debian repository is assigned a higher priority compared to a third-party source. This setup ensures that system-critical packages are sourced from trusted and stable repositories while still allowing less critical or alternative applications from external sources to be installed when necessary.

Another facet of repository management is handling package sources that might be temporarily disabled. For example, certain entries in the sources list can be commented out by prefacing them with a # symbol. This approach is useful during troubleshooting or when an external repository is known to be experiencing issues. Administrators can quickly reinstate the repository by removing the comment symbol after the issue has been resolved. An example entry might look like:

```
# deb http://example.com/debian unstable main
```

After future reactivation, the package index should again be updated to reflect the changes.

In environments where repositories are mirrored internally or customized for organizational requirements, maintaining a local mirror can be advantageous. A local mirror reduces bandwidth consumption, accelerates package retrieval times, and provides an added layer of control over software versions delivered across multiple systems. Configuring client systems to use an internal mirror involves replacing official repository URLs with the internal mirror's address in the /etc/apt/sources.list file. An internal mirror entry may appear as

74

follows:

```
deb http://internal-mirror.example.com/debian stable main contrib non
    -free
```

Regular synchronization of the internal mirror with the official repositories is essential to keep the local repository current with security updates and package releases.

Managing repository configurations effectively also encompasses routine maintenance tasks. Regular audits of the /etc/apt/sources.list
file and the /etc/apt/sources.list.d/ directory ensure that outdated or redundant entries are removed. This practice minimizes potential conflicts and decreases the risk of inadvertently installing packages from obsolete sources. Automated scripts can be deployed to periodically validate repository URLs and GPG keys. An example script
snippet that checks connectivity to a given repository URL might be:

```
#!/bin/bash
REPO_URL="http://deb.debian.org/debian/"
if curl --output /dev/null --silent --head --fail "$REPO_URL"; then
    echo "Repository is accessible."
else
    echo "Repository is not accessible."
fi
```

Maintaining a well-documented repository configuration process allows teams within an organization to standardize repository management practices. Documenting the source URLs, associated GPG keys,
pinning priorities, and any customizations ensures that configurations
can be reviewed and reproduced across multiple systems. Such documentation plays an essential role in enterprise environments where
consistency and compliance are critical.

In configuring software repositories, it is important to note the balance
between obtaining cutting-edge software and maintaining system stability. While repositories such as backports provide access to newer
packages, maintaining the core system on stable releases minimizes

the risk of incompatibilities. Administrators must evaluate organizational needs carefully before introducing repositories that might compromise the reliability of installed software.

As systems evolve, the repository configuration should be revisited regularly, particularly after major Debian releases or when significant changes are introduced in package management policies. Keeping abreast of updates from the Debian project and related community discussions assists in identifying recommendations for repository changes or adjustments to pinning priorities that may impact system behavior.

Configuring software repositories in Debian is a dynamic process that requires careful planning, continuous updates, and strict adherence to security practices. By implementing robust configurations that account for official repositories, security updates, backports, and custom sources, administrators can establish a reliable and secure software distribution model. The systematic approach described ensures that systems remain up-to-date, secure, and capable of delivering the latest software enhancements to users consistently.

2.6. Optimizing System Settings

Optimizing system settings in Debian is essential for achieving a balance between performance, resource utilization, and system stability. Following the installation and basic configuration phases, administrators can fine-tune kernel parameters, adjust hardware-specific settings, and configure system services to suit specialized workloads. This section discusses methods to optimize system performance through tuning kernel parameters, configuration of file descriptors and network settings, managing system services, and monitoring resource usage.

One of the primary methods for performance optimization is adjusting kernel parameters using the `sysctl` interface. The `/etc/sysctl.conf` file and supplementary files in `/etc/sysctl.d/` allow administrators to configure various runtime parameters. For instance, tuning memory management parameters such as `vm.swappiness` can improve performance, especially on systems with limited physical memory. Lowering the swappiness value reduces the likelihood of the kernel using swap space and favors physical memory usage. An exemplary configuration entry is:

```
vm.swappiness=10
```

After updating the configuration file, the settings can be applied immediately by executing:

```
sudo sysctl -p
```

In addition to memory settings, network performance can be enhanced by adjusting parameters such as the maximum number of file descriptors and TCP settings. For high-load web servers or database systems, increasing the limits on file descriptors is often necessary. Editing the file `/etc/security/limits.conf` allows for persistent changes to these settings. A sample configuration might include:

```
*               soft    nofile      4096
*               hard    nofile      8192
```

Furthermore, network parameters stored in `/etc/sysctl.conf` can be tuned for high throughput. For example, increasing the backlog for incoming connections and adjusting TCP window scaling can be beneficial. Sample entries include:

```
net.core.somaxconn=1024
net.ipv4.tcp_tw_reuse=1
net.ipv4.tcp_fin_timeout=15
```

These changes allow the system to handle a higher volume of simultaneous connections and reduce time spent in idle connection states.

Optimization efforts may also include configuring the I/O scheduler for storage devices. The choice of I/O scheduler can have a significant impact on disk performance. For modern solid-state drives (SSDs), the deadline or noop scheduler is often preferred over the default CFQ scheduler. To check the current I/O scheduler for a storage device, for example /dev/sda, the command is:

```
cat /sys/block/sda/queue/scheduler
```

Switching the scheduler to deadline may involve echoing the desired scheduler into the sysfs interface:

```
echo deadline | sudo tee /sys/block/sda/queue/scheduler
```

For a more permanent solution, administrators can configure udev rules or modify boot parameters in the GRUB configuration to set the desired scheduler at system start.

CPU performance optimization is another area of focus. CPU frequency scaling and governor settings can be managed using utilities such as cpufrequtils or directly through the /sys filesystem. To determine the available CPU governors, the following command can be used:

```
cat /sys/devices/system/cpu/cpu0/cpufreq/scaling_available_governors
```

A common performance-oriented setting is to switch the governor to performance mode, which sets the CPU at its highest frequency. This can be achieved by writing the setting for each CPU core as shown below:

```
for cpu in /sys/devices/system/cpu/cpu*/cpufreq/scaling_governor; do
    echo performance | sudo tee $cpu
done
```

Such adjustments are especially useful on systems performing compute-intensive tasks, though it is advisable to balance performance gains against increased power consumption and thermal output.

In addition to kernel and hardware parameters, proper configuration of system services is crucial. Systemd, the default init system on Debian, allows for fine-grained control over service behavior. Disabling unnecessary services that consume resources can yield measurable performance improvements. To view enabled services, administrators can use:

```
systemctl list-units --type=service --state=running
```

Services not required for the system's specific role should be disabled. For example, if a server does not require printing services, disabling the cups service is appropriate:

```
sudo systemctl disable cups
sudo systemctl stop cups
```

Furthermore, performance monitoring tools such as htop, iotop, and perf can assist in pinpointing resource-intensive processes. These utilities provide real-time insights into CPU, memory, and disk usage, allowing administrators to make data-driven decisions. An example command to invoke real-time CPU and memory monitoring is:

```
htop
```

Local system performance can also be enhanced by optimizing swap usage. Adjustments to swap configuration, including partitioning strategies and use of swap files, should be aligned with the system's expected workload. The swappiness parameter, as mentioned earlier, directly influences how aggressively the kernel uses swap space. In tandem with an appropriate swap partition or file, ensuring that swap is not over-utilized is vital for maintaining system responsiveness.

Beyond system kernel tuning, file system parameters can also impact performance. Modern file systems such as ext4, XFS, or Btrfs offer a range of mount options that can be tailored for performance. For instance, enabling data journaling and adjusting commit intervals in ext4 may improve write performance. An example entry in /etc/fstab for an ext4 partition with optimized mount options might be:

```
/dev/sda1    /    ext4    defaults,noatime,commit=60    0 1
```

The noatime option reduces overhead by minimizing disk writes related to file access metadata tracking. Such options are especially beneficial on systems running applications with high read/write frequency.

Tuning the system's scheduler and resource limits are additional avenues for optimization. The Linux kernel supports various scheduling policies that determine how processes are prioritized. Configuration of scheduler parameters can be done using sysfs or through scheduler-specific commands. For CPU-bound processes, setting real-time priorities using the chrt command may be advantageous in certain scenarios. An example invocation to set a process with a 'FIFO' scheduling policy is:

```
sudo chrt -f 99 <pid>
```

Such adjustments should be performed with care and a deep understanding of the workload, as improper use of real-time scheduling can lead to resource starvation for other processes.

Additionally, network tuning extends to the configuration of advanced parameters such as congestion control algorithms. Modifying the TCP congestion algorithm can help in optimizing performance under heavy network load. A common change is to switch from the default cubic algorithm to reno or bbr, depending on the network environment:

```
sudo sysctl -w net.ipv4.tcp_congestion_control=bbr
```

Persisting this change in /etc/sysctl.conf ensures that the selected algorithm is in effect after reboots.

Optimizing system settings is an iterative process that requires ongoing measurement and adjustment. Tools such as `sar` (from the sysstat package), `vmstat`, and `iostat` offer historical and real-time performance data, enabling administrators to correlate configuration changes with performance improvements. For instance, executing:

```
sar -u 1 5
```

provides insights into CPU utilization over a series of five-second intervals, aiding in diagnosing potential bottlenecks.

Empirical testing is an important part of the optimization process. Before applying any changes to a production system, it is prudent to test them in a controlled environment. Benchmarking tools, such as `fio` for disk I/O and `stress-ng` for overall system stress, can simulate real-world workloads and reveal the effects of tuning. For disk performance benchmarking, a command such as:

```
fio --name=randread --ioengine=libaio --iodepth=64 --rw=randread --bs
    =4k --direct=1 --size=2G --numjobs=4 --runtime=60 --
    group_reporting
```

provides a detailed report of disk read performance under load, which can be used to validate the impact of I/O scheduler changes or file system mount options.

Optimizing system settings also requires a comprehensive understanding of the workload. Different applications and user profiles demand unique configurations. Desktop environments may benefit from power-saving features and user-friendly performance adjustments, whereas server and compute clusters necessitate aggressive performance tuning. Detailed documentation, monitoring, and periodic review of system logs and metrics are integral to maintaining an optimal configuration over time.

Focusing on these adjustments not only enhances system performance but also contributes to greater stability, responsiveness, and scalability. By leveraging tools such as sysctl, systemd, and various benchmarking utilities, administrators can systematically address performance bottlenecks and ensure that the Debian system is tailored to meet specific operational demands. Continuous evaluation and refinement of these parameters allow the system to adapt to evolving workloads and technology advancements, cementing its suitability for both personal and enterprise use.

Chapter 3

Using the Command Line Interface

This chapter introduces essential command-line skills for efficiently navigating the Debian file system, managing files, and operating text editors. It covers process management, basic networking commands, and the use of shell operators for task automation. Additionally, it includes an introduction to Bash scripting, enabling users to automate routine tasks and enhance productivity within the command-line environment.

3.1. Navigating the File System

Navigating the Debian file system efficiently is vital for both users and administrators. The file system in Debian follows the Filesystem Hierarchy Standard, where each directory has a specific role and location in the overall hierarchy. Understanding this structure aids in maintaining an organized workflow and troubleshooting issues when they arise.

The primary commands for navigation include cd, pwd, and ls. The cd command, or *change directory*, is used to move between different directories in the file system. The command can be used with absolute paths, which specify the complete address of a directory starting from the root directory (denoted by a slash /), or relative paths, which describe a path relative to the current working directory. For example, one might use:

```
cd /usr/local/bin
```

to move to the /usr/local/bin directory using an absolute path. If the target directory is in a location relative to the present working directory, a command such as

```
cd documents/projects
```

facilitates quick traversal without retyping a complete path. Using cd .. allows moving one level upward in the hierarchy, which is especially useful for navigating nested directories.

The pwd command, standing for *print working directory*, is an essential tool to display the current directory in which the user is working. When issuing the command:

```
pwd
```

the terminal returns the absolute path of the current directory. This is particularly useful in command-line environments where visual context is minimal. Knowing your exact location within the file system helps prevent accidental operations in unintended directories and assists in scripting automations that rely on a known working directory.

Listing the contents of directories is commonly performed using the ls command. By default, ls displays a list of file and directory names within the current directory. However, its versatility is enhanced by

84

several options that can be combined to produce detailed output. For instance, the option -l provides a long listing format that includes permissions, ownership, size, and modification time:

```
ls -l
```

This command output delivers a tabulated view of directory entries, enabling detailed inspection of file attributes.

Another useful option is -a, which instructs ls to list all files, including hidden files whose names begin with a period:

```
ls -la
```

Hidden files typically store configuration settings and other metadata critical for system or application functionality. In environments where configuration management is paramount, quickly identifying hidden files can aid in diagnostics and form part of routine system audits.

The interplay of absolute and relative paths is crucial for efficiently navigating directories. Absolute paths provide a fixed reference starting from the root, whereas relative paths are used for dynamic movement based on the current location. For example, if the current directory is /home/user, executing:

```
cd /etc
```

transitions the user to the system configuration directory, independent of the current context. Conversely, a command such as:

```
cd ../../var/log
```

moves two levels up from the current directory and then enters the log directory within /var. Mastery of path types reduces both typing effort and the risk of errors during navigation.

A deep understanding of filesystem permissions also complements navigation proficiency. While the primary focus of this section is on navigating directories, knowing that every file and directory is associated with permission sets (read, write, execute) provides context when attempting to list or change directories. The long listing mode (`ls -l`) reveals these permissions, ensuring that users can verify their rights before performing file operations. For example, a sample output may appear as:

```
drwxr-xr-x  2 root root 4096 Apr 10 10:20 bin
```

This output indicates a directory with specific read and execute permissions assigned to the owner, group, and others. Awareness of such details prevents attempts to navigate into directories that the user may not have sufficient privileges to access.

The directory structure in Debian is designed to segment system files, user data, libraries, and executable binaries logically. As part of maintaining security and organization, understanding the roles of directories such as /etc for configuration files, /var for variable data, and /usr for user applications is essential. This hierarchy is not just philosophical; it allows for a compartmentalized view of the system where administrative tasks can be aligned with the appropriate directory paths to reduce errors and streamline operations.

Working within a multi-user environment, such as a server or development platform, frequently requires switching between directories belonging to different perspectives within the hierarchy. Efficient navigation becomes critical in these scenarios. Command line proficiency, including the precise use of `ls` options and `cd` operations, is indispensable for administrators tasked with maintaining system integrity. In addition, concise use of relative paths in scripts accelerates automation tasks, ensuring that scripts operate correctly regardless of their invocation point.

When combining navigation commands in scripts or complex command sequences, it is common to chain together several operations. For example, a script that catalogs directory information may include commands that both change directories and list their contents in a spe-

86

cific format:

```
#!/bin/bash
cd /var/log
ls -la > log_contents.txt
```

This script snippet illustrates a simple automation where after moving to the /var/log directory, the contents are listed in a detailed format and redirected to the file log_contents.txt. Such practices leverage the simplicity of the command line to build effective system management tools without relying on graphical interfaces.

The Debian file system's design and navigation mechanisms also facilitate troubleshooting. System administrators often need to examine log files, verify software installations, and modify configuration files. Quick navigation across different system partitions helps narrow down problems. The knowledge of how and when to use cd and ls underpins more advanced tasks such as batch file operations, software updates, and system backup procedures.

It is important to note that the utility of these commands extends beyond mere directory changes and listings; these fundamental operations serve as the building blocks for more advanced command-line operations and shell scripting. As command-line proficiency increases, users find that developing a habitual reliance on these simple yet powerful commands streamlines their workflow. Developers and administrators alike benefit from reduced complexity when executing frequent directory changes and file inspections as part of their daily routines.

By integrating these navigation commands into daily practice, users cultivate a more innate sense of the file system's layout. This built-in spatial awareness improves operational efficiency and reduces the risk associated with unexpected file operations. Furthermore, the knowledge of directory structures and their respective roles can guide more advanced system maintenance and troubleshooting tasks without additional guidance.

Combining these techniques with previously introduced concepts such as text editing and process management allows for a more rounded command-line experience. The ability to quickly locate and modify configuration files, manage running processes, and streamline workflows involves more than isolated commands—it is the synthesis of fundamental operations that enables proficient system interactions. The familiarity with cd, pwd, and ls sets the stage for deeper exploration into shell automations and network command utilities, ensuring that subsequent practices are built on a strong foundational understanding of navigating the Debian file system.

3.2. File Manipulation Commands

Manipulating files and directories is a fundamental skill for effective system management and automation in Debian. Building on the foundation of navigating the file system, this section delves into creating, deleting, and modifying files and directories using command-line utilities. Familiarity with these commands not only facilitates day-to-day tasks but also underpins more advanced system management and scripting techniques.

One of the simplest and most direct methods to create an empty file is through the touch command. When executed without additional parameters, touch updates the access and modification timestamps of the specified file. If the file does not exist, it is created. For instance:

```
touch newfile.txt
```

This command creates newfile.txt in the current directory. In scripting environments, touch is commonly used to ensure that a file exists before writing data to it, particularly when combined with redirection operators.

Creating directories is achieved with the mkdir command. Directories encapsulate files and subdirectories, thereby facilitating logical organization within the file system. The basic usage is:

```
mkdir new_directory
```

This command makes a new directory named `new_directory` in the current working directory. For creating nested directories where intermediate directories may not already exist, the -p flag proves advantageous:

```
mkdir -p parent_dir/child_dir/grandchild_dir
```

The -p option ensures that all necessary parent directories are created if they do not exist, simplifying the setup of complex directory structures.

Deleting files is performed using the `rm` command. Although straightforward, `rm` must be used with caution due to its irreversible nature. To remove a file, the command is:

```
rm file_to_delete.txt
```

For deletion of directories and their contents, the command requires the recursive flag -r. This flag causes `rm` to remove all files and subdirectories within the specified directory:

```
rm -r obsolete_directory
```

When combining with the -f flag for *force*, the command mitigates any interactive confirmations, thus permitting automated or scripted deletions:

```
rm -rf temp_directory
```

It is critical to verify the target directory and its contents before executing such powerful commands.

Renaming or moving files and directories is accomplished using the `mv` command. Its dual functionality allows users to either change the

89

name of a file or relocate it within the file system. For example, renaming a file is simple:

```
mv oldname.txt newname.txt
```

When moving a file into a different directory:

```
mv report.pdf /home/user/documents/
```

The mv command thus provides flexibility in managing file organization, whether for restructuring directories or updating naming conventions.

Copying files is handled by the cp command. Similar to mv, cp offers options for simple file duplication as well as recursive copying for directories. Copying a single file is executed as:

```
cp source.txt destination.txt
```

In scenarios where an entire directory, along with its contents, must be copied, recursion is enabled with the -r flag:

```
cp -r source_directory destination_directory
```

This command duplicates source_directory and all of its subdirectories and files into destination_directory. As with deletion, caution is advised when performing recursive operations to prevent unintentional overwrites.

Modifying files often involves text editing, which can be performed directly within the command line using editors such as nano or vim. While these commands extend the discussion into text editing utilities, understanding their invocation for file modification is essential. To open a file in nano, the command is:

```
nano file_to_edit.txt
```

Similarly, vim can be used for users who are comfortable with its mode-based editing system:

```
vim file_to_edit.txt
```

These editors facilitate direct changes within files, with `vim` offering advanced capabilities for regular expression search, substitution, and complex file manipulations.

File redirection and appending are instrumental in modifying file contents without opening an interactive editor. The redirection operator > overwrites existing file content, while >> appends new data. For example, to overwrite a file with new content:

```
echo "New content overwrites old content" > file.txt
```

Conversely, appending data to a file is accomplished with:

```
echo "Appended content" >> file.txt
```

These operations are integral in automating text modifications via scripts, such as logging events or updating configuration files.

Understanding file permissions is also crucial when modifying files and directories. The `chmod` command alters the permissions assigned to files or directories. For instance, to assign read, write, and execute permissions to the owner and read and execute to the group and others, one may use:

```
chmod 755 script.sh
```

The numerical representation of permissions (755 in this case) defines the access privileges. Additionally, changing ownership with `chown` may be necessary when managing multi-user environments:

```
chown user:group file.txt
```

Appropriate permission management ensures that files and directories can be modified by authorized users while preserving system security.

When developing scripts or automating tasks, combining these file manipulation commands into sequences enhances productivity and relia-bility. A practical example is maintaining a backup of critical configura-tion files. A script could combine copying files, appending time stamps, and organizing backups into dated folders:

```
#!/bin/bash
backup_dir="/backup/$(date +%F)"
mkdir -p "$backup_dir"
cp -r /etc "$backup_dir"
echo "Backup completed on $(date)" >> "$backup_dir/backup_log.txt"
```

In this script, the mkdir -p command creates a new backup directory with the current date, cp -r recursively copies the configuration di-rectory, and the echo command appends a log entry. This systematic approach to file manipulation demonstrates how multiple commands work together to achieve comprehensive administrative goals.

Advanced usage of these commands involves combining search opera-tions with manipulation tasks. For example, using find to locate files modified within a specific period and removing them, a command se-quence might be:

```
find /var/tmp -type f -mtime +30 -exec rm {} \;
```

Here, find searches for files in /var/tmp that have not been modified in over 30 days and deletes them. This integration of commands is powerful in maintenance routines such as cleaning up temporary files to free disk space or reduce clutter.

It is important to consistently verify operations performed by these commands. Viewing the results of file manipulations is facilitated by the ls command. For example, after creating a directory or copying files, listing the new structure ensures the intended changes have been made:

```
ls -l /path/to/directory
```

Furthermore, combining ls with -R for recursive listing provides a comprehensive tree view of a directory's structure:

```
ls -lR /path/to/directory
```

This verification step minimizes errors and provides confidence in the execution of file manipulation commands.

Modifying file contents can also be achieved via stream editors like sed or awk. Although these tools extend beyond basic file manipulation, they provide advanced means to modify large files without loading them fully into an interactive editor. A typical usage with sed might be:

```
sed -i 's/old_text/new_text/g' file.txt
```

This command replaces all occurrences of old_text with new_text directly within file.txt. The option -i specifies in-place editing, making sed an efficient option for systematic file modifications.

Investing time to understand these file manipulation commands enhances both manual operation and automated processes. The combination of creating, deleting, and modifying files and directories forms the backbone of system administration. Routine tasks such as backups, file archiving, and system cleanup become more efficient when these commands are employed with precision. The interplay of touch, mkdir, rm, mv, cp, and related utilities prepares users for more advanced operations, including scripting and process automation, which leverage command combinations to address complex administrative and developmental challenges.

Proficiency in these utilities forms the basis for a larger approach to system management that integrates navigation, editing, permission control, and automation. Daily tasks, such as monitoring file changes, updating configurations, and managing data storage, rely heavily on the precise execution of these commands. Users who master these file manipulation commands are better equipped to maintain system integrity and respond efficiently to operational challenges, ensuring that their systems remain robust and well-organized.

3.3. Using Text Editors

Command-line text editors serve as essential tools for editing configuration files, writing scripts, and quickly modifying documents in Debian. Building on earlier sections that discussed file manipulation and navigation, it is important to gain proficiency in editors such as Nano and Vim, which are widely available and vary significantly in design and functionality.

Nano is designed for simplicity and ease of use. It provides a straightforward editing environment with on-screen shortcuts that guide users through basic operations. When a file is opened in Nano by typing:

```
nano filename.txt
```

a screen is presented that displays the file content along with a list of common commands at the bottom. For instance, the shortcut ^O (Control-O) indicates how to save the file, while ^X (Control-X) is used to exit. This inline help makes Nano an excellent choice for users who are new to command-line editing. The interface minimizes distractions by displaying only the file contents and a simple command list, facilitating focused text modification.

Nano supports standard editing functions, such as cutting, copying, and pasting text. To cut a line, one can use ^K, and to paste it back, ^U is available. These operations are evident in the command menu, reducing the need for memorization. Nano also provides a search functionality that is invoked by the shortcut ^W. Entering a search query displays the first match and highlights it, thereby allowing users to quickly navigate to a particular section of the text.

94

The editor's configuration can be customized by modifying configuration files, such as /etc/nanorc or $HOME/.nanorc. Users can enable features like syntax highlighting and line numbering by editing these files. For example, adding the line:

```
set linenumbers
```

to the .nanorc file instructs Nano to display line numbers, which is particularly useful when debugging scripts or configuration files. This balance between functionality and simplicity has made Nano a standard tool in many Debian installations, especially in environments where ease of access and low overhead are prioritized.

In contrast, Vim is a modal text editor known for its efficiency and extensive feature set. Unlike Nano, Vim operates in multiple modes, the primary ones being Normal, Insert, and Visual. When starting Vim by executing:

```
vim filename.txt
```

the default mode is Normal, where keystrokes are interpreted as commands rather than direct text input. To insert text, one must switch to Insert mode by pressing i. In Insert mode, text entry behaves similarly to conventional editors until returning to Normal mode by pressing Esc. This modal system, although presenting a steeper learning curve initially, enables extensive customization and rapid command execution once mastered.

Vim provides powerful text manipulation capabilities. For example, in Normal mode, the command dd deletes an entire line, while yy (yank) copies the line into a buffer. The command p (paste) can then be used to insert the text at the desired location. These operations can be combined with counts to perform repetitive actions; for instance, 5dd deletes the next five lines, thereby improving productivity in large text files.

95

Navigation in Vim is optimized with keyboard shortcuts. The keys h, j, k, and l facilitate movement left, down, up, and right, respectively. Additional commands such as gg and G quickly transport the cursor to the beginning and end of the file. The combination of these navigation techniques supports efficient editing even in very large files. Vim's search functionality, invoked with / followed by a search pattern, allows for rapid location of specific text. For example, typing:

```
/pattern
```

searches forward for pattern and highlights the first occurrence. Pressing n continues the search in the same direction, providing a cohesive experience for sorting through extensive documents.

A key advantage of Vim lies in its deep extensibility and powerful command set. Users can define macros, customize key mappings, and utilize plugins to enhance functionality. The vimrc file, typically located in $HOME/.vimrc, serves as the configuration file where customization settings are stored. A common configuration might include enabling line numbering, syntax highlighting, and setting tabs to convert spaces:

```
set number
syntax on
set tabstop=4
set shiftwidth=4
set expandtab
```

These configurations optimize Vim for programming and system administration tasks, leading to a smoother editing experience. Additionally, many system administrators write and maintain scripts directly in Vim, benefiting from its robust text manipulation features.

Although Nano and Vim serve similar basic functions, their intended audiences differ. Nano is optimal for users seeking a lightweight and immediately accessible tool with minimal configuration requirements. In contrast, Vim is more suited for users who are willing to invest time in mastering its commands in exchange for advanced editing features.

Each editor has features that can be tailored to specific workflows. For instance, users dealing with quick edits and minor modifications may opt for Nano's simplicity, while those engaged in continuous editing of large codebases or configuration files might prefer Vim's efficiency.

Both Nano and Vim support features such as search and replace. In Nano, the combination ^\ (Control-Backslash) initiates a search and replace operation. The editor prompts for the text to be searched and the replacement text and, upon confirmation, applies changes throughout the document. In Vim, the search and replace command is executed in Normal mode using the command:

```
:%s/old_text/new_text/g
```

This command substitutes every occurrence of old_text with new_text across the entire file, controlled by the g flag for a global operation. These capabilities are especially useful in automated editing scenarios, where large-scale text modifications must be applied efficiently.

When discussing text editors in Debian, it is also important to consider contextual features like syntax highlighting and spell checking, which are common in both Nano and Vim. Syntax highlighting differentiates elements of text based on programming language or file type, thereby reducing syntax errors and improving readability. Vim generally excels in this area due to its extensive plugins and community-contributed scripts, though Nano also supports highlighting with appropriate configuration. Spell checking, while less common in command-line text editors than in graphical counterparts, can be integrated into Vim using plugins that point to system dictionaries, aiding in documentation editing.

Version control systems often integrate with text editors to streamline code review and commit processes. Vim, in particular, can be embedded within version control workflows. When editing commit messages with systems such as Git, Vim is frequently invoked as the default editor. This integration supports improved workflow consistency, allowing developers to edit, review, and commit changes without leaving the terminal environment. Nano can also be set as the default editor in version control systems, ensuring that a user's familiarity with simple text editing is maintained.

Advanced users of these editors often leverage macros or command sequences to automate routine editing tasks. In Vim, recording a macro is initiated with the q command followed by a register. For example, pressing:

```
qa
```

starts recording into register a. Commands executed afterward are stored until recording is stopped using q again. The macro can then be played back by entering:

```
@a
```

Such macros are invaluable for repetitive actions, such as formatting multiple lines of code or applying systematic modifications across a document.

Both Nano and Vim offer command history and undo/redo functions that further contribute to effective text editing. In Nano, each edit can be reversed with ^U after a cut operation or by using the undo feature if it is enabled through configuration. Vim includes an extensive undo tree that allows navigation through multiple changes. The command u undoes the most recent action, while Ctrl-R redoes an undone change. Advanced configurations enable persistent undo history by specifying a file to store the undo tree, thereby preserving changes across sessions.

Collaborative environments often require simultaneous editing and versioning of documents. In such scenarios, the choice of text editor can affect the fluidity of contributions. Vim's non-destructive editing and the ability to split windows allow users to work on multiple parts of a document concurrently. Splitting a window vertically can be done with:

```
:vs filename.txt
```

This command opens `filename.txt` in a split view, providing a means to compare files line by line or edit configuration files in concert. Nano, while more limited in window management, can still open multiple files in different terminal sessions or tabs, which is sufficient for simpler tasks.

Understanding the strengths and limitations of these text editors enables users to select the appropriate tool based on task complexity and personal proficiency. Nano's simplicity ensures that newcomers to the Debian environment can quickly adapt without encountering the steep learning curve associated with mode-based logic. Vim, on the other hand, offers a higher ceiling for efficiency that is well-suited for experienced users who require advanced editing capabilities, scripting, and integration with development tools.

The use of command-line text editors is not solely confined to manual file editing; they also serve as integral components in automation workflows. When embedded in scripts or integrated with configuration management tools, these editors facilitate bulk modifications and provide consistent output across different systems. Mastery over these tools inherently contributes to better system administration, as users are empowered to rapidly iterate over configuration files and source code in a controlled, predictable manner.

Command-line text editors, therefore, constitute a critical skill set for any Debian user, bridging the gap between simple file manipulation and advanced system customization.

3.4. Managing Processes

Process management is a critical aspect of system administration and performance tuning in Debian. The ability to view, control, and adjust running processes enables users to diagnose issues, optimize system resources, and automate routine tasks. Process management in Debian utilizes a spectrum of command-line tools that provide detailed information about active processes, allow for process termination, and enable dynamic control over process priority and execution.

At the foundation of process management is the ps command, which lists processes running on the system. By default, executing:

```
ps
```

displays processes associated with the current terminal session. For a more comprehensive view that includes processes from all sessions, the aux options are commonly used:

```
ps aux
```

This command outputs columns detailing the user, process ID (PID), CPU and memory usage, and the command used to initiate each process. The output serves as an immediate snapshot of the system's workload, providing administrators with crucial performance metrics for each process.

In addition to static snapshots provided by ps, dynamic monitoring tools such as top present a continuously updated view of processes. When top is run:

```
top
```

a terminal-based real-time display is shown where processes are sorted by CPU utilization by default. In top, interactive commands allow users to adjust sorting criteria—for instance, pressing M reorders processes by memory consumption. htop, an enhanced version of top, offers a user-friendly interface with color-coding and improved navigation. Although htop may require additional installation, its intuitive design facilitates tasks such as process selection and termination by simply moving a cursor to highlight the targeted process.

Understanding the concept of process identifiers (PIDs) is essential when managing processes. Commands like ps, top, and htop provide access to these identifiers, which are then used to send signals to processes. The kill command stands as the primary utility for terminating processes or sending other signals. For example, to gracefully terminate a process with a PID of 1234, one would use:

```
kill 1234
```

This command sends the default signal SIGTERM, requesting a process to terminate. In cases where a process does not respond to a termination request, a stronger signal such as SIGKILL can be issued:

```
kill -9 1234
```

Using -9 forces the termination and immediately stops the process, although it bypasses cleanup routines that a normal shutdown might perform.

Beyond singular processes, the killall and pkill commands provide mechanisms to broadcast signals based on process names or patterns. For instance, to terminate all instances of a service with the identifier firefox, the command is:

```
killall firefox
```

Alternatively, pkill allows for more flexible matching using regular expressions. For example:

```
pkill -f some_process_pattern
```

sends the termination signal to all processes matching the given pattern. Such commands are efficient in environments where multiple instances of a process exist and need to be managed collectively.

Managing processes also involves controlling the scheduling priority to optimize CPU allocation. The nice command launches processes with incremented niceness levels, which influence the process scheduler's decisions. A higher niceness value reduces the process's scheduling priority. For example:

```
nice -n 10 command_to_run
```

starts a process with a niceness of 10, ensuring that it receives proportionally less CPU time relative to processes with lower niceness values. Conversely, the renice command modifies the niceness of a running process. To adjust the priority of a process with PID 1234 to a niceness of -5 (requiring administrative privileges), one would execute:

```
renice -n -5 -p 1234
```

This dynamic adjustment is particularly useful in multitasking environments where process behavior must be tuned in real time to ensure system responsiveness.

Effective process management extends to job control and background execution. Many command-line tasks are executed in the foreground by default, thereby monopolizing the terminal session. Appending an ampersand (&) to a command launches it in the background:

```
long_running_command &
```

This allows the terminal to be available for additional commands while the background process continues its execution. Once running in the background, the jobs command lists these processes alongside information about their status—whether running, stopped, or completed. In scenarios where a background job has been suspended using Ctrl+Z, users can resume the process by entering:

```
bg
```

to continue in the background, or:

```
fg
```

to bring the job to the foreground. This job control mechanism is essential for juggling multiple tasks in an interactive shell and for managing long-running processes effectively.

Signals also play a central role in controlling process behavior beyond termination. For example, the SIGSTOP signal can suspend a process without terminating the communication channels or the state within the system. While SIGSTOP cannot be caught or ignored by a process, it informs the system that the process should be halted:

```
kill -SIGSTOP 1234
```

Subsequently, resuming the process is achieved by sending the SIGCONT signal:

```
kill -SIGCONT 1234
```

This approach is valuable when temporary suspension of resource-intensive tasks is necessary during periods of high system load.

For operations requiring in-depth process inspection, additional utilities such as pstree provide a hierarchical view of process relationships. Executing:

```
pstree -p
```

displays a tree-like diagram where each process is shown along with its PID, emphasizing parent-child relationships. This visualization aids in understanding process lineage and dependencies, which is fundamental when troubleshooting cascading failures or orphaned processes.

The management of processes in Debian is significantly enhanced by scripting. Automating process monitoring and control tasks can be achieved through shell scripts that integrate multiple command-line tools. For example, a script to monitor CPU-intensive processes and adjust their priority might be written as:

```
#!/bin/bash
for pid in $(ps aux | awk '$3>50 {print $2}'); do
    echo "Adjusting priority for process $pid"
    renice -n 10 -p $pid
done
```

In this snippet, ps aux and awk are used to filter processes exceeding a specified CPU usage threshold. The resulting process identifiers are then iterated over to lower their priority, thereby redistributing CPU resources to other tasks. Such automation is critical in high-load systems where manual intervention is impractical.

Developers and system administrators also leverage log file analysis in tandem with process management to diagnose issues. Logging outputs from commands like top or ps over time enables trend analysis and performance benchmarking. Redirecting the output of top to a file on a periodic basis via a cron job is one such strategy:

```
top -b -n 1 >> /var/log/top_snapshot.log
```

Here, the -b flag runs top in batch mode, and -n 1 specifies a single iteration. This data can be later analyzed to identify processes that consistently overuse system resources.

Another advanced tool is lsof (list open files), which provides insight into the files associated with active processes. Given that processes interact with files and network sockets, lsof reveals these relationships, often critical in debugging file descriptor leaks or resource contention. For instance, executing:

```
lsof -p 1234
```

lists all open files for the process with PID 1234, offering a comprehensive look at the process's interactions with system resources.

Process management in Debian is not static but requires continuous review, adjustment, and the application of best practices. System administrators must be vigilant in monitoring rogue processes, ensuring that resource allocation aligns with service-level agreements. Proper use of logging, monitoring utilities, and commands for process control helps maintain system stability, efficiency, and security. The techniques discussed here form an interconnected framework that combines real-time monitoring with automated control, granting users the flexibility to manage processes under a wide range of conditions.

Understanding these dynamic process management tools, including ps, top, htop, kill, renice, and others, is essential for successful system administration. Mastery of these tools, and their application through both manual commands and scripts, empowers users to maintain responsive and resource-efficient environments in Debian. The cumulative knowledge of process identification, signal handling, job control, and scheduling priorities supports a proactive approach to system management, ensuring that operations proceed smoothly even under varying workloads.

3.5. Basic Network Commands

Understanding network configuration and troubleshooting from the command line is essential for any Debian user. This section focuses on key network-related commands that allow administrators and users to inspect, configure, and debug network connections. Building on the skills developed previously in file manipulation and process management, these commands facilitate robust interaction with network interfaces and services.

One of the foundational tools for network configuration is the ip utility, which has largely supplanted older utilities such as ifconfig in modern Debian distributions. The ip addr command displays current network interface configurations, revealing critical details such as IP addresses, subnet masks, and interface status. For example, executing:

```
ip addr show
```

produces a detailed readout of each network interface, including logical interfaces such as loopback and physical interfaces like Ethernet or Wi-Fi. This output guides users in verifying that their interfaces are configured correctly and are up and running.

Configuration adjustments can also be managed using the ip command. To assign a new IP address to an interface temporarily, one might execute:

```
sudo ip addr add 192.168.1.100/24 dev eth0
```

This command attaches the IP address 192.168.1.100 with a subnet mask of /24 to the interface named eth0. Removing an IP address follows a similar pattern:

```
sudo ip addr del 192.168.1.100/24 dev eth0
```

These commands are invaluable in situations where a quick test or reconfiguration is required without modifying persistent configuration files.

Another crucial command is ip route, which displays the system's routing table. The routing table is fundamental in determining where network traffic is directed. By running:

```
ip route show
```

users can discern the default gateway, connected networks, and specific routes. To modify routes, administrators can add new routes or change the default gateway; for instance:

```
sudo ip route add default via 192.168.1.1
```

This command sets the default gateway to 192.168.1.1, directing packets with no specific route to this address.

For quickly verifying connectivity to remote hosts, the `ping` command is indispensable. By sending Internet Control Message Protocol (ICMP) echo requests, `ping` helps diagnose whether a host is reachable:

```
ping -c 4 www.example.com
```

The `-c 4` flag limits the command to four packets, allowing for a concise check of both network connectivity and latency. The output displays packet loss, round-trip times, and thus helps in identifying potential network congestion or connectivity issues.

Complementing `ping` is `traceroute` (or `tracepath` as an alternative on some systems), which maps the path that packets take to reach a destination. This tool breaks down each hop between the source and the destination and is useful in diagnosing routing problems:

```
traceroute www.example.com
```

The resulting output shows the IP addresses (or hostnames) of routers along the packet's path along with the time taken for each leg. Analyzing this information helps to pinpoint bottlenecks or misconfigured routers that may be causing delays.

The `netstat` utility, although being gradually replaced in some scenarios by `ss`, remains a powerful tool for monitoring network connections. When invoked as:

```
netstat -tulpn
```

the command outputs a list of active TCP and UDP connections along with the processes (PIDs) that are listening on specific ports. The options –t and –u filter TCP and UDP sockets respectively, while –l lists only listening sockets, –p shows the process identifier, and –n displays numerical addresses, avoiding DNS lookups that can delay the output.

For environments requiring more granular network statistics, the `ss` command provides similar functionality to `netstat` but with enhanced performance and options. For example:

```
ss -tulw
```

This command lists TCP and UDP listener sockets with additional information that may be needed for debugging port usage or identifying network service conflicts.

DNS resolution commands such as `nslookup` and `dig` are instrumental in verifying and diagnosing domain name system configurations. The command:

```
nslookup www.example.com
```

retrieves the IP address associated with the domain name, making it possible to confirm that DNS servers are returning correct responses. Similarly, `dig` provides a more detailed query breakdown:

```
dig www.example.com
```

The output from `dig` includes information about query time, authoritative answers, and additional DNS records, making it suitable for thorough DNS diagnostics.

File transfer and network communication also leverage command-line tools. The `curl` command is a versatile tool for interacting with HTTP, FTP, and other protocols. To fetch the content of a web page, one may use:

```
curl -v http://www.example.com
```

The `-v` flag triggers verbose mode, which prints detailed information about the request and response exchange. This is particularly useful for debugging web service endpoints or checking for proper server responses.

Similarly, wget serves as a command-line utility designed for non-interactive file downloads. By executing:

```
wget http://www.example.com/file.tar.gz
```

users can download files directly to the system. wget supports resumption of interrupted downloads and can be integrated into scripts for batch file downloads.

Remote connectivity to other machines, especially in server environments, is achieved with ssh. For example:

```
ssh user@remotehost
```

establishes a secure connection to the remote system, allowing for remote command execution and file management. The scp command, closely related to ssh, facilitates secure file transfers between the local and remote systems:

```
scp localfile.txt user@remotehost:/path/to/destination
```

These commands are essential in modern network administration where remote access and secure file transfers for configuration purposes are routine.

In scenarios where network configuration changes require persistence across reboots, Debian utilizes configuration files located in directories like /etc/network and /etc/NetworkManager. Editing these files directly using text editors discussed in previous sections (for example, with nano or vim) allows administrators to establish static IP configurations, define network bridges, or set up advanced routing rules. A typical configuration file entry for a static IP interface might appear as:

```
auto eth0
iface eth0 inet static
    address 192.168.1.100
    netmask 255.255.255.0
    gateway 192.168.1.1
```

Such configurations ensure that the network settings persist across system reboots and are a core part of configuring servers for production environments.

Firewall management and packet filtering are also integral aspects of network commands in Debian. The `iptables` utility provides command-line control over the Linux kernel firewall. For example, to list all current `iptables` rules, one would use:

```
sudo iptables -L -v -n
```

This command shows detailed statistics, such as packet counts and byte counts, for each rule in a concise format. More advanced configurations, including rules for NAT (Network Address Translation) and port forwarding, can also be defined with `iptables`, making it a versatile tool for network security and traffic management.

Troubleshooting connectivity issues may involve a combination of the aforementioned commands. For instance, if a web service is not reachable, an administrator might first verify network interface settings with `ip addr`, then check for active routes with `ip route`, and finally use `ping` or `curl` to validate external connectivity. Logging outputs using these utilities enables systematic diagnosis; combining commands in a script may periodically sample network statistics and alert administrators to anomalies:

```
#!/bin/bash
if ! ping -c 1 8.8.8.8 &>/dev/null; then
    echo "Network connectivity issue detected at $(date)" >> /var/log
    /network_issue.log
fi
```

This script monitors connectivity to a well-known public DNS server and logs any failures along with a timestamp, paving the way for automated network monitoring solutions.

Additionally, tools such as `ethtool` offer insights into the physical layer of network interfaces. Running:

```
sudo ethtool eth0
```

displays hardware-specific settings, such as speed, duplex mode, and link status. These diagnostics are useful when troubleshooting physical connectivity problems, verifying that hardware is operating at expected parameters, or checking for compatibility issues with newer network technologies.

The integration of these network commands within scripts and automated tasks is central to maintaining a secure and reliably connected system. Commands such as ip, ping, traceroute, netstat, ss, curl, and iptables collectively form a comprehensive toolkit for diagnosing and configuring network connections in Debian. Mastery of these commands not only enhances troubleshooting efficiencies but also prepares administrators to manage complex network configurations and respond to connectivity anomalies promptly.

In environments ranging from personal desktops to enterprise servers, leveraging command-line network utilities ensures rapid response to issues and contributes to overall system reliability. Continuous monitoring, configuration management, and the ability to automate routine network tasks create a proactive approach to system maintenance, yielding a resilient network architecture that supports the diverse needs of modern computing environments.

3.6.   Using Shell Operators and Redirection

The shell in Debian offers a powerful set of tools that allow the chaining of commands and the management of input/output streams. Mastery of shell operators and redirection techniques increases efficiency by reducing repetitive actions and enabling the automation of complex tasks. These operators manipulate the execution flow, combine outputs from multiple commands, and channel data between processes seamlessly.

At the most fundamental level, command chaining permits sequential execution of discrete commands. The semicolon operator (;) enables the execution of commands one after another regardless of the outcome of each individual command. For example, consider the following sequence:

```
echo "Starting process"; ls -l; echo "Process complete"
```

In this example, the echo command is executed to display a starting message, followed by a detailed list of directory contents via ls -l, and finally another message is printed. The semicolon ensures that each command runs in sequence without dependency on the success or failure of its predecessor.

Logical operators extend this concept by introducing conditional execution. The logical AND operator (&&) executes the subsequent command only if the preceding command succeeds. This is particularly useful when the execution of a subsequent command depends on the successful completion of the previous one. An illustration of this is:

```
mkdir new_folder && cd new_folder
```

Here, the cd command is executed only if mkdir new_folder completes successfully. Conversely, the logical OR operator (||) executes the following command only if the previous command fails. For example:

```
grep "pattern" file.txt || echo "Pattern not found"
```

In this scenario, if grep does not find the specified pattern, the shell will execute the echo command to indicate the absence of a match. Together, these conditional operators foster a responsive script or command-line session that adapts to each command's outcome.

Redirection is a versatile feature that manipulates the standard input (stdin), standard output (stdout), and standard error (stderr) streams of processes. The output redirection operator (>) directs the output of a command into a file, effectively overwriting its previous contents. For instance:

```
echo "This is a new file" > file.txt
```

This command writes the string, replacing any existing content in file.txt. If the goal is to preserve existing file content and append the new output, the append operator (>>) should be used:

```
echo "Appended text" >> file.txt
```

This subtle yet significant difference between > and >> allows for precise control over file content manipulation, which is essential in tasks such as logging and data aggregation.

Input redirection is equally critical. By using the operator (<), the shell can feed the content of a file as input to a command that typically reads from stdin. For example:

```
sort < unsorted_list.txt
```

This command reads data from unsorted_list.txt and sorts its contents. Combining input and output redirection in a single command further enhances productivity, as illustrated below:

```
sort < unsorted_list.txt > sorted_list.txt
```

This single line leverages redirection to both ingest data from a file and output the sorted result into another file, streamlining workflows that would otherwise require multiple steps.

Piping is a cornerstone feature of Unix-like systems. The pipe operator (|) transfers the stdout of one command directly into the stdin of another. This creates a chain of operations where each command performs a specific task on the data. For example:

```
ps aux | grep apache
```

In this chain, the output from ps aux is filtered by grep apache to display only those processes related to Apache. Piping is highly effective when dealing with large outputs that need real-time filtering or transformation. Multiple commands can be chained together using several pipes, such as:

```
cat logfile.log | grep "ERROR" | sort | uniq -c | sort -nr
```

Here, the content of a log file is first piped to grep to filter error messages, then sorted, aggregated by unique occurrences with counts, and finally sorted in numerical reverse order to highlight the most frequent errors. This multi-stage process underscores the flexibility and power of pipelines in transforming complex data streams.

Standard error redirection is an important yet often overlooked aspect. The standard error stream, identified as file descriptor 2, can be redirected independently of standard output. To combine both output streams, a common approach is:

```
command > output.log 2>&1
```

This command directs both standard output and standard error to output.log. Alternatively, testing error conditions may require separating them into distinct files:

```
command > output.log 2> error.log
```

By doing so, successful outputs are captured in one file while error messages are stored in another, simplifying the debugging process.

Command substitution is another powerful operator in shell scripting. It allows the output of a command to be used as an argument in another command. The syntax for command substitution can be achieved using either backticks or the preferred $() notation. For example:

114

```
current_dir=$(pwd)
echo "You are in: $current_dir"
```

In this instance, the shell substitutes the output of pwd into the variable current_dir before the echo command is executed. This feature is fundamental in creating dynamic scripts where the context influences the behavior of subsequent commands.

Grouping commands is also essential for managing more complex instructions. Parentheses (()) execute a group of commands in a subshell, isolating any changes in environment or directory context from the main shell session. For example:

```
(cd /tmp && ls) > tmp_listing.txt
```

In this command, the directory change to /tmp is confined to the subshell created by the parentheses. Once the commands inside the group are executed, the output of ls is redirected into tmp_listing.txt without affecting the current working directory of the main shell. Alternatively, curly braces ({}) allow multiple commands to be executed in the current shell:

```
{ echo "Start"; date; echo "End"; } > session_info.txt
```

Here, all three commands are executed in sequence within the same shell, and the output is captured in a single file.

Combining these operators enables the construction of more elaborate command sequences. Consider a scenario where an administrator needs to archive and compress log files while also documenting the operation:

```
tar -czf logs.tar.gz /var/log && echo "Archive created on $(date)" >>
    /var/log/archive.log
```

In this example, the tar command creates a compressed archive of the /var/log directory. Only upon successful completion, indicated by the use of &&, does the script append a timestamped message to an archive log file. This one-line command elegantly combines file archiving, compression, command chaining, and redirection.

Shell operators are critical in error handling and ensuring robustness in scripts. When writing scripts, it is often necessary to verify the success of preceding commands before executing subsequent ones. The use of && and || in tandem can create error-handling constructs. For example:

```
command && echo "Command succeeded" || echo "Command failed"
```

This construction ensures that feedback is provided based on the outcome of command. However, care must be taken as the use of both operators in one line may lead to unexpected behaviors if not structured correctly, especially when commands have complex interdependencies.

Pipe operators may also be combined with logical operators to generate scripts that can process data and conditionally handle errors based on output content. For example, if a file search via grep finds no matches, a fallback action can be triggered:

```
grep "search_term" file.txt | tee result.txt | wc -l | { read count;
    test "$count" -gt 0 && echo "Matches found" || echo "No matches
    found"; }
```

This compound command searches for a term in file.txt, duplicates the result into result.txt via tee, counts the number of matching lines, and then uses a grouping construct to read the count and conditionally output a message. The integration of pipes, command substitution, and conditional operators here demonstrates the depth of control the shell offers.

Another aspect of mastering shell operators is understanding their interplay with background processes. The ampersand (&) allows commands to run in the background, thereby freeing up the shell for other tasks while processes execute concurrently. For example:

116

```
long_running_task &
```

When combined with redirection, background processes can log outputs independently:

```
long_running_task > task_output.log 2>&1 &
```

This command runs `long_running_task` in the background while both its stdout and stderr are captured in `task_output.log`. Such patterns are indispensable when managing tasks on systems with concurrent workloads.

Advanced usages include chaining multiple redirection operators to form more sophisticated I/O management schemes. Process substitution, introduced with the syntax `<(command)`, enables the output of a command to be treated as a file. For instance:

```
diff <(sort file1.txt) <(sort file2.txt)
```

In this command, the sorted contents of `file1.txt` and `file2.txt` are compared using `diff` without needing to create temporary files. This not only simplifies the command structure but also enhances performance by minimizing disk I/O.

The ability to combine these various operators empowers users to perform complex operations with minimal code. Whether filtering data streams through pipes, redirecting outputs to log files, or managing conditional execution with logical operators, shell operators and redirection streamline many facets of system administration. The syntax may appear terse at first, but with practice, it becomes a concise language for expressing intricate workflows.

Understanding and applying these techniques is essential for users who seek efficiency and precision in the command-line environment. The operators discussed in this section form the backbone of many advanced scripts and one-liner commands that are routinely used by system administrators and developers alike. Through diligent practice, users will find that these tools can transform simple commands into robust, dynamic operations that significantly enhance productivity in Debian.

3.7. Introduction to Bash Shell Scripting

Bash scripting provides a method for automating repetitive tasks and extending command-line operations by consolidating multiple commands into a single file. Bash scripts supplement interactive command usage and enable system administrators and users to focus on higher-level tasks while the script handles routine operations. These scripts are text files containing a series of shell commands executed sequentially, and they often incorporate control structures, variable manipulation, and modular code structures to achieve complex behaviors with minimal user intervention.

A Bash script begins with a shebang line that designates the interpreter responsible for executing the script. This line is conventionally written as:

```
#!/bin/bash
```

Placing the shebang at the start of the file guarantees that the script is interpreted by Bash, regardless of the user's default shell environment. This practice contributes to predictable script behavior.

Comments in Bash scripts, introduced with the # symbol, are crucial for documentation. They offer insights into the purpose, logic, and specific behaviors of the script without affecting execution. For example:

```
#!/bin/bash
# This script performs a system backup and logs the operation.
```

Comments not only enhance maintainability but also facilitate collaboration when multiple administrators or developers review the code.

Variables in Bash are used to store data, such as strings, numbers, and command outputs, which can later be retrieved or manipulated. The syntax is straightforward, and variables are typically assigned without spaces around the equal sign:

```
backup_dir="/backup/$(date +%F)"
```

This example creates a variable `backup_dir` that incorporates the current date into its value. Variables can later be referenced by preceding their name with a dollar sign:

```
echo "Backup directory is set to \$backup_dir"
```

Using variables consistently not only prevents redundancy but also makes scripts easier to update.

The inclusion of control structures such as conditional statements and loops allows Bash scripts to react dynamically under varying circumstances. A common control structure is the `if` statement, which executes commands based on the evaluation of an expression. For instance:

```
if [ -d "$backup_dir" ]; then
    echo "Backup directory already exists."
else
    mkdir -p "$backup_dir"
    echo "Backup directory created."
fi
```

In this example, the script checks for the existence of a directory before attempting to create it, ensuring the script behaves correctly even if run multiple times.

Loops are similarly essential for managing repetitive tasks. The `for` loop iterates over a list of items, processing each element in turn. Consider a script section that processes multiple log files:

```
for logfile in /var/log/*.log; do
```

```
      echo "Archiving \$logfile"
      gzip "\$logfile"
done
```

This loop scans the /var/log directory for files ending with .log, compressing each one with gzip. The design of the loop removes the necessity for manual intervention when handling large numbers of files.

While the for loop is straightforward, the while loop also proves useful, especially when responding to data streams. For example, reading user input continuously until a specified termination condition is met can be achieved as follows:

```
echo "Enter text (type 'quit' to exit):"
while read line; do
    if [ "\$line" = "quit" ]; then
        break
    fi
    echo "You entered: \$line"
done
```

Such loops are instrumental in creating interactive scripts that take input from users or process command output iteratively.

Functions in Bash allow for the encapsulation of code into reusable modules. Defining a function helps break a script into manageable blocks, reducing redundancy and improving clarity. A typical function definition is illustrated below:

```
backup_files() {
    echo "Starting backup..."
    tar -czf "\$backup_dir/files_backup.tar.gz" /home/user/documents
    echo "Backup completed."
}
```

This function, backup_files, encapsulates the logic for archiving user documents. Later in the script, invoking the function is as simple as calling its name:

```
backup_files
```

120

Functions thus provide a means to reuse code segments, helping to maintain consistent behavior across different parts of a script.

Error handling is another important aspect of robust Bash scripting. By evaluating command exit statuses, scripts can gracefully handle failures and prevent cascading errors. The exit status of a command in Bash is represented by the $? variable immediately after a command runs. For instance:

```
tar -czf "\$backup_dir/archive.tar.gz" /etc
if [ \$? -eq 0 ]; then
    echo "Archive created successfully."
else
    echo "Error creating archive." >&2
fi
```

Alternatively, the logical operator && can be employed for a more concise form of error checking:

```
tar -czf "\$backup_dir/archive.tar.gz" /etc && echo "Archive created
    successfully." || echo "Error creating archive." >&2
```

This pattern succinctly combines command execution with conditional output, thereby improving script readability.

Bash scripting also leverages shell operators and redirection, concepts introduced earlier. Redirection operators allow a script to channel output to files or other commands. For example, logging the output of a script is achieved by appending redirection operators to commands:

```
echo "Backup started at \$(date)" >> "\$backup_dir/backup.log"
tar -czf "\$backup_dir/archive.tar.gz" /etc >> "\$backup_dir/backup.
    log" 2>&1
```

Here, both standard output and standard error from the tar command are directed into a log file, ensuring that any issues are recorded for later analysis.

In addition to standard utilities, Bash scripts often incorporate miscellaneous commands for dynamic functionality based on real-time system information. For instance, a script may be designed to monitor system disk usage and send alerts when usage exceeds a certain threshold:

```
#!/bin/bash
threshold=90
disk_usage=\$(df / | tail -1 | awk '{print \$5}' | sed 's/%//')
if [ "\$disk_usage" -gt "\$threshold" ]; then
    echo "Warning: Disk usage at \${disk_usage}\%."
else
    echo "Disk usage is under control at \${disk_usage}\%."
fi
```

In this example, the script uses a combination of df, tail, awk, and sed to extract the percentage of disk usage, comparing it against a predefined threshold. Such dynamic assessments automate monitoring tasks that otherwise require manual checks.

Bash scripting supports incorporating external configuration files to centralize information and simplify maintenance. Often, scripts source configuration files using the source command or the dot operator (.), which imports variables and functions defined in an external file:

```
#!/bin/bash
source /etc/my_script.conf
echo "Configuration loaded for backup directory: \$backup_dir"
```

This approach decouples configuration parameters from the script logic, making it easier for administrators to adapt scripts to various environments without altering the code directly.

Debugging Bash scripts is a vital part of the development process. Bash provides options such as -x to enable a trace of the script's execution. Running a script with:

```
bash -x myscript.sh
```

displays each command along with its arguments, thereby facilitating the identification of logic errors or syntax issues. Incorporating temporary debugging statements such as:

```
set -x
```

at the beginning of a problematic section can further help isolate issues by printing variable values and command outputs during execution.

Best practices in Bash scripting emphasize the importance of readability and maintainability. Consistent indentation, descriptive variable names, and thorough comments contribute significantly to the long-term usability of a script. Organizing code into well-defined functions and separating configuration from logic are additional measures that simplify future enhancements and troubleshooting.

A simple real-world example that combines many of these concepts is a Bash script designed to automate the backup of key system directories. Consider the following script:

```
#!/bin/bash
# Automated system backup script

# Set backup directory with current date
backup_dir="/backup/\$(date +%F)"
mkdir -p "\$backup_dir"

# Log the start of the backup
echo "Backup started at \$(date)" >> "\$backup_dir/backup.log"

# Function to backup a directory
backup_directory() {
    local dir_path=\$1
    local backup_name=\$(basename "\$dir_path")
    tar -czf "\$backup_dir/\${backup_name}.tar.gz" "\$dir_path"
    if [ \$? -eq 0 ]; then
        echo "Successfully backed up \$dir_path" >> "\$backup_dir/
     backup.log"
    else
        echo "Error backing up \$dir_path" >> "\$backup_dir/backup.
     log"
    fi
}

# Backup several important directories
backup_directory /etc
backup_directory /home
```

```
backup_directory /var/log

# Log the completion of the backup
echo "Backup completed at \$(date)" >> "\$backup_dir/backup.log"
```

This script demonstrates the use of functions, variable assignments, conditional checks, and redirection in a cohesive manner. By encapsulating backup operations within a function, the script reduces redundancy and simplifies error handling. Each command is logged with appropriate timestamps, ensuring a record of actions that can be referenced during troubleshooting.

Constructing and refining Bash scripts offers a pathway to enhanced efficiency in system administration tasks. Through the consolidation of routine commands into executable files, users can schedule tasks using cron, integrate complex logic into command-line workflows, and develop custom tools tailored to specific operational needs.

The transition from interactive command-line use to automated script execution represents a significant advancement in productivity and reliability. Embracing Bash scripting encourages a structured approach to problem-solving, where common tasks are automated, potential errors are managed gracefully, and overall system management becomes more predictable. In environments where repeated tasks are the norm, the skills gained from writing even simple Bash scripts build a foundation for more advanced scripting techniques and overall system optimization.

Chapter 4

Managing Software Packages with APT

This chapter details the use of APT for efficient software package management in Debian. It covers installing, removing, updating, and upgrading packages while ensuring dependency management. Users learn to search for packages and configure repositories, including adding third-party sources. Advanced topics include package locking and troubleshooting APT issues, empowering users to maintain a well-managed and up-to-date system environment.

4.1. Understanding APT and Package Management

The Advanced Packaging Tool (APT) is the cornerstone of software management in Debian-based systems. It streamlines the processes of software installation, upgrading, and removal by abstracting away the complexities of package dependency management and repository configuration. Building upon the foundational knowledge received in prior sections, this section delves into the internal workings of APT and examines how it contributes to an efficient and robust system management framework.

APT operates on a repository model, where packages are stored in remote or local repositories, and metadata about available software is maintained to inform package selection and dependency resolution. The primary configuration file, /etc/apt/sources.list, along with supplemental files in /etc/apt/sources.list.d/, defines which repositories APT consults. This separation ensures that packages come only from authenticated sources and that security risks are minimized. The metadata in these repositories includes package versions, dependencies, and the description of the package contents, which APT uses to construct a dependency graph for packages during installation or upgrading.

One primary advantage of APT is its ability to manage complex dependencies automatically. Before any package is installed, APT examines its dependencies to ensure that any required libraries or ancillary packages are also present. This prevents runtime errors that could occur when an application attempts to use a missing component. For example, when installing a text editor like nano, a simple command triggers a cascade of dependency checks and installations:

```
sudo apt-get install nano
```

APT begins by consulting its local package database, which is periodically updated using the following command:

```
sudo apt-get update
```

This synchronization process downloads the latest package lists from the configured repositories, ensuring that subsequent operations are carried out on the most current data available. The upgrade process then leverages this updated database to replace outdated packages with the newer versions, all while taking into account the intricate web of interdependencies.

An important feature of APT is its handling of package removal. When a package is no longer needed, APT not only removes the selected package but also computes which orphaned packages can be safely eliminated. This is particularly useful for removing libraries installed solely as dependencies for a package that has been uninstalled. The command to perform such housekeeping is:

```
sudo apt-get autoremove
```

This command mitigates the risk of leaving behind unnecessary files that could clutter the system, ensuring that the environment remains lean and efficient.

APT provides two levels of command interfaces: the traditional apt-get and the more user-friendly apt. Although these commands overlap in functionality, apt consolidates commands and output formats to make interaction more intuitive for new users. While the underlying mechanisms remain the same, this interface improvement contributes to both system administration efficiency and the reduction of the learning curve for newcomers.

The dependency resolution mechanism within APT relies on a precise algorithm that identifies necessary packages and conflicts by examining various metadata files stored locally in the directory /var/lib/apt/lists/. These files, refreshed during the update process, contain detailed package indices and ensure that each package installation is executed with the correct versions and associated dependencies. The algorithm compares candidate packages with those already installed, ensuring that version changes are managed correctly, and handles pre- and post-installation scripts that configure packages according to system requirements.

In addition to handling dependencies, APT verifies the integrity and authenticity of packages through cryptographic signatures associated with repository metadata. This is achieved by using public key infrastructure mechanisms; repository maintainers sign their metadata and packages, and APT checks these signatures against a trusted list of keys stored locally. This process is critical in protecting the system from inadvertent installation of tampered or malicious software. If the signatures do not match, APT will refuse to install or update the package, thereby preserving the integrity of the software ecosystem.

APT also supports a caching mechanism that stores packages in a local repository cache, typically found in the directory `/var/cache/apt/archives/`. This mechanism reduces redundant downloads for packages that are frequently installed or reinstalled, optimizing the operation of package management functions, especially in environments where bandwidth is a concern. The cache can be manually cleaned or configured to discard old packages after successful operations to maintain system hygiene.

Another nuanced aspect of APT is its flexibility in handling repository prioritization. Through the use of pinning, system administrators can assign priorities to packages from different repositories. This feature is particularly useful in situations where packages from experimental or third-party repositories might otherwise interfere with system stability. The pinning mechanism is specified in configuration files under `/etc/apt/preferences.d/`, where package versions can be assigned specific priorities, influencing which version is preferred during installations or upgrades. An example configuration snippet might appear as follows:

```
Package: *
Pin: release a=stable
Pin-Priority: 900

Package: *
Pin: release a=unstable
```

```
Pin-Priority: 300
```

This configuration ensures that stable repository packages are favored over those from unstable repositories, unless explicitly requested, thereby maintaining overall system reliability.

APT's design also accommodates the need for non-interactive environments, such as automated scripts or provisioning systems. The tool can be operated in a fully automated mode by using specific command flags to suppress interactive prompts. For instance, the following command demonstrates how to install a package without needing manual confirmation:

```
sudo apt-get install -y curl
```

This non-interactive installation is particularly useful when scripts are deployed during system provisioning or when managing multiple systems simultaneously.

The modularity and extensibility of APT have led to its adoption in numerous derivative distributions, making it a fundamental tool within the Linux ecosystem. Its capacity to combine a robust dependency resolution engine with secure package verification, flexible configuration options, and support for automated system management renders it a pivotal asset in modern system administration. The integration of these features simplifies the otherwise intricate process of maintaining an up-to-date and secure operating system.

APT's structured approach is further bolstered by its ability to integrate alternative sources of software. This is evident in the handling of personal package archives (PPAs) and third-party repositories, which, when properly configured and authenticated, provide users and administrators access to a broader range of software than those available in the default repositories. Proper care must be taken when adding these repositories, as improper configuration can lead to conflicts or potential security issues. The process involves appending repository information to /etc/apt/sources.list or placing a dedicated file within /etc/apt/sources.list.d/ followed by a subsequent update. For instance, to add a repository, one might execute the following:

```
echo "deb http://example.com/debian stable main" | sudo tee /etc/apt/
    sources.list.d/example.list
sudo apt-get update
```

This procedure illustrates the ease with which new sources can be incorporated into the system, while APT's internal consistency checks further ensure that only valid and verified packages are considered for installation.

Central to the philosophy of APT is its emphasis on ensuring system stability without sacrificing the ease of package management. The systemic checks, from verifying signatures to resolving dependencies, contribute to creating a reliable operational environment that is resistant to common pitfalls such as dependency hell. Users and administrators benefit structurally from a system that not only simplifies package management tasks but also inherently incorporates measures to prevent the propagation of errors through its tightly integrated framework.

APT therefore represents a paradigm in system administration by embodying principles of modularity, automation, and security. Its comprehensive design addresses both the needs of novice users who benefit from its simplified command interfaces and that of expert administrators who require granular control over package sources, priorities, and dependencies. The ability to manage packages seamlessly with minimal manual intervention demonstrates APT's effectiveness in handling the complex requirements of software management in modern Debian systems.

By leveraging the full spectrum of APT features—from simple installation commands to advanced configuration for repository pinning and non-interactive operations—the tool empowers system administrators to maintain robust, secure, and well-organized environments. Its adoption and continuous evolution underscore the importance of having an intelligently designed package management system that can adapt to diverse operational requirements and evolving software landscapes.

4.2. Installing and Removing Packages

APT offers a robust framework for installing and removing software packages while automatically managing dependencies that applications require. This section expands upon previous discussions of APT's internal architecture by focusing on the practical operations of package installation and removal. These operations ensure that a Debian-based system remains consistent in functionality and minimizes the common issues associated with unmet dependencies.

When installing a package, APT performs several critical tasks. Primarily, it analyzes the package metadata to determine the required libraries and supporting software components. This dependency resolution is crucial, as it guarantees that every application has access to the necessary system resources without manual intervention. For example, installing a common package like `curl` triggers APT to check for any dependencies related to networking libraries and SSL protocols. The process is initiated via the command:

```
sudo apt-get install curl
```

Upon execution, APT queries the locally cached package database, constructs a dependency tree, and schedules the installation of both the requested package and its associated libraries. This tree ensures that the configuration of a package is complete and that all referenced components are available in compatible versions.

APT's capability to resolve dependencies reduces the likelihood of the so-called "dependency hell," a common problem in software environments where interdependent packages may conflict. By automatically managing dependencies, APT alleviates the administrator from the burden of manual dependency tracking. This mechanism is particularly vital in large-scale deployments where manual oversight is impractical. The automated resolution process saves time and prevents installation failures, ensuring that the system remains stable and fully functional.

In addition to installing packages individually, administrators often need to install multiple packages simultaneously. APT accommodates this requirement by allowing several package names to be listed in a single command. For example, to install both curl and wget concurrently, one may use:

```
sudo apt-get install curl wget
```

APT processes the list as a whole, analyzing the combined dependencies and resolving any common requirements only once. This efficiency enhances system performance and reduces redundant operations.

APT also supports the usage of more modern command syntaxes and enhanced output. The apt command, which provides a simplified interface for common tasks, is functionally equivalent to apt-get for most package management tasks. The modern syntax can sometimes be clearer for new users, as it consolidates command options and provides more user-friendly feedback. An example using the apt command is as follows:

```
sudo apt install curl
```

Beyond the standard installation, there are alternatives and options within the installation process that cater to varying administrative needs. For instance, the flag -y can be appended to the installation command to automatically provide confirmation for the installation process, making it suitable for scripted or automated operations.

```
sudo apt-get install -y curl
```

Non-interactive installations are critical in environments where human interaction is impractical, such as automated provisioning systems or continuous deployment pipelines. These scenarios rely on APT's ability to operate without interactive prompts, ensuring that installations proceed without pause or error.

Removing packages is handled with a similar set of precautions as installation. The removal process is designed to deconstruct the dependency structure established during the installation. When an application is no longer required, it is essential to remove it in a manner that does not compromise the dependencies of other packages. The basic removal command is:

```
sudo apt-get remove curl
```

This command uninstalls the selected package while preserving its configuration files. In circumstances where a complete clean-up is required—removing both the package and its configuration files—the following command can be used:

```
sudo apt-get purge curl
```

The purge option ensures that residual configuration files, which might factor into future package conflicts or misconfigurations, are eradicated.

A notable feature inherent to APT's package removal process is its aptitude to recognize dependencies that were installed as a consequence of installing the removed package. These dependencies, often not required by any other software, are considered orphaned packages. APT provides a specific command to clean up these additional packages:

```
sudo apt-get autoremove
```

This command traverses the dependency graph to identify and remove

133

orphaned packages. By doing so, the system avoids unnecessary consumption of disk space and potential software conflicts that could arise from outdated or redundant packages lingering in the repository.

When confronting package removal, administrators may also encounter situations where dependencies are not in a clean state. For example, if a package removal breaks another package's dependency chain, APT will typically abort the process until the administrator addresses the conflict. In such cases, manual intervention is required to either adjust the dependency list or reinstall necessary packages. One common remedial action is to attempt a configuration fix using:

```
sudo dpkg --configure -a
```

This command instructs the package management system to configure all unpacked but unconfigured packages, thereby resolving interrupted or incomplete installations that might interfere with subsequent operations.

APT also integrates well with higher-level package management workflows. For example, when a system upgrade is prepared, a package's removal may be coordinated with the installation of a newer version, ensuring that dependencies match the system's current state. An administrator can combine removal and installation within a single command to handle such transitional states, streamlining the upgrade process.

The flexibility of APT in handling complex operations stems from its detailed logging and output mechanism. During installation and removal, APT provides verbose output that can be redirected to log files for later analysis. This feature is especially useful when troubleshooting installation failures or dependency conflicts. An example of capturing output on an installation operation is:

```
sudo apt-get install curl 2>&1 | tee install.log
```

Such logging practices help ensure that administrators have historical data that can diagnose issues, thus improving the overall reliability of system maintenance operations.

For users managing systems with specific package version require-ments, APT provides fine-grained controls such as holding and lock-ing packages. With these mechanisms, an administrator can prevent undesired upgrades that might otherwise introduce incompatibilities or instability. Even though these operations extend beyond simple in-stallation and removal, they are inherently tied to the command struc-ture discussed in this section. The commands to hold a package are designed to signal to APT that certain packages should not be automat-ically updated during a system upgrade, thus preserving a known good state.

Error handling is an important aspect of both installation and removal procedures. APT is equipped with built-in checks that prompt the user if a command might disrupt system stability. For instance, if a package is core to the system and its removal might trigger a cascade of depen-dency issues, APT outputs a warning detailing the potential impact. In such cases, a careful review of the planned operation is critical before confirming the command.

APT also interacts with the dpkg system, serving as a higher level in-terface. While dpkg operates at the level of individual packages, APT's integration with dpkg allows for comprehensive actions that span mul-tiple interdependent packages. This hierarchical relationship between APT and dpkg is central to the overall reliability of the Debian package management system. Should an error arise during an installation—such as a misconfiguration or interrupted operation—APT defers to dpkg for low-level operations and provides the necessary tools for cor-rective actions.

In practice, consistent use of APT for both installation and removal contributes to a system that remains consistent, verifiable, and secure. Its automated dependency management relieves administrators from manual resolution of complex relationships between packages, thereby reducing the risk of inadvertently breaking system functionality. Whether in the context of a personal workstation or a large-scale server environment, the principles governing APT's installation and removal operations are indispensable for maintaining operational integrity.

Both routine package installation and strategic package removal form the basis of effective system administration. They preserve the delicate balance between software utility and system stability. This balance is achieved through intelligent defaults, automated checks, and extensive configurability—all of which are embodied in the behavior of APT. By leveraging these mechanisms appropriately, system administrators can significantly reduce maintenance overhead while ensuring that their systems remain both secure and efficient.

The thoughtful design of APT, combining ease of use with powerful automation, transforms the process of package management into a streamlined and error-resistant activity. Administrators who master these operations not only enhance system performance but also safeguard against the inadvertent introduction of vulnerabilities or redundant components. Such expertise in installing and removing packages is therefore central to realizing the full potential of Debian-based systems in varied operational environments.

4.3. Updating and Upgrading Software

Maintaining an up-to-date system is critical for ensuring that software packages contain the latest features, performance improvements, and essential security patches. The Advanced Package Tool (APT) offers a suite of commands that facilitate frequent updates and robust upgrades. This section details the underlying processes, best practices, and command-line tools used for updating repository data, upgrading installed packages, and addressing security patches with precision.

The primary command for refreshing the package database is apt update. This command downloads the latest package information from repositories configured in the system. The downloaded metadata includes package versions, dependencies, and security updates. It is important to understand that the command does not alter installed packages; rather, it synchronizes the local package state with the remote repositories. This operation is essential prior to any upgrade procedure to ensure that decisions are made based on the most recent data.

```
sudo apt update
```

After running apt update, the system's local cache is refreshed. This cache provides the necessary reference against which upgrade actions are determined. Reviewing the output of the update process is advisable since it often includes information about repository changes, potential issues with certain sources, or warnings regarding outdated repository keys. Should any discrepancies or errors be observed, it is recommended to correct the repository configuration.

Upgrading installed packages is typically achieved with the command apt upgrade. This command examines the stored data from the update step and determines which packages have new versions available. When executed, APT downloads and installs the updated packages while respecting dependency constraints. The upgrade process is designed to replace only the files of packages already installed, without removing or installing new packages that might be introduced by dependencies. This conservative approach minimizes the changes applied to the system and reduces the risk of unexpected behavior.

```
sudo apt upgrade
```

A critical aspect of performing an upgrade is understanding the difference between apt upgrade and apt full-upgrade (or its equivalent, apt-get dist-upgrade). The apt full-upgrade command goes further by managing dependency changes that require the removal of obsolete packages or the installation of additional packages. This contrast emphasizes that while apt upgrade is typically sufficient for routine updates, the full-upgrade option is necessary when significant changes in package dependencies are expected, often as a result of larger distribution updates or major software version changes.

```
sudo apt full-upgrade
```

Careful reading of the command-line feedback during both upgrade and full-upgrade cycles is paramount. APT clearly indicates if the process would remove, install, or upgrade certain packages, providing users the opportunity to review and confirm these changes. This transparency helps prevent inadvertent modifications that might lead to system instability.

APT also enables the selection of specific packages for upgrades, allowing administrators to focus on critical software components. For example, to update only the security patches for a given package, a user might list details about available updates and manually trigger a selective upgrade. Although this functionality requires more direct intervention, it reinforces the importance of technically managing software environments, particularly when security is of utmost concern.

APT's security mechanisms further complement the update process by enforcing cryptographic signature verification. Each package repository is generally signed using GnuPG keys, helping to ensure that only authentic packages are installed. Should the update process reveal issues with missing or outdated keys, an administrator must retrieve and install updated repository keys from trusted sources. Following these protocols reinforces the system's security posture by preventing the installation of unverified software.

Automation can play a valuable role in sustaining system reliability. For systems that require frequent updates, implementing automated scripts or cron jobs to periodically execute the update and upgrade commands mitigates the risk of overlooking critical patches. Attention must be paid to configuration, logging, and error handling. These scheduled operations provide a consistent update routine, especially in enterprise environments. The example below illustrates a simple cron job entry that performs an automatic update every day at 2 AM:

```
0 2 * * * /usr/bin/sudo /usr/bin/apt update && /usr/bin/sudo /usr/bin
    /apt upgrade -y
```

In configuring such automatic actions, the use of the -y flag with apt upgrade is common as it bypasses user confirmation. While convenient, this practice should be adopted with caution because automatic approval may inadvertently accept unwanted changes if issues arise with repository configurations or package conflicts. Logging results from these automated tasks is recommended to allow periodic review and troubleshooting.

Security patches represent a special category of updates aimed at mitigating vulnerabilities. Keeping systems updated against known security vulnerabilities is a best practice supported by APT through timely updates. Advanced system administrators often integrate security-focused repositories or verify patches through dedicated tools that monitor vulnerability databases. In many cases, the policies governing system maintenance prioritize the immediate application of security patches over feature updates, thereby aligning the upgrade procedures with organizational security standards.

APT can also be combined with additional options that help in verifying system health during the upgrade process. For instance, performing a simulation using the --simulate flag allows users to preview the outcome of an upgrade operation without making any changes to the system. The simulation feature is particularly useful for diagnosing potential issues and for planning maintenance on critical servers where downtime is expensive.

```
sudo apt upgrade --simulate
```

Another useful diagnostic tool is the apt list --upgradable command, which provides a concise list of packages that have newer versions available. This output enables administrators to quickly assess the scope of pending upgrades. The information serves as a checklist to ensure that all important security and functionality updates are accounted for.

```
sudo apt list --upgradable
```

Managing pending upgrades also includes strategies for handling packages with fixed versions. In scenarios where a specific package must remain at a determined version due to compatibility reasons, administrators can place a hold on that package. This procedure prevents the automated process from upgrading it when running standard commands. The syntax for placing a hold is straightforward and integrates well into the broader update strategy. Once the hold is no longer needed, it can be removed to allow normal upgrade procedures.

During the upgrade phase, it is common to encounter problems related to broken dependencies or conflicts between packages. APT is equipped to handle many of these cases, and it provides detailed error messages that indicate the source of the conflict. In such scenarios, it is advisable to attempt a correction using the apt --fix-broken install command, which addresses dependency issues by reconfiguring the package system to resolve conflicts. This troubleshooting step is vital to maintain system integrity and ensure consistent package behavior.

```
sudo apt --fix-broken install
```

Understanding the nuances of package priorities, release cycles, and repository configurations further enhances the upgrade strategy. Systems managed under long-term support (LTS) releases often receive backported security fixes without a complete package version upgrade. Such policies ensure that critical security footprints are addressed while preserving overall system stability. Likewise, administrators overseeing systems with rolling releases might observe frequent package changes and more aggressive upgrade paths, which demand diligent review of package logs and configuration settings.

For environments that face complex upgrade requirements, such as systems heavily modified from their default state or those with specialized repositories, maintaining detailed logs during update and upgrade cycles is crucial. These logs offer historical context and pave the way for troubleshooting when discrepancies arise between expected and actual system states. Integrating these logs with centralized monitoring systems can further streamline the process, ensuring that any inconsistencies are flagged for immediate review.

The procedures discussed reinforce the significance of a methodical and informed approach to system maintenance. By leveraging the capabilities of APT, users gain granular control over both standard updates and more significant system upgrades. The combination of simulation, logging, and differential upgrade strategies forms the foundation of an effective maintenance routine designed to align with both operational requirements and security standards.

This focused assessment of system update and upgrade processes emphasizes the imperative nature of staying current with package repositories. Routine execution of these mechanisms, supported by proper diagnostic and automation tools, minimizes vulnerability exposure while enhancing system performance and reliability.

4.4. Searching for Packages

The ability to search for packages is critical for managing system software efficiently in Debian. Mastery of package search techniques empowers users to locate exactly the software they require, whether it be new applications, libraries, or system utilities. This section details various command-line tools and strategies for searching within Debian repositories, building upon prior discussions regarding package installation and repository management.

APT provides several commands designed to search for packages. The apt search command is one of the primary tools available. When executed, it scans the local package cache for names and descriptions that match a provided search pattern. The search functionality supports a wide range of queries, including simple keywords and more complex regular expressions. This command not only enhances discoverability but also offers a quick method to verify the availability of software before proceeding with an installation.

```
sudo apt update     % Ensure the local package database is current
apt search editor
```

In this example, the search query editor returns results from packages with the word in their name or description. The output typically includes package names, brief descriptions, and version details. Analyzing this output can help users decide if a package meets their needs.

Another widely used command is apt-cache search. Although similar to apt search, apt-cache search is part of the underlying APT utilities designed to directly query the package cache. It is particularly useful when a more granular search is required, as it returns a list of candidate packages along with a concise summary of each package's functionality.

```
apt-cache search web server
```

142

The two commands apt search and apt-cache search complement each other. Although both methods scan the package cache, the output format of apt search is generally more modern and may incorporate color coding and additional formatting improvements, making it easier to read and analyze.

Often, users require more detailed information regarding a package beyond its basic description. The apt show command fulfills this need by displaying comprehensive package metadata. Running apt show with the package name provides details such as version number, dependencies, maintainers, and a full description. This information is critical for understanding the implications of installing or upgrading a package and facilitates informed decision-making regarding system configuration.

```
apt show nano
```

Another useful command in the package search arsenal is apt list. When used with the --installed flag, the command lists all packages currently installed on the system. Conversely, when executed without filtering options, it can display available packages including potential updates. Combining apt list with piping and command-line filtering utilities such as grep allows users to perform refined searches.

```
apt list --installed | grep lib
```

Using common shell functionalities like pipelining and regular expressions enhances the versatility of package searches. For example, combining apt search with grep offers advanced filtering beyond what APT commands provide by default.

```
apt search python | grep -i "django"
```

The combination of native APT commands and shell utilities provides significant flexibility. For users who regularly need to search for packages, creating useful aliases in the shell configuration can streamline the process. For example, placing an alias in the $HOME/.bashrc file can reduce repetitive typing and simplify package searches.

```
alias psearch='apt search'
```

After adding this alias, invoking psearch in the terminal replicates the behavior of apt search. Customizing shell environments in this manner is a common practice among system administrators to improve efficiency when managing packages.

In addition to these command-line tools, understanding package naming conventions and metadata is crucial for effective searching. Debian packages are often named in a manner that reflects their functionality. For instance, package names that begin with lib tend to be libraries, while names that include -dev indicate development-related packages. Recognizing these conventions facilitates more targeted searches. A user might search for a development library by combining these naming patterns in their query:

```
apt search libxml2 | grep dev
```

Exploring the available options in depth highlights additional command-line switches that refine package searches. The -n or --names-only option for the apt search command limits results to package names, omitting descriptions. This narrower output is beneficial in environments where only the package identifier is required for further processing or scripting.

Subtle differences between apt search and apt-cache search also warrant attention. While apt search benefits from the latest enhancements in the APT ecosystem, apt-cache search remains an important tool in scenarios where legacy scripts or environments are in use. Understanding both commands provides resilience and flexibility when working across different Debian releases and system configurations.

Another scenario encountered in package management involves

searching for packages based on their installation status. The command dpkg-query -l offers a systematic method for listing installed packages, thereby supporting maintenance tasks that ensure system integrity. Using this command in combination with regular expressions or additional filtering tools further refines the output. For instance, an administrator might search for all packages from a particular vendor or repository, which is instrumental in troubleshooting or performing targeted upgrades.

```
dpkg-query -l | grep firefox
```

Beyond simple searches, advanced users may need to verify the installation source and candidate version for a package. The apt policy command is designed to display detailed repository information for a given package, such as the installed version, available versions, and priority scores assigned by APT. This output is particularly valuable when discrepancies between expected and actual package versions occur, as it reveals the influence of pinning or repository configurations.

```
apt policy curl
```

The command reveals which repository provides the latest version and indicates if the package is pinned to a particular version. Such detailed scrutiny enables administrators to manage complex software environments where package versions are tightly controlled for compatibility or security reasons.

Exploring package metadata is further enhanced by the integration of search commands into scripts. Automated routines can parse output from apt search, apt show, and apt policy to maintain system consistency or perform scheduled audits of installed software. For example, a custom script might automatically verify that all installed packages are at the recommended version, flagging any discrepancies for manual review. Integrating logging mechanisms in these scripts ensures that any anomalies are documented for later analysis.

Utilizing APT's robust search capabilities requires a methodical approach. Users must exercise care to interpret results accurately, paying close attention to package names, version numbers, and descriptions. The decision to install a package is not solely based on its availability, but also on a comprehensive understanding of its dependencies, repository source, and potential impacts on system stability. In this respect, commands such as `apt show` and `apt policy` serve as indispensable tools when making informed installation choices.

Even as the toolset evolves, the fundamental principles of searching for packages remain consistent. Familiarity with these core commands, combined with an understanding of shell-based utilities, equips users to navigate the Debian repository with confidence. Through regular practice and thoughtful customization of search parameters, administrators and users alike can reduce troubleshooting time and maintain system integrity.

Integrating these search techniques into everyday operations also prepares users for more complex package management tasks. Frequent use of these commands instills best practices, such as updating the package cache before conducting a search to ensure that the data reflects the most recent repository state. Moreover, combining multiple search commands builds a layered understanding of available options, enabling precise control over software discovery.

The continuity between package searching, installation, updating, and other management tasks reinforces a systematic approach to maintaining a Debian system. As users progress in their familiarity with APT and associated tools, the ability to efficiently search for, review, and analyze packages translates into enhanced system performance and security. The coherent integration of these techniques, supported by reliable command-line tools and shell customizations, forms a comprehensive framework for effective package management in Debian environments.

4.5. Working with Package Repositories

APT repositories constitute the backbone of Debian's package management, defining the sources from which software packages, security patches, and updates are retrieved. Understanding the configuration and management of these repositories is essential for customizing the system's software landscape, incorporating third-party packages, and ensuring secure delivery of updates. Repositories are typically defined in configuration files located in /etc/apt/sources.list and in the /etc/apt/sources.list.d/ directory, where each line specifies a component of the repository including its type, URI, distribution, and sections.

In the default configuration file /etc/apt/sources.list, repository entries follow a clear syntax. Each entry begins with the type field, for example, deb for binary packages and deb-src for source packages. The subsequent fields indicate the repository server's URI, the distribution (which often reflects the Debian codename), and the package sections (such as main, contrib, non-free). An example entry might appear as follows:

```
deb http://deb.debian.org/debian bullseye main contrib non-free
```

Adding new repositories involves appending similar entries either directly to /etc/apt/sources.list or as separate files within the /etc/apt/sources.list.d/ directory. The latter method is preferred for modularity and ease of management. For instance, to add a third-party repository that provides bleeding-edge software not available in the official distribution, one would create a new file with a descriptive name. A repository file might start with the following content:

```
deb http://example.com/debian stable main
```

After adding the repository configuration, it is imperative to update the package cache using the apt update command. This operation synchronizes the local cache with the package lists defined in the new repository entry, allowing new or updated packages to be discovered.

Handling repository keys is another critical aspect of repository management. Repositories are signed using cryptographic keys to ensure that the packages they provide have not been tampered with. Traditionally, the apt-key command was used to import public keys associated with repositories. However, modern practices recommend placing key files in the /etc/apt/trusted.gpg.d/ directory to improve security and management. An administrator may download the key and add it as follows:

```
wget -qO - https://example.com/repo-key.gpg | sudo tee /etc/apt/
    trusted.gpg.d/example.gpg
```

This command uses wget to retrieve the repository key, which is then piped into tee to save it in the trusted key directory. The presence of a trusted key reassures APT that packages from the repository are valid and have been verified by the provider. Errors related to repository keys during the apt update stage are indicative of either expired keys or misconfigured repositories, so frequent validation of these keys is important.

Advanced repository configuration may involve setting specific options to control package selection. One such option is repository pinning, which allows administrators to prioritize specific repositories or restrict upgrades from certain sources. The configuration for pinning is maintained in the file /etc/apt/preferences or within files inside /etc/apt/preferences.d/. A sample pinning configuration is illustrated below:

```
Package: *
Pin: origin "deb.debian.org"
Pin-Priority: 900

Package: *
Pin: origin "example.com"
Pin-Priority: 400
```

In this configuration, packages originating from deb.debian.org are assigned a higher priority than those from a third-party repository at example.com. Pinning ensures that the system adheres to preferred sources for updates, while still allowing installation of packages from alternative sources if explicitly requested.

Another facet of repository management involves dealing with repository components designed to offer source code. While binary packages are typically the focus of system administrators, source repositories are fundamental for developers and those wishing to compile applications from source. Enabling or disabling these source repositories is as simple as commenting or uncommenting the respective deb-src entries in the repository configuration file. As such, maintaining consistency between binary and source entries is advisable when both forms of package distribution are relevant.

The ability to add third-party repositories expands the breadth of available software beyond what the official Debian repositories offer. When incorporating a third-party source, it is crucial to verify the reliability of the source. Integrating official PPAs (Personal Package Archives) or repositories maintained by known vendors minimizes risks associated with untrusted software. Before adding any third-party repository, administrators should review the repository's documentation, check for security advisories, and ensure that the provided GPG keys correspond to the expected signer.

APT repositories can also be temporarily disabled without removing their configuration entries. This is particularly useful during troubleshooting or when there is a need to restrict updates from a specific source for an interval of time. Disabling a repository can be achieved by commenting out the relevant line in the configuration file. For example, using a text editor, an administrator may insert a # at the beginning of the line as follows:

```
# deb http://example.com/debian stable main
```

Following modifications to repository configurations, running apt update is necessary to refresh the local package cache and apply the updated repository settings.

In enterprise or multi-user environments, managing repositories with care is essential for compliance and controlled updates. System automation tools and configuration management systems often maintain repository configuration files as part of their standard procedure. These tools ensure that repository settings remain consistent across multiple systems, minimizing the risk of configuration drift. Moreover, centralized logging of repository updates and key management activities can enhance oversight, allowing administrators to audit repository changes and remediate any issues quickly.

The role of repositories in maintaining security cannot be understated. Repositories frequently provide essential security updates vital for protecting systems against newly identified vulnerabilities. Administrators must ensure that both main repositories and any additional third-party repositories are updated regularly to obtain the latest security patches. The occasional need to refresh keys, update repository URLs, or remove outdated repository entries is part of a broader security maintenance strategy. In scenarios where repository keys expire or repository URLs change, prompt administrative intervention is necessary to prevent interruptions in system updates.

When dealing with unrated packages or non-standard repositories, it is advisable to incorporate testing practices before deployment. Creating a test environment, replicating the proposed repository configuration, and simulating an upgrade can help identify potential conflicts or dependency issues introduced by third-party sources. APT's simulation feature using the --simulate flag can aid in this analysis:

```
sudo apt update --simulate
```

Such simulations allow administrators to predict the outcomes of various repository changes without impacting the stable production environment. It is a precautionary measure that enhances confidence in modifications made to the repository configuration.

Maintaining a robust repository configuration requires a proactive and systematic approach. Educating users about repository structure and configuration empowers them to adopt best practices in package management. Furthermore, leveraging the capabilities of APT through command-line flags and configuration files bridges the gap between system administration and software development, ensuring that both security and functionality are upheld.

Regular audits of repository configuration files, including inspections of the primary /etc/apt/sources.list and files in /etc/apt/sources.list.d/, help prevent issues arising from outdated or misconfigured entries. Implementing automated checks, coupled with the use of monitoring systems, assists in maintaining the integrity of repository configurations over time. Together, these practices form a comprehensive framework for managing and configuring APT repositories in diverse environments.

Through careful configuration, proactive key management, and vigilant auditing, administrators can harness the full potential of Debian repositories. The resulting system is not only secure but also flexible enough to incorporate a broad spectrum of software from both official and trusted third-party sources, thus ensuring consistent performance and reliability in system updates and package management.

4.6. Locking and Holding Packages

Locking and holding packages is a valuable technique in Debian-based systems for managing system stability and ensuring specific software versions remain unchanged. This section discusses methods for pre-

venting packages from being updated or removed, strategies for holding package versions, and the implications of these practices on system
maintenance. The discussion builds on prior analyses of package updates, upgrades, and repository management by introducing control
mechanisms that allow administrators to fine-tune package behavior.

A common scenario that necessitates package locking is when a package update may introduce incompatibility with custom configurations
or third-party applications. By locking a package, administrators can
preserve a known working version, thereby ensuring minimal disruption in environments where stability is paramount. The command
apt-mark hold is the primary tool for such operations in Debian.
When a package is held, subsequent calls to update or upgrade commands will bypass the package, preserving its current installed version.

```
sudo apt-mark hold package-name
```

In this example, replacing package-name with the name of the targeted
package instructs APT to exclude this package from performing an upgrade. The state can be verified by executing the following command:

```
apt-mark showhold
```

The output lists all packages marked to be held, thus providing immediate feedback on which packages are locked from change. This process
is crucial before proceeding with system upgrades, particularly in environments with complex dependency trees or highly customized setups.

Conversely, when the need for a package to remain at a specific version has ended, administrators can unhold it, allowing APT to include
the package in routine update operations. The unholding command is
equally straightforward:

```
sudo apt-mark unhold package-name
```

Returning a package to normal maintenance status ensures that it will
receive improvements and security updates available in the reposito-

ries. The flexibility to toggle the hold status dynamically is an essential aspect of managing packages in a controlled manner.

Beyond the straightforward usage of apt-mark hold, Debian provides other mechanisms to lock package versions and restrict their behavior. Repository pinning, which was discussed in the context of repository management, also facilitates package locking. Pinning modifies the priority of packages based on their repository of origin, effectively controlling which versions are eligible for installation or upgrade. Configuration for pinning is maintained in /etc/apt/preferences or within separate files under /etc/apt/preferences.d/. An administrator may specify that a particular package should only be sourced from a designated repository by setting an exceptionally high pin priority.

```
Package: package-name
Pin: version 1.2.3-4
Pin-Priority: 1001
```

A Pin-Priority value exceeding 1000 forces the installation of the specified version even if a newer version is available in the repository. This method, while more intricate, offers granular control especially in systems requiring precise versioning for software compatibility. It is essential to recognize that package pinning can interact with the normal update process, so configurations must be documented and reviewed periodically.

Another scenario that might require locking packages involves dependencies where an update to one package could cascade into multiple changes in the system. In such cases, holding a package limits the propagation of updates and mitigates the risk associated with a widespread upgrade. By isolating these packages, administrators create a controlled environment where only selected components are updated. This selective update strategy, when combined with regular monitoring of package statuses and changelogs, reinforces system reliability.

Managing package locks through either `apt-mark` or pinning configurations can introduce complexities in dependency resolution. Administrators may encounter situations where a held package is required as a dependency for another package scheduled for an upgrade. In such events, APT will display a dependency conflict error. Addressing these conflicts requires careful analysis of dependency chains. The decision to override a hold might involve temporary unholding, upgrading dependent packages, or modifying the pinning configuration. Documenting such interventions is critical for maintaining a clear historical record of changes in system maintenance.

Verifying the effect of package holds is critical when troubleshooting update anomalies. Commands like `apt-cache policy package-name` provide insights into the current version, available candidate versions, and the held status of the package. The output of this command serves as a diagnostic tool ensuring that the release version remains as intended. An example diagnostic command is provided below:

```
apt-cache policy package-name
```

This command reveals the currently installed version, the pinned candidate, and any potential conflicts that might arise during the upgrade process. Administrators should routinely employ such verification tools to monitor the health of locked packages.

Furthermore, complex environments may require maintaining a list of packages that are intentionally held across multiple systems. Configuration management tools such as Ansible, Puppet, or Chef can be integrated to apply package hold statuses uniformly. An example Ansible task that holds a package is illustrated below:

```
- name: Hold package
  apt:
    name: package-name
    state: present
    force: yes
    mark_hold: yes
```

154

Such automation ensures consistency across a fleet of Debian systems, reducing manual errors and facilitating centralized oversight. The automation of package holds also contributes to predictable upgrade paths, where only packages authorized for change are updated during system maintenance windows.

It is important to consider the implications of holding packages on system security. While holding a package might preserve critical functionality, it also prevents the application of security patches that may be released in subsequent updates. Administrators must balance the need for stability with the requirement for security. In certain cases, it may be advisable to hold a package temporarily while assessing the impact of a security update. Once the necessary compatibility checks are completed, the hold should be removed so that the package can be updated to a secure version. This trade-off between immediate system stability and long-term security necessitates a comprehensive review of each hold decision.

Documentation and change management play significant roles in environments with held or locked packages. Comprehensive records—detailing the reasons for holding packages, the duration of holds, and any related dependency configurations—assist in future troubleshooting and upgrade planning. Maintaining detailed logs and integrating them with configuration management databases can also facilitate audits and ensure that security standards are not inadvertently compromised by prolonged holds.

Locking and holding packages on a Debian system is a critical practice for managing package versions and preserving system stability, especially in complex, interdependent environments. The use of `apt-mark hold` and repository pinning are two primary methods that provide control over package updates. Tools such as `apt-cache policy` and automation frameworks help enforce these configurations consistently while providing diagnostic insights during upgrades. Through deliberate configuration and continuous monitoring, system administrators can ensure that essential packages remain at defined versions, thereby reducing the risk of unintended system changes while retaining the ability to promptly apply security patches when deemed safe.

4.7. Troubleshooting APT Issues

Managing software with APT is generally reliable, yet several common issues can disrupt its operation. System administrators and users must be familiar with diagnostic techniques and resolutions to maintain system stability. Problems range from repository key errors and lock file conflicts to network issues, broken dependencies, and misconfigurations in repository files. A methodical approach, starting by carefully reading error messages and examining logs, is essential to isolate and resolve the underlying causes.

Frequently, errors occur during repository updates when APT encounters signature verification failures. Error messages such as "The following signatures were invalid" or "NO_PUBKEY" indicate that the cryptographic trust model has been compromised. This situation may arise if repository keys are missing, expired, or not imported correctly. A typical resolution involves re-importing or updating the repository key. For example, if a key is reported missing, a command such as the following resolves the issue:

```
wget -qO - https://example.com/repo-key.gpg | sudo tee /etc/apt/
    trusted.gpg.d/example.gpg
```

After importing the key, running `apt update` should proceed without signature warnings. It is advisable to verify repository URLs and key sources for authenticity, ensuring that they match officially trusted sources.

Another common challenge involves lock files, which can prevent simultaneous APT operations. When an APT command fails with a message indicating it could not get a lock (e.g., Could not get lock /var/lib/dpkg/lock-frontend or E: Unable to lock the administration directory), it often means that either another package management process is running or a previous process terminated unexpectedly, leaving a stale lock file. To diagnose the issue, list the active package management processes using:

```
ps aux | grep -E "apt|dpkg"
```

If no active processes are found, it may be necessary to remove the stale lock files manually:

```
sudo rm /var/lib/dpkg/lock-frontend
sudo rm /var/lib/dpkg/lock
sudo rm /var/cache/apt/archives/lock
```

After removing these files, run the configuration command to ensure that the package database is consistent:

```
sudo dpkg --configure -a
```

Dependency issues are also common when managing packages. Errors such as "dependency problems - leaving unconfigured" or messages about held broken packages may arise when updates cause conflicts between packages. To address these issues, using APT's built-in fix command is usually effective:

```
sudo apt --fix-broken install
```

This command attempts to automatically resolve dependencies, install missing packages, and configure partially installed ones. Sometimes, held packages might be interfering with the dependency resolution. To check which packages are held, use:

```
apt-mark showhold
```

If necessary, release a held package that is causing conflicts:

```
sudo apt-mark unhold problematic-package
```

Network connectivity issues also interfere with APT operations. When errors such as "Failed to fetch" or "Network is unreachable" appear, verifying the network connection is essential. Testing connectivity can be accomplished by using the `ping` command:

```
ping deb.debian.org
```

Should the network be operational, reviewing proxy configurations in /etc/apt/apt.conf or environment variables like http_proxy and https_proxy is important. Incorrect proxy settings can result in time-outs and failed connections. Temporarily disabling or correctly config-uring proxy parameters often resolves such issues.

At times, corrupted package lists can lead to errors such as "Hash Sum mismatch" during the execution of apt update. This error is gener-ally due to outdated or corrupted cache files. Clearing the local cache compels APT to retrieve fresh metadata from the repositories:

```
sudo rm -rf /var/lib/apt/lists/*
sudo apt update
```

This process downloads new package lists, often resolving checksum discrepancies that result from caching issues or mirror synchroniza-tion delays.

Misconfigurations within repository files in /etc/apt/sources.list or within /etc/apt/sources.list.d/ can lead to problems as well. Syntax errors—in the form of incorrect repository URLs, missing fields, or stray characters—can cause APT to misinterpret the repository data. It is prudent to edit these files using a text editor, verify that the repos-itory entries adhere to the correct format, and remove any extraneous characters. For example, a correct repository entry appears as:

```
deb http://deb.debian.org/debian bullseye main contrib non-free
```

After editing, re-run the update operation to confirm that the configuration errors have been resolved:

```
sudo apt update
```

Sometimes, APT may report conflicts related to package versions, particularly when repository pinning or held packages are involved. In such scenarios, using the apt-cache policy command reveals the current status of a package, including installed versions, candidate versions, and repository priorities:

```
apt-cache policy package-name
```

This output is invaluable for diagnosing version conflicts, as it shows whether the intended version is being blocked by pinning policies or conflicting dependencies.

In more advanced troubleshooting scenarios, simulating operations without making changes can provide insights into potential issues. The --simulate flag with commands such as apt upgrade allows administrators to inspect what changes APT would perform without actually altering the system:

```
sudo apt upgrade --simulate
```

This dry-run approach helps identify problematic packages, dependency cycles, and conflicts before performing a full upgrade.

Another useful strategy involves reconfiguring the package database. Occasionally, the internal state of APT or dpkg might become inconsistent due to interrupted operations or manual interventions. Running the following command helps restore consistency:

```
sudo dpkg --configure -a
```

This command searches for half-installed or broken packages and attempts to complete their configuration. Following up with an apt install of the missing dependencies completes the resolution process.

Log files also provide critical context when troubleshooting APT issues. Files in /var/log/apt/ and the system log (/var/log/syslog or /var/log/messages) should be examined to uncover recurring errors or patterns that may have gone unnoticed. For example, reviewing the APT logs can help track down intermittent connectivity issues or repeated failures in signature verification.

For automated diagnosis, crafting simple shell scripts to monitor APT operations can alert administrators to emerging issues. An example script is provided below:

```
#!/bin/bash
LOGFILE="/tmp/apt_update.log"
sudo apt update > "$LOGFILE" 2>&1
if grep -i "error" "$LOGFILE"; then
    echo "Errors detected during apt update. Please review $LOGFILE
     for details."
else
    echo "apt update completed without errors."
fi
```

Scheduled execution of such scripts using cron can ensure continuous monitoring, enabling rapid response to new issues before they escalate.

When troubleshooting APT, it is crucial to consider problems that arise from third-party repositories. Such repositories may occasionally provide packages that are not fully aligned with Debian standards or that conflict with packages from official sources. In these cases, revisiting repository configurations, verifying the authenticity of GPG keys, and temporarily disabling third-party sources can help isolate the issue. Reverting to a simplified repository configuration temporarily and gradually reintroducing third-party entries allows administrators to pinpoint which repository is responsible for the conflict.

The interplay between APT and other package management tools also merits attention. Tools that wrap around APT, such as graphical frontends or configuration management systems, might behave differently when underlying errors occur. Ensuring that these tools are updated and configured to handle advanced APT diagnostics contributes to a more resilient management environment.

By adopting a comprehensive troubleshooting framework that includes verifying cryptographic keys, managing lock files, resolving dependency issues, addressing network problems, and correcting configuration errors, users can maintain a smoothly operating Debian system. Each of these strategies contributes to a robust set of practices that not only address immediate issues but also prevent future occurrences. Through careful monitoring, simulation of operations, and methodical resolution of errors, administrators ensure that APT continues to serve as a reliable and secure package management solution.

The detailed inspection of APT issues reinforces the importance of proactive maintenance and thorough documentation. Consistent logging, rigorous validation of repository sources, and automated diagnostics are core components of a sustainable system management strategy. This disciplined approach ultimately reduces downtime, minimizes disruption during critical updates, and fortifies system security against evolving software vulnerabilities.

Chapter 5

System Administration and Management

This chapter provides comprehensive insights into user and group management, system monitoring, and performance tuning. It explains managing services, scheduling tasks, and implementing effective backup and restore strategies. The chapter includes guidelines on handling system logs and configuring hardware, equipping administrators with essential tools and techniques to maintain and optimize Debian systems efficiently and securely.

5.1. User and Group Management

Effective control over user accounts and groups is fundamental to maintaining system security and operational efficiency. In Debian systems, each user account is associated with a unique identifier (UID) and has corresponding entries in files such as /etc/passwd

163

and /etc/shadow. Similarly, group management is handled through /etc/group, which organizes users into logical collections to simplify permission management. The management of these entities not only simplifies administrative tasks but also plays a key role in controlling access and defining user privileges.

User creation is typically performed using the useradd command. This tool provides various options that allow administrators to create new accounts with specific configurations, including the creation of a home directory, assignment of a default shell, and specification of a primary group. An example of creating a new user with a home directory and a Bash shell is illustrated below:

```
sudo useradd -m -s /bin/bash newuser
```

This command creates the user newuser, generating a corresponding home directory and setting the login shell to /bin/bash. In environments where security policies demand strict password management, it is essential to enforce password aging. The chage command facilitates this process by setting attributes such as maximum password age and warning periods. For instance, to set password aging policies for a user one might execute:

```
sudo chage -M 90 -W 7 newuser
```

Here, the maximum number of days a password remains valid is set to 90, with a 7-day warning period prior to expiration.

While the useradd command is used to initialize user accounts, modifying existing user attributes is accomplished through the usermod command. This utility enables administrators to change parameters such as the login name, home directory, and default group. For example, to change the default shell for an existing user, one can use:

```
sudo usermod -s /bin/zsh newuser
```

Verification of the updated configuration is straightforward with the

164

id command. Executing `id newuser` outputs the user's UID, primary group, and any supplementary groups. An execution sample might look as follows:

```
uid=1001(newuser) gid=1001(newuser) groups=1001(newuser),27(sudo)
```

Proper group management is equally critical. Groups facilitate the enforcement of access controls by allowing multiple users to share common permissions on files, directories, and system processes. The command `groupadd` provides an efficient approach to creating groups. For example, to create a new group for developers, one would issue:

```
sudo groupadd developers
```

To assign users to supplementary groups and thus extend their privileges, the `usermod` command is again utilized with the `-aG` option. Adding a user to the newly created group is executed as follows:

```
sudo usermod -aG developers newuser
```

The listing confirms that the user is associated not only with the primary group but also with the `developers` group. This association allows finer control over file permissions and access to shared resources, as files created with group write permissions in the working directory of the `developers` group become accessible to all its members.

Understanding file permission semantics in Unix-like systems complements user and group management. Every file and directory is associated with a set of permissions governing the operations that various categories of users—owner, group, and others—can perform. Administrators can modify these permissions using the `chmod` command, and changing file ownership is accomplished with the `chown` command. The interplay between file permissions and group assignments is crucial in designing secure access policies, particularly in multi-user environments where data integrity and confidentiality must be preserved.

165

Beyond administrative commands, manual verification and file inspection supplement system configuration. Critical files such as /etc/passwd, /etc/shadow, and /etc/group contain essential information and are structured in a format that is both human- and machine-readable. Editing these files directly is not recommended because mistakes can lead to system instability; however, familiarity with their structure assists administrators in troubleshooting and verifying the system's state. For instance, the /etc/group file typically contains entries structured as:

```
group_name:x:group_id:user1,user2,user3
```

This notation delineates the group name, a placeholder for the encrypted password (commonly x when password management is offloaded to /etc/gshadow), the group identifier, and a comma-separated list of users who belong to the group.

In addition to these command-line mechanisms, Debian provides graphical user interfaces and specialized management tools that streamline common tasks. Nevertheless, command-line proficiency remains indispensable for systems administrators. The flexibility of command-line utilities permits automation through scripts, which is beneficial for managing large-scale systems or environments where rapid deployment of user accounts and groups is necessary. A practical script example for bulk user creation can be implemented using a shell loop:

```bash
#!/bin/bash
for user in user1 user2 user3; do
    sudo useradd -m -s /bin/bash "$user"
    sudo passwd "$user"
done
```

This script iterates over a predefined list of usernames, creates accounts with a home directory and default shell, and then prompts for password configuration. Such automation reduces manual workload and enforces consistency across system configurations.

Beyond individual account management, effective security practices necessitate regular reviews of user and group configurations. Administrators should periodically audit the system to identify inactive accounts, redundant groups, or incorrect permissions that could potentially expose the system to unauthorized access. Tools such as `lastlog` or `faillog` assist in tracking user activities, while log files provide additional insight into authentication attempts. Combining these tools and techniques creates a comprehensive framework for system security.

It is crucial to recognize that managing users and groups is not a static task. The dynamic nature of organizational needs often requires modifications such as altering group memberships or updating user configurations to reflect changes in roles or responsibilities. Thus, understanding the underlying configuration files, command-line utilities, and best practices is essential for maintaining robust system security. Regular updates to policies and practices, as well as careful planning when implementing changes, help mitigate risks associated with configuration errors and unauthorized access.

Integrating these practices within the broader context of system administration ensures that user and group management is performed with precision and foresight. A consistent approach to account management, periodic audits, and adherence to system security policies form the backbone of an effective administrative strategy. Administrators must remain vigilant in responding to organizational changes and ensure that account configurations are aligned with current operational requirements. The structure and design of Debian's user and group management tools provide a reliable foundation for such tasks, allowing for scalable and secure system administration.

The processes described are integral to maintaining a stable and secure Debian system. Mastery of these tools and concepts provides a platform for further exploration of system performance and service management, reinforcing the importance of structured access control in both individual and enterprise environments.

5.2. System Monitoring and Performance Tuning

System monitoring and performance tuning are crucial for ensuring that a Debian system operates within optimal parameters. The identification and analysis of performance bottlenecks, alongside proactive resource management strategies, contribute directly to overall system stability and responsiveness. Tools designed for monitoring various system attributes, when combined with appropriate tuning techniques, provide administrators with the necessary guidance to make informed decisions. Building on earlier discussions regarding system security and resource access, these practices integrate into the broader scope of effective system administration.

One of the primary tools for real-time system monitoring is top. This command offers a dynamic view of processor activity, displaying all running processes along with CPU usage, memory consumption, and load averages. The output from top allows administrators to identify resource-intensive processes quickly. An invocation of the command appears as follows:

```
top
```

Within top, continuous updates provide a snapshot of system performance. Specific numeric thresholds, such as CPU load averages and memory utilization percentages, help administrators discern whether immediate intervention is required. Alternative tools such as htop present a more user-friendly interface with additional features like process tree visualization and enhanced color coding. These tools are particularly useful for environments where quick identification of perfor-

168

mance issues is essential.

Memory management is a critical focus area for performance tuning. The `free` command supplies a concise summary of the system's
memory state, detailing used and available memory, swap usage, and
buffers. For instance, executing:

```
free -h
```

yields human-readable figures, providing immediate insight into the
system's memory health. The output may resemble:

```
               total       used       free     shared  buff/cache   availab
le
Mem:            15G         8G         2G       500M        5G          6G
Swap:          2.0G       1.0G       1.0G
```

This command gives the administrator a clear perspective on whether
the system is approaching its memory limits, prompting potential
strategies such as increasing swap space, adjusting application memory consumption, or optimizing service configurations.

Monitoring disk I/O is another fundamental aspect of system performance. The `iostat` utility, provided by the sysstat package, offers detailed statistics on disk activity and can help locate I/O constrained
devices. A sample command to check disk performance is illustrated
below:

```
iostat -xz 1 10
```

This command provides comprehensive statistics including CPU utilization and extended disk statistics over ten reporting intervals. Analysis of metrics such as the `await` time (the average time for I/O requests
to be completed) and `%util` (the percentage of time the device was active) can reveal disk bottlenecks and guide decisions for load balancing
or hardware upgrades.

Network performance is equally important. Utilities like `iftop` and

169

nload serve to monitor bandwidth usage and network traffic in real time. Monitoring network throughput can be indispensable in systems where services are sensitive to latency and bandwidth variations. For example, iftop provides an immediate view of the ongoing network connections and their bandwidth consumption:

```
sudo iftop -i eth0
```

The information displayed by iftop assists administrators in pinpointing network-intensive processes or potential anomalies that may indicate a security breach or misconfiguration.

In addition to these command-line utilities, log files play a vital role in performance monitoring. System logs maintain a historical record of events, errors, and anomalies. The utility journalctl allows administrators to query and filter logs in systems that use systemd. A command such as:

```
journalctl -p err -b
```

retrieves error logs from the current boot session. Regular review of these logs facilitates the early detection of system problems that might otherwise degrade performance over time.

Monitoring tools often include the ability to collect historical data, which supports trend analysis over extended periods. Tools like Munin or Zabbix, and even more comprehensive monitoring solutions such as Prometheus, store time-series data that can be analyzed graphically. The resulting trends provide valuable insights into resource usage patterns, which are essential for preemptively tuning the system configuration.

The process of performance tuning involves both reactive and proactive measures. Reactive tuning is concerned with resolving issues as they are identified, such as terminating runaway processes or addressing memory leaks. Proactive tuning, on the other hand, encompasses configuring system parameters to prevent performance degradation. For instance, tuning the kernel's parameters through the /etc/sysctl.conf file can optimize network settings, memory management policies, and file system behaviors. An example entry in this file reads:

```
# Increase the maximum number of open files
fs.file-max = 100000
```

After saving changes, the new settings are applied with the command:

```
sudo sysctl -p
```

Examining the system's file descriptor usage via lsof and monitoring system limits using ulimit ensures that the adjustments are effective and that applications do not encounter unexpected resource constraints.

Central processing unit (CPU) performance also benefits from fine-tuning. Load balancing, process scheduling, and CPU affinity settings can be modified to improve overall efficiency. Tools such as taskset allow administrators to assign specific CPU cores to processes, minimizing contention with other running applications. An illustrative command might be:

```
sudo taskset -c 0,1 myapp
```

This command confines myapp to cores 0 and 1, potentially reducing cache thrashing and enhancing application responsiveness. The decision to bind processes to particular CPUs should be made after carefully analyzing workload characteristics and system architecture.

Disk performance may also require tuning at the file system level. Adjustments to mount options and periodic defragmentation (where applicable) contribute to an optimized disk I/O environment. File systems such as ext4 offer flexibility through options like write barriers and journaling modes, and tuning these settings may result in significant performance improvements under certain workloads. Performance testing using benchmarking tools such as `fio` can quantify the impact of these changes:

```
fio --name=benchmark --ioengine=libaio --iodepth=16 --rw=randread --
    bs=4k --direct=1 --size=1G --numjobs=4 --runtime=60 --
    group_reporting
```

The output from `fio` supplies detailed statistics on I/O performance, which administrators can use as a basis for tuning file system parameters and disk configurations.

Integrating these techniques into routine system maintenance is essential. Scheduled monitoring tasks can be automated through cron jobs, collecting system statistics at predefined intervals. Such automation not only ensures continuous oversight but also assists in capturing data that may explain transient performance issues. A simple cron job to append output from `vmstat` to a log file every five minutes may be written as:

```
*/5 * * * * /usr/bin/vmstat >> /var/log/vmstat.log
```

Periodic analysis of these logs facilitates a deeper understanding of system behavior over time, helping to identify patterns that precede performance slowdowns.

Maintaining a balance between performance and security is a continuous challenge. Proper configuration and regular monitoring are central to this balance. Tuning parameters in isolation may lead to improvements in one area while inadvertently degrading performance or security in another. Comprehensive system testing and verification must accompany any tuning efforts.

Monitoring systems are not static; their configurations require periodic review as new software is installed and workloads evolve. Administrators should establish baselines for normal performance, then identify deviations that may warrant further investigation. Leveraging historical monitoring data, along with current system checks, creates a robust framework for proactive performance management.

Understanding the interplay between hardware capabilities and software demands underpins effective performance tuning. Adequate monitoring, combined with deliberate adjustments to system settings, forms a robust strategy for maintaining a high-performance, stable computing environment. The methods described here allow for both rapid troubleshooting and long-term system stability, reinforcing the importance of detailed oversight in modern system administration.

5.3. Managing Services and Daemons

Effective management of system services and daemons is essential for maintaining a reliable and secure operating environment on Debian systems. System services and daemons run in the background, providing critical functionality ranging from networking and web servers to logging and scheduling tasks. A firm understanding of the tools and commands that interact with these services is a prerequisite for any system administrator. In newer Debian releases, the `systemctl` command is central to managing these components, while legacy compatibility is maintained through the `service` command. Mastery of these tools allows administrators to control service states, configure startup behavior, and troubleshoot issues in real time.

The evolution from traditional SysV init systems to systemd has brought a unified and robust approach to service management. With systemd, services are defined by unit files that describe how daemons are started, stopped, reloaded, and monitored. The basic syntax of the `systemctl` command permits status queries, state changes, and the modification of how services behave on boot. For example, checking the status of the SSH daemon is achieved by running:

```
sudo systemctl status ssh
```

173

This command displays detailed information about the SSH service, including its process ID, memory usage, and any recent log entries. The output, typically presented in a structured format, facilitates rapid diagnosis of issues such as service failures or misconfigured dependencies.

For administrators accustomed to the `service` command, Debian ensures backward compatibility. The `service` utility acts as a front-end to systemd, abstracting the complexity of unit files for routine tasks. For instance, obtaining the status of the Apache web server can be done through:

```
sudo service apache2 status
```

Despite its simplicity, the `service` command offers a practical interface for quick checks and minor adjustments in service state. However, advanced configuration and troubleshooting typically require direct interaction with systemd unit files and the richer options provided by `systemctl`.

Configuring the startup behavior of services is another aspect of daemon management that contributes to the stability of the system. Services can be enabled or disabled, which determines whether they automatically start during boot. To enable a service, such as the MySQL database server, the following command schedules it for startup:

```
sudo systemctl enable mysql
```

Similarly, if a particular service is not required on boot or if it interferes with other processes, it can be disabled with:

```
sudo systemctl disable mysql
```

These commands modify symbolic links in system directories that dictate the boot process. In some cases, administrators may choose to permanently mask a service to prevent it from being started manually or by dependency:

```
sudo systemctl mask service_name
```

Such masking is often used in environments where certain services are known to cause conflicts with essential system components.

Managing the state of services is a routine operation for administrators. Starting, stopping, and restarting services are fundamental actions that can address transient errors or configuration changes. To start a service, for instance:

```
sudo systemctl start cron
```

Stopping a service is similarly straightforward:

```
sudo systemctl stop cron
```

Restarting, which is particularly useful after modifying configuration files, is accomplished by:

```
sudo systemctl restart cron
```

Some services support reloading their configuration files without a full restart, preserving service continuity. In such cases, the reload option is preferred:

```
sudo systemctl reload nginx
```

This set of commands provides the basic building blocks for controlling the state of daemons, ensuring that changes in configuration or environmental conditions are reflected immediately in the process state.

System logs play a pivotal role in managing services, as they offer insight into the behavior of daemons over time. The journalctl command, part of the systemd ecosystem, enables administrators to query log messages generated by services. For example, to display error messages from the Samba daemon, one might use:

175

```
sudo journalctl -u smbd -p err
```

Such filtered queries assist in isolating issues and understanding error conditions without sifting through extraneous log entries. Administrators often integrate log analysis into their troubleshooting routines to ensure that lingering problems with startup scripts or misconfigured services are promptly addressed.

One of the advanced aspects of managing system services is the creation and customization of systemd unit files. A unit file defines how a service should behave under various circumstances. Administrators may need to create custom unit files for bespoke applications or adapt existing ones to suit their deployment environments. Below is an example of a simple service unit file that describes a daemon running a custom application:

```
[Unit]
Description=Custom Application Service
After=network.target

[Service]
Type=simple
ExecStart=/usr/local/bin/custom-app --config /etc/custom-app.conf
Restart=on-failure
RestartSec=5

[Install]
WantedBy=multi-user.target
```

This unit file is structured into sections that detail dependencies, execution parameters, and installation targets. The [Unit] section establishes a dependency on network availability to ensure that the service does not start prematurely. The [Service] section specifies that the service is a simple process, defines the command that launches the daemon, and sets policies for restarting if the process fails. The [Install] section determines the target in which the service is activated during boot, typically aligning with multi-user operation.

After creating or modifying a unit file, administrators must reload the systemd configuration to incorporate the changes. This is done by executing:

```
sudo systemctl daemon-reload
```

Once reloaded, the custom service can be started, stopped, or enabled like any other systemd service. This flexibility allows for rapid deployment of new services and adjustments to existing daemons without extensive system reboots or manual intervention.

Service dependency management is another critical aspect that ensures the orderly startup and shutdown of interrelated components. Unit files can specify dependencies using directives like `After=` and `Requires=`. This means that a service will wait for the successful initialization of its dependencies before starting. Such orchestration is vital in complex systems where multiple services rely on each other for data exchange or security context.

Management of services extends into the monitoring of their runtime behavior. The command `systemctl list-units --type=service` displays a comprehensive list of active services, which is beneficial when performing a system-wide analysis. For example:

```
sudo systemctl list-units --type=service
```

This command provides a snapshot of the current state of all services, making it easier to identify those that have failed or are in a degraded state. Pairing this with system logs results in a powerful diagnostic toolset that helps administrators maintain the integrity and performance of the system.

In environments with high service demand or critical uptime requirements, it is common to configure services for automatic recovery. The directives within unit files, such as `Restart=always` or `Restart=on-abort`, facilitate automatic restarts. These options reduce downtime by enabling the system to recover from transient failures without human intervention. However, improper configuration of these options can lead to rapid restart loops that may further destabilize the system. It is crucial that service restart policies are designed with the nature of the workload and the potential causes of failure in mind.

For services that require a more controlled shutdown, a graceful termination policy may be implemented. The `TimeoutStopSec=` directive within a unit file allows the service to perform cleanup operations before termination. When combined with a signal such as SIGTERM, which is less forceful than SIGKILL, administrators have a buffer period to ensure that process termination does not result in data corruption or loss.

The role of service management in system administration is not solely limited to runtime control but also encompasses security. Properly configured services help prevent unauthorized access by ensuring that unnecessary daemons are disabled and that critical services are only accessible through secure channels. The process of scrutinizing startup behavior and audit logs helps maintain a minimal attack surface, reducing the risk of exploitation.

Ensuring that new or updated services are properly integrated into the system's startup sequence is an ongoing responsibility. Administrators should routinely verify that all critical services are enabled and operating as expected. The complementary use of the `systemctl` and `service` commands enhances both routine maintenance and in-depth troubleshooting procedures. By combining direct command-line interactions with customized unit file configurations, system administrators can achieve an effective balance between operational robustness and flexibility.

5.4. Scheduling Tasks with Cron and Anacron

Automation of recurring tasks is a fundamental aspect of effective system administration. Debian provides robust scheduling utilities, primarily cron and anacron, which enable administrators to execute commands and scripts without manual intervention. These tools cater to various scheduling needs, with cron suited for regularly occurring tasks on systems that run continuously, and anacron designed for systems that may be intermittently powered off. Mastery of these tools not only enhances productivity but also ensures timely execution of critical maintenance operations, backups, and other recurring tasks.

The cron daemon is responsible for running scheduled tasks at specified times. Its configuration is managed through crontab files, which define the schedule and command to be executed. Each user on a Debian system can have their own crontab file. Editing a crontab is performed via the crontab -e command, which opens the file in a text editor configured by the system. The structure of a crontab file consists of five fields that specify the minute, hour, day of the month, month, and day of the week, followed by the command to be executed. For example:

```
# m h  dom mon dow   command
30 2 * * * /usr/local/bin/backup.sh
```

In this example, the script backup.sh is executed daily at 2:30 AM. The scheduling syntax provides fine-grained control, including the use of asterisks to represent wildcards and commas to specify multiple values. Additionally, hyphens can define ranges for a time field. Understanding this syntax is crucial for correctly scheduling tasks that may have complex timing requirements.

A central feature of cron is its ability to run tasks with minimal overhead. The daemon routinely checks the crontab files, comparing the

179

current system time with scheduled entries, and executes tasks when a match is found. Since the cron daemon parses multiple crontabs, it is essential for administrators to be cautious when editing these files to avoid syntax errors that could prevent scheduled tasks from running. A quick test of a new crontab entry can be made by scheduling a command to output a timestamp to a log file. For instance:

```
* * * * * date >> /home/user/cron_test.log
```

This entry appends the current date and time to cron_test.log every minute, providing a practical means to verify that the scheduling system is operational.

In addition to individual user crontabs, system-wide crontab files exist. The file /etc/crontab is maintained by the system and includes an extra field that specifies the user under which the command should be executed. A typical entry might be:

```
# m h dom mon dow user   command
15 1 * * * root /usr/local/bin/daily_maintenance.sh
```

This entry ensures that the maintenance script is run daily at 1:15 AM under the root user, illustrating how system-level tasks are managed separately from user-specific jobs.

While cron is ideal for tasks on systems that are continuously powered on, it does not account for downtime. In environments where the system may not run 24/7, scheduled tasks might be missed if the system is off when a task is supposed to occur. This limitation is addressed by anacron. Anacron is implemented to ensure that periodic tasks, especially those scheduled on a daily, weekly, or monthly basis, are executed when the system is next available. The configuration files for anacron typically reside in /etc/anacrontab.

The format of an anacrontab file is slightly different. It defines the period in days, a delay in minutes, a unique identifier for the task, and the command to be run. For example:

```
# period   delay   job-identifier   command
1          10       cron.daily       run-parts /etc/cron.daily
7          20       cron.weekly      run-parts /etc/cron.weekly
30         30       cron.monthly     run-parts /etc/cron.monthly
```

In this configuration, tasks defined in /etc/cron.daily will execute with a 10-minute delay if they have not run during the previous day. The delay parameter allows the system to complete its boot process and handle other startup routines before initiating scheduled commands.

Managing tasks via both cron and anacron requires attention to logging and error handling. Many administrators redirect the output of scheduled commands to log files or use system logging facilities to capture errors. For instance, appending standard output and error to a logfile is a common practice:

```
30 2 * * * /usr/local/bin/backup.sh >> /var/log/backup.log 2>&1
```

This entry ensures that all output from the backup script is recorded in backup.log, simplifying troubleshooting in case the task fails or produces unexpected results. The use of redirection operators (>> and 2>&1) consolidates both standard output and error streams.

Integration of scheduled tasks with monitoring tools can further enhance system reliability. By combining scheduled tasks with log monitoring or notification systems, administrators can be alerted to failures in nearly real time. For example, a backup failure might trigger an email notification to alert the responsible administrator, minimizing downtime or data loss.

Editing and maintaining crontab files is facilitated by a variety of command-line options. The crontab -l command lists the current user's scheduled tasks, while crontab -r removes the user's crontab file entirely. When making modifications, it is advisable to create backups of existing crontab configurations. A simple approach involves redirecting the output of the `crontab -l` command into a backup file:

```
crontab -l > ~/my_cron_backup.txt
```

Restoring a crontab file can be achieved by piping the backup file back into the `crontab` command:

```
crontab ~/my_cron_backup.txt
```

Such practices ensure that administrators can recover from accidental deletions or misconfigurations efficiently.

Combining `cron` and `anacron` in a cohesive scheduling strategy requires a clear understanding of the operational environment. On systems that are rarely shut down, `cron` can easily handle all periodic tasks. Conversely, `anacron` excels in desktop environments or servers that may experience unplanned downtime. Developers and system administrators often employ a hybrid approach, using `cron` for minute- or hour-based tasks and deferring longer, less frequent tasks to `anacron`.

It is critical to consider the security implications of scheduled tasks. Scripts executed by `cron` may run with elevated privileges, especially when defined in the system-wide crontab. Therefore, rigorous testing and security audits of script contents are essential to prevent unauthorized code execution. Environment variables, user permissions, and the current working directory when `cron` initiates a script can differ significantly from a standard interactive session. Including explicit environment configurations at the top of a script or within the crontab can mitigate many potential issues. For example, one might specify the PATH variable explicitly:

```
PATH=/usr/local/sbin:/usr/local/bin:/usr/sbin:/usr/bin:/sbin:/bin
```

Placing this at the beginning of a crontab file ensures that all scheduled commands execute within a consistent environment.

Detailed documentation and regular reviews of scheduled tasks are integral to system sanity. Over time, obsolete or redundant entries can accumulate, leading to conflicts or resource overuse. Best practices advocate for periodic audits of both user and system-wide crontabs. These reviews should cross-reference scheduled tasks with current operational requirements, ensuring that each entry has a documented purpose. A centralized log of scheduled task changes can further assist in troubleshooting and historical analysis.

Debian's integration of `cron` and `anacron` supports a wide range of automation needs, from simple reminders to complex system maintenance tasks. By leveraging scheduled tasks, system administrators can offload routine maintenance work, focus on strategic system improvements, and maintain a proactive stance towards system reliability. The mechanisms for configuring, monitoring, and auditing these tasks are well-documented and provide a secure and efficient method for managing a diverse set of operations.

The ability to effectively schedule tasks is a cornerstone of operational efficiency. The structured approach offered by `cron` and `anacron` allows for granular control over task execution timing, a feature that is critical in optimizing system performance. As systems evolve, the proper management of scheduled tasks remains indispensable. Ensuring that these tasks are executed reliably and securely directly impacts overall system stability and contributes to the broader goals of effective system administration.

5.5. Logging and Log Management

Proper logging and log management are critical for maintaining oversight of system operations, troubleshooting issues, and ensuring security. Debian systems generate a variety of logs that record system events, application activities, and security-related information. Administrators must know how to locate these logs, interpret their content, manage logging services, and configure log rotation policies to prevent disk space exhaustion and facilitate historical analysis.

System logs are typically stored in the /var/log directory. Conventional logs such as /var/log/syslog, /var/log/auth.log, and /var/log/daemon.log capture real-time events generated by system components. For instance, /var/log/auth.log contains authentication messages which are essential for identifying unauthorized access attempts, while /var/log/syslog collects a wide range of system messages. Viewing these logs from the command line can be accomplished with commands such as:

```
sudo less /var/log/syslog
```

or

```
sudo tail -f /var/log/auth.log
```

The first command allows for scrolling through the entire file, whereas the second provides a real-time update of new log entries. Such commands are vital for both immediate troubleshooting and periodic audit procedures.

In recent versions of Debian, the systemd journal has become the centralized logging mechanism, complementing traditional syslog facilities. The journalctl utility offers an efficient way to query and filter log data from these sources. For example, to display all log entries for a particular service such as the SSH daemon, an administrator can use:

```
sudo journalctl -u ssh
```

This command extracts logs specific to the SSH service, enabling targeted analysis of connection attempts, configuration issues, and service restarts. Additional flags, such as -p err to filter error messages or -b to show messages since the last boot, yield further granularity:

```
sudo journalctl -u ssh -p err -b
```

184

This provides a concise set of log entries that are critical for diagnosing service-related problems.

Understanding the format of log messages is essential for effective log management. Most logs follow a standardized format comprising a timestamp, the host name, the software component, and the message content. For example, an entry from /var/log/syslog may appear as:

```
Oct 10 09:15:42 debian kernel: [12345.678901] eth0: Link is Up - 1Gbps/Full -
flow control off
```

This format facilitates both manual inspection and automated processing. Parsing logs with command-line tools such as grep, awk, or more specialized utilities enables administrators to extract pertinent information quickly. For instance, to filter messages related to the kernel, the command can be executed:

```
grep "kernel:" /var/log/syslog
```

Such filters assist in isolating relevant details, which is particularly useful when analyzing events during system failures or security incidents.

The management of logging services is another vital component of system administration. In Debian, logging services such as rsyslog or systemd-journald are responsible for collecting and storing log data. The rsyslog service, highly configurable via its configuration files found in /etc/rsyslog.conf and /etc/rsyslog.d/, directs log messages based on facility and severity into designated files or remote servers. Modifications in these configuration files can redirect logs, filter out excessive verbosity, or implement custom logging rules. Following any configuration change, the rsyslog service must be restarted to apply the new settings:

```
sudo systemctl restart rsyslog
```

By managing logging services effectively, administrators ensure that significant events are captured reliably and made available for review during audits.

Customized log rotation is integral to maintaining an efficient logging practice. Without proper rotation, log files can grow indefinitely, consuming excessive disk space and making log analysis cumbersome. Debian employs `logrotate` for this purpose. The primary configuration file, `/etc/logrotate.conf`, outlines overall rotation policies, while specific packages often include their own rotation policies in `/etc/logrotate.d/`. A typical configuration directive in an individual file might appear as:

```
/var/log/apache2/*.log {
    daily
    missingok
    rotate 14
    compress
    delaycompress
    notifempty
    create 640 root adm
    sharedscripts
    postrotate
        if /etc/init.d/apache2 status > /dev/null ; then \
            /etc/init.d/apache2 reload > /dev/null; \
        fi;
    endscript
}
```

In this configuration, Apache log files are rotated daily. The `rotate 14` directive keeps logs for 14 days before deletion. The `compress` option saves disk space by compressing older logs while the `notifempty` option prevents log rotation if the file is empty. The `postrotate` block ensures that the Apache service reloads after log rotation, guaranteeing that the logging continues without interruption.

Understanding log rotation policies is critical to system longevity and performance. Several considerations include the rotation frequency (daily, weekly, monthly), the number of rotations retained, and the use of compression to save space. Administrators should tailor these

186

settings to match the specific load and operational demands of their systems. Logging important events over longer periods can be beneficial for compliance and forensic analysis; however, overly aggressive retention can lead to unnecessary disk usage.

Automation of log management extends beyond basic rotation. Implementing customized scripts that monitor disk usage and trigger alerts can help preempt issues arising from growing log volumes. For example, a script that checks log file sizes and sends an email alert when thresholds are exceeded can be scheduled as a cron job:

```bash
#!/bin/bash
LOG_DIR="/var/log"
THRESHOLD=50000000  # 50MB as an example

for file in $(find $LOG_DIR -type f -name "*.log"); do
    size=$(stat -c%s "$file")
    if [ $size -gt $THRESHOLD ]; then
        echo "Warning: $file size is $(($size / 1048576)) MB" | mail
     -s "Log File Size Alert" admin@example.com
    fi
done
```

This script routinely inspects log file sizes and notifies administrators if a file exceeds a predetermined limit, thereby allowing timely intervention before disk space issues arise.

Effective interpretation of logs is not limited to hardware or system issues. Application logs are equally significant in diagnosing problems with web servers, database systems, or custom applications. A unified logging strategy that integrates both system-level entries and application-specific logs can provide comprehensive insights into the entire system's state. Tools like the Elastic Stack (Elasticsearch, Logstash, and Kibana) are often employed in larger environments to aggregate, parse, and visualize log data from diverse sources. While such tools extend beyond the standard Debian installation, they highlight the importance of centralized log management in complex environments.

In practice, maintaining a secure environment demands regular monitoring of logs for unusual or potentially malicious activity. Automated log analysis tools can parse routine logs to detect duplicates, failed login attempts, unauthorized access patterns, or anomalous service restarts. Administrators can pair these tools with alert systems that notify them immediately upon detecting suspicious events. By correlating log data across multiple files and sources, it becomes possible to build a proactive defense against evolving threats.

The configuration files governing log management and rotation are integral to an efficient system. Regular audits of these configuration files, including testing new settings in a staging environment, ensure that logging behaves as expected. Backing up configuration files before making changes is a prudent measure. Simple version control systems or diff tools can assist in tracking changes over time, providing a record of modifications that can be crucial during audits or security investigations.

Effective log management is an ongoing process that encompasses not only the tools mentioned but also policies and procedures. Establishing clear guidelines for log retention, access control, and periodic audits fosters a disciplined approach to system monitoring. In scenarios where regulatory compliance is required, meticulous log management becomes even more critical, as logs serve as verifiable records of system activities and changes.

Ensuring that logs are both accurate and accessible involves proper configuration and rigorous maintenance. Validation of logging configurations, regular review of log files, and systematic rotation all contribute to a reliable logging system. The cumulative effect of these practices is a comprehensive snapshot of system activity over time, which underpins troubleshooting, security analysis, and performance optimization efforts.

An integrated approach to logging and log management creates a stable environment where system operations are continuously monitored, evaluated, and refined. By systematically locating, interpreting, and rotating logs, administrators maintain a granular view of system performance, detect anomalies early, and ensure that system history is preserved for future analysis. This methodical approach supports better decision-making and reinforces a proactive stance in system administration.

5.6. Backup and Restore Strategies

Robust backup and restore strategies are essential to safeguard against data loss, system failures, and security breaches. In Debian systems, a variety of tools and techniques can be employed to perform backups, each tailored to the specific requirements and constraints of the environment. Understanding the differences between full, incremental, and differential backups, as well as the appropriate use of utilities such as `tar`, `rsync`, and filesystem snapshots, is crucial for establishing comprehensive data protection.

The strategy selection often starts with identifying the critical data that needs to be preserved. This data might include system configuration files, application data, user home directories, and database contents. Based on the frequency of changes and the system's role, administrators must decide between a complete backup and an incremental approach. A full backup creates a copy of all designated data, which simplifies restoration but may require significant storage and time. Conversely, incremental backups capture only the changes made since the last backup, conserving storage space and reducing backup times, albeit at the cost of more complex restoration procedures.

A common approach to full backups is to use the `tar` utility. This utility provides a straightforward mechanism to archive files and directories, preserving the directory structure and permissions. For example, backing up the /etc directory can be accomplished with:

```
sudo tar -czvf /backup/etc-backup.tar.gz /etc
```

In this command, the -c option creates an archive, the -z option compresses it using gzip, the -v option enables verbose output, and the -f option specifies the filename for the archive. The resulting file can then be stored on a local or remote backup server.

For incremental backups, rsync is a favored tool due to its efficiency in copying only changed files. By maintaining a previous snapshot of the data, rsync computes differences and transfers only the modifications. A typical command might look like:

```
rsync -av --delete /home/user/ /backup/home/user/
```

Here, the -a option preserves file attributes and permissions, while the -v option provides verbose output. The --delete flag ensures that files removed from the source are also deleted in the backup, maintaining consistency between the two locations. This command is particularly useful for regularly syncing important files and can be complemented with scheduled tasks through cron.

In addition to local backups, network-based solutions offer the advantage of storing data remotely. Tools such as rsnapshot build on rsync to provide automated, incremental backups with minimal configuration. Its use of hard links for unchanged files significantly reduces storage consumption while organizing backups in a directory hierarchy that reflects the backup intervals. This hierarchical approach facilitates quick restoration and versioning of data over several periods.

Database backups require special consideration because of the need to capture consistent snapshots while the database is running. Utilities like mysqldump for MySQL or pg_dump for PostgreSQL are designed to extract safe, transaction-consistent backups of database contents. A typical backup command for MySQL might resemble:

```
mysqldump -u root -p mydatabase > /backup/mydatabase.sql
```

This command prompts for the database password and writes the SQL dump to a file. In production systems, it is common to schedule this command to run during periods of low activity and to securely store the output, often compressing it to save space.

Restoration is as critical as the backup process itself. A well-documented restore procedure enables administrators to recover data quickly in the event of hardware failure, human error, or malicious activity. For instance, extracting files from a tar archive is straightforward:

```
sudo tar -xzvf /backup/etc-backup.tar.gz -C /restore_directory
```

The `-C` option specifies the directory to which the files should be extracted. This process highlights the importance of maintaining organized backup repositories and clear documentation regarding the location and contents of backup files.

An often overlooked component of a backup strategy is the scheduling and automation of backup tasks. Automated backups minimize the risk of human error and ensure regular data preservation. With tools like `cron`, backups can be scheduled to run at fixed intervals. A sample crontab entry to automate a nightly backup using `tar` might be:

```
0 3 * * * /usr/local/bin/backup_script.sh >> /var/log/backup.log 2>&1
```

This entry schedules the backup script to execute at 3:00 AM every day and directs both standard output and error messages to a log file. Logging the backup process is essential to verify successful completion or to troubleshoot potential failures.

In environments where downtime must be minimized, snapshot-based backups provide a dynamic solution. Filesystems like Btrfs and LVM support snapshot functionality, allowing point-in-time snapshots with minimal performance impact. A snapshot can be taken instantaneously, providing a consistent backup state that is especially useful when coupled with applications that require continuous availability. For example, creating an LVM snapshot might involve:

```
sudo lvcreate --size 1G --snapshot --name lv_snapshot /dev/vg0/
    lv_data
```

Snapshots are typically temporary, and it is common to schedule their removal after a backup job has safely copied the data from the snapshot to long-term storage.

Backup and restore strategies must also account for security. Backups can contain sensitive data, and it is critical to ensure that they are stored securely. Encrypting backup files using tools like gpg adds a layer of protection. For instance, after creating a backup archive, an administrator can encrypt the file with:

```
gpg --symmetric --cipher-algo AES256 /backup/etc-backup.tar.gz
```

This command prompts for a passphrase and produces an encrypted version of the backup file, reducing the risk that stolen backup files lead to data breaches. Similarly, secure transmission protocols such as SSH and SCP can safeguard backups sent over a network. A sample SCP command to transfer a backup file to a remote server is:

```
scp /backup/etc-backup.tar.gz user@backupserver:/remote_backup/
```

Using encrypted connections ensures that transmitted backup data remains confidential.

Verifying backup integrity is equally important to ensure that data can be restored successfully when needed. Many backup strategies include periodic verification, wherein the backup set is compared against the original data or subjected to a test restoration. Tools such as md5sum or sha256sum can generate checksums to detect file corruption. A routine verification might involve the following commands:

```
md5sum /backup/etc-backup.tar.gz > /backup/etc-backup.md5
md5sum -c /backup/etc-backup.md5
```

These commands create a checksum file and then compare the current checksum of the backup file with the saved value. Regular integrity checks help identify corruption before a restore becomes necessary.

Operational considerations, such as backup rotation and retention policies, further influence backup strategies. Retaining too many backups can lead to storage exhaustion, while too few may leave gaps in historical data. Configuring automated deletion of outdated backups using tools such as `logrotate` or custom scripts is a common practice. For example, a script to delete backups older than 30 days might incorporate the `find` command:

```
find /backup -type f -mtime +30 -exec rm {} \;
```

This command deletes files in the `/backup` directory that have not been modified in the last 30 days, ensuring that storage is managed efficiently.

Integrating backup strategies within the overall system administration framework requires careful planning. Documentation of backup locations, schedules, encryption keys, and restoration procedures must be maintained in a secure location. Testing these procedures on a regular basis ensures that, when needed, backups can be restored quickly and accurately, minimizing downtime and mitigating the impact of data loss.

A comprehensive approach to backup and restore strategies recognizes the importance of layered defenses. Local backups, network backups, encrypted archives, and snapshots collectively form a resilient protection mechanism. Such an approach not only protects against hardware failures and accidental deletions but also addresses the growing threat of cyberattacks, where ransomware or data breaches can compromise critical information.

By combining automated scheduling, secure data transmission, regular integrity verification, and thorough documentation, system administrators can implement a backup and restore strategy that meets both operational and security requirements. The tools and techniques discussed in this section represent a cohesive framework for ensuring data continuity in a dynamic computing environment. This thorough methodology bolsters system resilience and contributes significantly to the long-term stability of Debian systems.

5.7. Configuring Hardware and Peripherals

Debian systems provide a comprehensive set of command-line utilities for detecting, configuring, and managing hardware devices and peripherals. Effective hardware configuration begins with identifying the available devices, understanding their properties, and then applying the appropriate drivers and settings to ensure proper operation. The following discussion examines the most commonly used tools for hardware detection, driver management, and peripheral configuration, thereby ensuring a well-integrated system environment.

To begin with, hardware detection is fundamental for any configuration activity. Several utilities offer detailed insights into the connected devices. The lspci command, for instance, lists all PCI buses and the devices connected to them. This is particularly useful for identifying graphics cards, network adapters, and other internal components:

```
sudo lspci
```

Similarly, the lsusb command enumerates all USB devices attached to the system. This tool is crucial for peripherals such as external storage, printers, or input devices:

```
lsusb
```

For a more comprehensive overview, lshw presents detailed information regarding the hardware configuration, including capabilities, configuration settings, and resource usage. Running the command with the -short flag provides a succinct summary:

```
sudo lshw -short
```

Kernel messages also provide essential clues about hardware events during system startup and operation. The dmesg command outputs kernel ring buffer messages which can reveal errors, firmware loading activities, or device initialization events:

```
dmesg | less
```

Interpreting kernel logs through dmesg aids in diagnosing hardware issues, especially when paired with filtering. For example, filtering messages related to a specific device can be achieved using:

```
dmesg | grep -i usb
```

Once devices have been detected, configuring them typically involves managing kernel modules and setting up appropriate driver parameters. The lsmod command lists currently loaded modules, which helps verify that the required drivers for detected hardware components are active:

```
lsmod
```

In cases where a necessary module is not loaded, modprobe is used to load it dynamically. Conversely, if a module is causing conflicts or is no longer required, it can be unloaded:

```
sudo modprobe module_name    # To load a module
sudo modprobe -r module_name # To remove a module
```

For hardware that must be present at every boot, the module name

195

can be added to the /etc/modules file. This ensures that the module is loaded automatically during system startup. Additionally, options specific to a module can be set by creating or modifying configuration files in the /etc/modprobe.d/ directory.

Peripheral configuration extends beyond basic device detection and driver management. Many peripherals require custom settings to enhance performance or compatibility. For example, network interfaces on Debian can be configured using the ip suite of commands. Listing all network interfaces is easily accomplished by:

```
ip link show
```

To assign an IP address to an interface and activate it, the following commands might be used:

```
sudo ip addr add 192.168.1.100/24 dev eth0
sudo ip link set eth0 up
```

These commands not only configure the network interface but also ensure that the system can communicate on the network immediately. For persistent network configuration, administrators often edit configuration files in /etc/network/interfaces or use tools such as NetworkManager in desktop environments.

Storage devices and other peripherals also require careful management. The lsblk command provides a tree view of available block devices, along with their mount points and partition schemes:

```
lsblk
```

When additional partitioning or formatting is required, tools like fdisk or parted are invoked. For example, listing partition tables with fdisk is performed via:

```
sudo fdisk -l
```

In environments where performance and reliability are critical, administrators may wish to leverage the capabilities of modern filesystems that support snapshotting and advanced configurations. Accessing diagnostic information, such as SMART data, through tools like smartctl from the smartmontools package, further ensures the health of storage devices:

```
sudo smartctl -a /dev/sda
```

Peripheral devices such as printers, scanners, and other USB-connected instruments also benefit from command-line configuration. For example, the Common UNIX Printing System (CUPS) is configurable via terminal commands, and examining printer status can be conducted using:

```
lpstat -t
```

For input devices such as keyboards and mice, Linux provides tools like xinput (commonly used in graphical environments) to list and configure input properties. A sample command to list input devices is:

```
xinput list
```

Even in headless or non-graphical environments, many peripheral settings can be adjusted via file-based configuration and low-level system interfaces available within the /proc or /sys filesystem. Monitoring and altering hardware parameters in these virtual filesystems allow fine-tuned control over system components.

Another critical component in peripheral configuration is udev, the device manager for the Linux kernel. Udev dynamically creates and removes device nodes from the /dev directory and can apply custom rules based on device attributes. Custom udev rules reside in the /etc/udev/rules.d/ directory and can automate tasks when a device is added. An example of a udev rule might be:

```
SUBSYSTEM=="usb", ATTR{idVendor}=="1234", ATTR{idProduct}=="5678",
    MODE="0666", GROUP="users"
```

This rule assigns a specific permission and group ownership to a USB device with designated vendor and product IDs, thereby automating its configuration when connected. Such rules are invaluable in multi-user environments where device access control is necessary.

Troubleshooting hardware and peripheral configurations often involves interpreting system logs and re-evaluating device statuses. Commands like dmesg and journalctl help administrators trace issues to their source. For example, if a peripheral is not recognized, filtering the kernel log can provide clues:

```
dmesg | grep -i usb
```

Similarly, udev interactions can be monitored using:

```
udevadm monitor --environment --udev
```

This command provides a real-time stream of device events, which is particularly useful for identifying configuration errors or verifying that udev rules are triggered correctly.

In some cases, peripheral management extends into power management and performance tuning for hardware devices. Adjusting CPU frequency scaling or configuring fan control for thermal management ensures that hardware operates within safe parameters. Tools like cpufreq-info and fancontrol assist in monitoring and adjusting these parameters. For instance, determining the current CPU governor configuration is achieved with:

```
cpufreq-info
```

Subsequent adjustments may be applied by modifying configuration files or using specific commands to set an appropriate governor profile.

Overall, configuring hardware and peripherals on Debian systems requires a combination of accurate detection, dynamic configuration of drivers and modules, and the implementation of custom rules where

198

necessary. The use of command-line utilities such as `lspci`, `lsusb`, `lshw`, and `dmesg` lays the foundation for understanding the available hardware. Ensuring that appropriate drivers are loaded and configured via `modprobe` and managing device-specific settings with udev fosters an environment where hardware resources are fully leveraged.

In addition, the configuration of peripheral devices such as network interfaces, storage devices, and input devices benefits from dedicated utilities like `ip`, `lsblk`, and `xinput`. By integrating these tools with automated scripts, structured configuration files, and real-time monitoring of system logs, administrators are well-equipped to manage a wide range of hardware scenarios. This integrated approach not only simplifies troubleshooting but also ensures that system performance is optimized through precise control over hardware behavior.

The discipline of hardware configuration also involves regular documentation and verification of system settings. Maintaining backups of configuration files, recording changes to udev rules, and monitoring kernel messages over time contributes to a resilient system infrastructure. In environments where hardware configurations may change frequently due to updates, peripheral additions, or system upgrades, a structured approach to hardware management reduces downtime and minimizes the risk of misconfigurations.

In summary, the effective management of hardware and peripherals in Debian relies on a blend of detection, configuration, and continuous monitoring. Command-line utilities provide the transparency necessary to fully understand system hardware, while modules, udev rules, and device-specific configuration tools empower administrators to customize peripheral behavior in line with organizational requirements. This holistic approach to hardware management is an indispensable component of maintaining secure, high-performance, and stable Debian systems.

Chapter 6

Networking and Remote Access

This chapter covers configuring network interfaces, managing connections, and understanding IP addressing and subnetting. It includes setting up firewalls, using SSH for secure remote access, and configuring Samba for file sharing. Additionally, it addresses the use of VPNs for private networking, offering comprehensive guidance on establishing secure and effective network and remote access solutions in Debian environments.

6.1. Configuring Network Interfaces

Configuring network interfaces in Debian is both an essential and versatile task that underpins effective network management. In this section, the focus is on configuring interfaces using a dual approach: manual configuration through system files and the utilization of graphical tools. This detailed discussion integrates technical aspects with practical examples and code snippets to demonstrate the configuration process in Debian environments.

The Debian operating system uses the `/etc/network/interfaces` file as the primary source for interface definitions. This file prescribes how individual network interfaces are initialized during startup. Manual configuration provides granular control over each interface and can be particularly useful in server environments or on systems where minimal interfaces are desired. The fundamental syntax of this configuration file involves defining each interface with a set of options such as the method of network address assignment, whether via Dynamic Host Configuration Protocol (DHCP) or static IP addressing.

A common configuration for an interface that obtains its IP address from a DHCP server can be expressed as follows:

```
# The loopback network interface
auto lo
iface lo inet loopback

# Primary network interface using DHCP
auto eth0
iface eth0 inet dhcp
```

In the above snippet, the loopback interface (`lo`) is configured for internal communication using the loopback driver. The primary interface (`eth0`) is configured to obtain its network parameters automatically via DHCP. The use of the `auto` directive instructs Debian to bring the specified interface up at startup.

When a static IP configuration is preferred, it becomes necessary to specify details such as the IP address, netmask, gateway, and potentially nameservers. An example of static configuration is illustrated below:

```
auto eth0
iface eth0 inet static
    address 192.168.1.10
```

```
netmask 255.255.255.0
gateway 192.168.1.1
dns-nameservers 8.8.8.8 8.8.4.4
```

This static configuration assigns a fixed IP address to the interface. It explicitly defines the network mask (which determines the network's size), the default gateway (used for external communications), and the DNS servers to resolve hostnames. The indentation maintained under the `iface` declaration underscores the hierarchical relationship between the interface and its options.

Manual configuration is advantageous when precise network control is required, such as setting up multiple interfaces with different routing needs. Debian's configuration also supports more advanced directives. For example, aliasing an interface allows a single physical connection to be associated with multiple IP addresses, commonly used in hosting environments. This can be configured by referencing a primary interface definition and then adding additional identifiers:

```
auto eth0:0
iface eth0:0 inet static
    address 192.168.1.20
    netmask 255.255.255.0
```

Implementing such configurations requires careful consideration of network design; improper configurations can lead to routing conflicts or service interruptions. Each change made to the `/etc/network/interfaces` file necessitates a restart of the networking service to take effect. This can be achieved using commands such as:

```
sudo systemctl restart networking
```

or, on older systems,

```
sudo /etc/init.d/networking restart
```

These commands cause Debian to reevaluate the network interface definitions and reinitialize the network interfaces according to the changes made.

Graphical tools offer an alternative approach that can simplify network interface configuration, particularly for desktop users or those inexperienced with editing configuration files. One such tool is NetworkManager, which provides a graphical user interface (GUI) for configuring network parameters. Debian typically installs NetworkManager with a system tray applet that makes it possible to easily switch between networks, update configurations, and troubleshoot connectivity issues without any command-line interaction.

NetworkManager abstracts the lower-level details of the /etc/network/interfaces file but still writes necessary configurations to ensure consistency with the system state. It offers an accessible strategy for enabling or disabling interfaces, managing wireless connections, and securing networks through an intuitive interface. While it is particularly useful in environments with frequent network changes, system administrators often prefer manual configuration on servers or in environments that require a deterministic network setup.

When using graphical tools, one must understand that changes made through the GUI have an underlying translation to the configuration files. It is essential to ensure that graphical tools and manual configurations do not introduce conflicting directives. To mitigate such risks, it is recommended to maintain a backup of existing configuration files and periodically verify the system state using command-line utilities such as ifconfig or ip addr show. For instance, after making changes through NetworkManager, verifying the active configuration using:

```
ip addr show eth0
```

confirms that the intended IP address and interface status are in effect. The command output might resemble the following:

```
2: eth0: <BROADCAST,MULTICAST,UP,LOWER_UP> mtu 1500 qdisc mq state UP mode DE
FAULT group default qlen 1000
    link/ether 08:00:27:4a:be:2f brd ff:ff:ff:ff:ff:ff
    inet 192.168.1.10/24 brd 192.168.1.255 scope global dynamic eth0
       valid_lft 86400sec preferred_lft 86400sec
```

The output provides essential details: the interface state, hardware address, assigned IP address, and its configuration parameters. This immediate feedback allows users to ascertain network correctness and troubleshoot any anomalies.

For users who need to adapt configurations dynamically, integrating scripting mechanisms with network configuration is beneficial. Advanced users can write scripts that modify /etc/network/interfaces entries based on environmental variables or network conditions. Combining Bash scripting with network utilities can automate reconfiguration tasks. An illustrative example is presented below:

```bash
#!/bin/bash
INTERFACE="eth0"

# Check if interface is currently up
if ip link show "$INTERFACE" | grep -q "UP"; then
    echo "$INTERFACE is currently up. Restarting network service."
    sudo systemctl restart networking
else
    echo "$INTERFACE is down. Bringing up the interface."
    sudo ifup "$INTERFACE"
fi
```

This script checks the current state of the specified interface and uses system commands to either restart the network or bring the interface up. Automation through such scripts can be scheduled with cron jobs or invoked by system events, providing a robust solution for environments that require frequent network adjustments.

Understanding the nuances of network interface configuration is further enhanced by considering the variations across hardware types. For instance, wireless interfaces often require supplementary parameters such as SSID and security keys, which differ from wired configuration. When configuring wireless interfaces manually, additional options like wpa-ssid and wpa-psk can be specified within the configuration file as shown below:

```
auto wlan0
iface wlan0 inet dhcp
    wpa-ssid "DebianNetwork"
    wpa-psk "securepassword"
```

This configuration assigns a dynamic IP to a wireless interface while embedding the necessary credentials for authentication via the WPA protocol. Such examples underscore the importance of tailoring configurations to the type of network interface and the security requirements of the network itself.

It is noteworthy that while manual configurations offer extensive control, they require a foundational understanding of networking concepts such as subnetting, routing, and DNS resolution. The manual approach is primarily favored in controlled environments where each network change is documented and validated. In contrast, graphical tools streamline the process for those who prefer a visual representation of network parameters and may not require granular control over every detail.

Combining manual and graphical methods is feasible and sometimes beneficial in complex network environments. Administrators may configure core settings manually for predictability and use graphical utilities to manage transient settings or monitor network performance. Understanding the interplay between these methods allows system administrators to ensure consistency across various layers of network management, thereby reducing the likelihood of configuration conflicts.

Learning to configure network interfaces effectively in Debian will empower users to adapt to diverse network conditions while maintaining robust network security and connectivity. The interplay between manual configurations and graphical tools is integral to creating a resilient network infrastructure. Mastery of both approaches ensures that system administrators are well-equipped to troubleshoot and optimize network performance in a range of operational scenarios.

6.2. Managing Network Connections

Effective management of network connections is essential for both wired and wireless environments in Debian. The extensive suite of networking tools and utilities available in Debian allows administrators and users to monitor, manage, and test connectivity reliably. This section delves into the practical methods for managing network connections, emphasizing both command-line and graphical utilities that complement the manual configuration strategies previously discussed.

In wired environments, the physical connection generally remains constant; however, configuration and management remain critical. Utilities such as ifconfig and ip provide direct insights into the state of network interfaces. The ip command, in particular, is favored in modern Debian systems due to its versatility and detailed output. For example, executing:

```
ip addr show
```

displays a comprehensive list of network interfaces and their associated configurations. This command offers insights into the current IP addresses, link status, and network parameters for each interface, ensuring that any deviations from expected states can be quickly identified.

Wireless connections introduce additional layers of complexity. Unlike wired connections, wireless interfaces demand authentication credentials and are subject to environmental factors such as signal strength and interference. Tools such as `iwconfig` and `iwlist` are common utilities for inspecting and adjusting wireless parameters. One can verify the status of a wireless interface by invoking:

```
iwconfig wlan0
```

This command returns details such as the network's ESSID, frequency, bit rate, and signal quality, which are critical for troubleshooting connectivity issues. In environments where dynamic changes occur—for example, shifting from one access point to another—the real-time output of `iwconfig` assists in ensuring that the correct network parameters are maintained.

Graphical utilities augment these command-line tools and simplify management, particularly for desktop users. `NetworkManager` provides an integrated graphical interface where users can view available networks, manage connection profiles, and monitor performance at a glance. The utility enables users to switch among wired and wireless networks seamlessly. Despite its graphical nature, `NetworkManager` is designed to be consistent with underlying Debian configurations, ensuring that changes made via the GUI are reflected in system files. This dual approach facilitates redundancy in management, which is especially useful during periods of network troubleshooting or reconfiguration.

The command-line counterpart to `NetworkManager` is `nmcli`, a command-line tool that offers full control over network settings without leaving the terminal. For example, listing available connections can be performed with the command:

```
nmcli connection show
```

The output from this command might be:

```
NAME        UUID                          TYPE     DEVICE
```

```
Wired-eth0   3f9a39db-c5d2-4c18-bc7b-0a9e2173d945  ethernet  eth0
WiFi-Home    8b0d3c2d-d3c4-45d2-87e4-1f3a64456c09  wifi      wlan0
```

This detailed listing allows administrators to verify which network profiles are active, understand their unique identifiers, and manage any
necessary modifications. Creating a new wireless connection profile
can be achieved with:

```
nmcli dev wifi connect "WiFi-Home" password "securepass"
```

This command securely associates the wireless interface wlan0 with the
network named WiFi-Home using the specified password. The use of
nmcli streamlines the process by integrating scanning, authentication,
and connection management in a single command.

Testing network connectivity is fundamental to the management process. The ping command is the most basic tool for verifying connectivity between hosts. For instance, sending ICMP echo requests to a
remote host is accomplished through:

```
ping -c 4 8.8.8.8
```

The flag -c 4 limits the command to four packets. A typical output
from this command is:

```
PING 8.8.8.8 (8.8.8.8) 56(84) bytes of data.
64 bytes from 8.8.8.8: icmp_seq=1 ttl=117 time=14.2 ms
64 bytes from 8.8.8.8: icmp_seq=2 ttl=117 time=14.1 ms
64 bytes from 8.8.8.8: icmp_seq=3 ttl=117 time=14.3 ms
64 bytes from 8.8.8.8: icmp_seq=4 ttl=117 time=14.3 ms

--- 8.8.8.8 ping statistics ---
4 packets transmitted, 4 received, 0\% packet loss, time 3004ms
rtt min/avg/max/mdev = 14.105/14.224/14.349/0.095 ms
```

The results confirm network responsiveness and packet round-trip
times. In addition to ping, the traceroute utility is invaluable for diagnosing the path between source and destination. Running:

209

```
sudo traceroute google.com
```

reveals the series of network hops that packets traverse. This insight assists in identifying network bottlenecks or problematic routing configurations.

Advanced testing tools such as `mtr` merge the functionality of `ping` and `traceroute` to provide real-time metrics on network performance. The command:

```
mtr -rw google.com
```

provides a continuously updating report of latency and packet loss across each hop, making it an ideal choice for diagnosing intermittent connectivity issues. The interactive nature of these tools allows system administrators to make informed decisions regarding network health and performance improvements.

Furthermore, the `netstat` and `ss` utilities are utilized to inspect active network connections and listening ports. While `netstat` offers a legacy method, `ss` is recognized for its faster performance and more detailed output. An example command is:

```
ss -tuln
```

This command lists TCP and UDP ports that are currently open, along with associated details. Such information is critical for ensuring that only the expected services are running and that there are no unexpected connections which might indicate security issues.

Managing connections also involves monitoring wireless networks to ensure that signal strength and noise levels remain within acceptable thresholds. Tools designed for wireless analysis, including `wavemon` and `nmcli dev wifi list`, can be used to evaluate factors such as signal quality and interference. For example, executing:

```
nmcli dev wifi list
```

produces an output similar to:

```
IN-USE SSID            MODE  CHAN RATE        SIGNAL BARS SECURITY
*      DebianNetwork   Infra 6    130 Mbit/s  75      _   WPA2
       GuestNetwork    Infra 11   130 Mbit/s  60      _   WPA1 WP
A2
```

This detailed overview assists in selecting the optimal network based on performance metrics. It also provides a direct method to identify any potentially conflicting networks in crowded environments.

Automation is another critical aspect of connection management. Administrators often develop scripts to routinely monitor network status, perform connectivity tests, or re-establish connections when they drop. An example Bash script for automated connectivity testing is:

```
#!/bin/bash
TARGET="8.8.8.8"
LOGFILE="/var/log/network_ping.log"

if ping -c 1 $TARGET &>/dev/null; then
    echo "$(date): $TARGET is reachable" >> $LOGFILE
else
    echo "$(date): $TARGET is unreachable" >> $LOGFILE
    # Optionally, restart the network service or perform other
     recovery steps
    sudo systemctl restart networking
fi
```

This script pings a remote host and logs the results. In scenarios where the test fails, it can trigger corrective measures such as restarting the network service automatically. Logs maintained by such scripts contribute to historical data analytics, guiding future adjustments to network configurations and troubleshooting routines.

Comprehensive management of network connections also involves understanding the status of hardware components, such as network interface cards (NICs). The lspci command assists by revealing detailed

211

hardware information. For example, running:

```
lspci | grep -i ethernet
```

generates output that identifies Ethernet controllers present within the system. This data is useful when diagnosing hardware-level connectivity issues, ensuring that the drivers and firmware are up to date.

Maintaining a balance between manual intervention and automated management is crucial in minimizing downtime.   Graphical tools simplify everyday tasks by providing real-time monitoring, while command-line utilities and scripts offer precision and repeatability. The coexistence of both approaches empowers users to adapt their management strategies based on the complexity and requirements of their network environment.

Consolidating the management of wired and wireless connections under a unified suite of tools reduces the risk of configuration errors. Accurate testing and continuous monitoring preempt potential issues, reinforcing the stability and performance of the network.   The synergy between the utilities discussed provides a robust framework that can adapt efficiently to both planned changes and unexpected disruptions, ensuring effective network administration across Debian deployments.

6.3.   Understanding IP Addressing and Subnetting

A thorough comprehension of IP addressing and subnetting is central to efficient network management. At its core, IP addressing serves as the identification mechanism for devices connected to a network, while subnetting organizes these addresses into logical segments. This section builds on previous discussions on network interface configuration and connection management by delving into the theoretical and practical aspects of IP addressing, subnet masks, and network segmentation.

IP addresses in IPv4 format consist of 32 bits, generally represented in dotted decimal notation. For instance, an IP address such as 192.168.1.10 comprises four octets, each ranging from 0 to 255. Each address is divided into two main components: the network portion and the host portion. The subnet mask determines the separation between these two components. A common subnet mask of 255.255.255.0 indicates that the initial 24 bits represent the network address while the final 8 bits designate individual hosts within that network.

The binary representation of the address and mask emphasizes this division. For example, the IP address 192.168.1.10 is represented in binary as:

```
11000000.10101000.00000001.00001010
```

while the corresponding subnet mask 255.255.255.0 translates to:

```
11111111.11111111.11111111.00000000
```

The use of the subnet mask effectively isolates the network portion, ensuring that all devices with an IP address beginning with the same fixed 24 bits can communicate directly within that local subnet, while devices in different subnets are distinguished by differing bits in their host portion.

CIDR (Classless Inter-Domain Routing) notation is an efficient way to express subnet masks and network sizes. The notation appends a forward slash followed by the number of bits in the network portion. In the previous example, the notation 192.168.1.10/24 indicates that 24 bits are used to define the network. This approach is both concise and flexible, as it allows administrators to define networks with varying sizes, ranging from very large to highly segmented small networks.

The process of subnetting involves dividing a larger network into

213

smaller, more manageable segments. This division not only optimizes address allocation but also enhances network performance by limiting broadcast domains. Consider a network 192.168.1.0/24. By creating subnets within this network, it is possible to allocate addresses to different departments in an organization. For example, if one were to subdivide the /24 network into four equally sized subnets, each subnet would have a /26 prefix. The available subnets would be listed as follows:

```
Subnet 1: 192.168.1.0/26    (Addresses: 192.168.1.1 - 192.168.1.62)
Subnet 2: 192.168.1.64/26   (Addresses: 192.168.1.65 - 192.168.1.126)
Subnet 3: 192.168.1.128/26  (Addresses: 192.168.1.129 - 192.168.1.190)
Subnet 4: 192.168.1.192/26  (Addresses: 192.168.1.193 - 192.168.1.254)
```

Each subnet reserves two addresses for network and broadcast purposes, thereby defining the range of usable addresses for hosts. Careful planning and allocation of these addresses help prevent overlaps and ensure efficient use of address space.

The role of a broadcast address is essential in IPv4 configurations. It is the highest address in any subnet and is used to communicate with all hosts on that subnet simultaneously. For a subnet such as 192.168.1.0/24, the broadcast address is 192.168.1.255. This address is reserved and never assigned to individual devices. Similarly, the network address, which in the preceding example would be 192.168.1.0, identifies the subnet itself and is also reserved.

When manually configuring network interfaces in Debian, it is critical to correctly specify both IP addresses and subnet masks. An interface configured with a static IP address must include the subnet mask to ensure accurate interpretation of the network scope. An example configuration in /etc/network/interfaces is shown below:

```
auto eth0
iface eth0 inet static
    address 192.168.1.10
    netmask 255.255.255.0
    gateway 192.168.1.1
```

In the above configuration, the static IP address is paired with a standard subnet mask, ensuring that the device correctly identifies the network and the associated broadcast address. Additionally, the gateway directive points to the router which facilitates communication with external networks.

A common challenge in network configuration is determining the correct subnet notation for various requirements. Tools such as ipcalc simplify these calculations by computing network, broadcast, and host ranges based on a given IP address and subnet mask. For example, executing:

```
ipcalc 192.168.1.10/24
```

produces output similar to:

```
Address:   192.168.1.10       11000000.10101000.00000001.00001010
Netmask:   255.255.255.0 = 24 11111111.11111111.11111111.00000000
Wildcard:  0.0.0.255          00000000.00000000.00000000.11111111
Network:   192.168.1.0/24     11000000.10101000.00000001.00000000
Broadcast: 192.168.1.255      11000000.10101000.00000001.11111111
HostMin:   192.168.1.1
HostMax:   192.168.1.254
Hosts/Net: 254
```

By providing both a visual and numerical dissection of the network, such tools reinforce the understanding of how addresses are partitioned and used in practical settings.

Efficient network management also involves planning for future expansion. Allocating subnets using flexible CIDR notations, such as /22 or /23, may cater to larger departmental needs while keeping the network segmented. This foresight is essential when users or devices proliferate and bandwidth demands increase. Modular and scalable subnetting strategies allow for easier adjustments in routing policies and troubleshooting while minimizing the impact on the existing network structure.

In complex network environments, route summarization (or supernetting) is a technique that reduces the number of routing table entries by aggregating multiple routes into one. For example, if multiple subnets within the 192.168.1.0/24 network are being used across various segments, it may be possible to summarize these routes under a single larger network if they are contiguous. This practice decreases the complexity of routing protocols and improves overall network efficiency.

IPv6 addressing, though not the primary focus of this discussion, shares a number of conceptual similarities with IPv4 addressing but introduces a vastly larger address space. The principles of network segmentation, though, remain rooted in the idea of prefix length and the division between network and host portions. For administrators accustomed to IPv4, these similarities serve as a bridge to understanding IPv6 network configuration and its associated subnetting strategies.

The relationship between IP addressing and routing is another crucial factor. Routing protocols rely on the proper configuration of IP addresses and subnet masks to determine the best path for data packets. In Debian, tools like `ip route` allow administrators to view and manipulate routing tables:

```
ip route show
```

This command provides detailed information on routes, emphasizing how subnet definitions influence packet forwarding decisions. Configuring static routes explicitly using the IP addressing scheme reinforces the importance of structured network segmentation within the broader system topology.

A deep understanding of subnetting also aids in troubleshooting connectivity issues. For instance, mismatched subnet masks between devices can lead to scenarios where hosts believe they are on different networks, leading to unreachable services or dropped packets. Verification of the IP addressing scheme via utilities like `ifconfig` or `ip`

216

addr show is an essential step in diagnosing such issues. Comparing the subnet masks and network addresses across devices ensures consistency and compatibility.

An advanced approach for administrators includes employing network simulation tools to visualize the impacts of different subnetting schemes. Software such as GNS3 or NetSim allows configuration of virtual networks, providing a sandbox environment for testing configurations before they are deployed in production settings. These simulations offer an opportunity to experiment with various subnet masks, CIDR notations, and route summarizations without risking network downtime.

In configuring networks for scalable and secure operations, it is essential to document every addressing and subnetting decision. This documentation facilitates future audits and ensures that any modifications to the network can be implemented with full awareness of their impact on network architecture. The correlation between IP addressing, subnetting, and connectivity underscores how deliberate network planning contributes to overall system stability and operational performance.

Understanding IP addressing and subnetting brings together a range of practical skills and theoretical knowledge critical for efficient network configuration and management. The ability to calculate ranges, derive proper subnet masks, and implement address planning directly influences the effectiveness of network deployments and security measures. Such foundations enable system administrators to design resilient networks that can adapt to expanding needs and evolving technology without compromising performance or accessibility.

6.4.   Setting Up a Basic Firewall

Enhancing system security in Debian involves implementing a basic firewall to filter incoming and outgoing network traffic. This section focuses on setting up a firewall using two primary tools: UFW (Uncomplicated Firewall) and iptables. Both utilities offer robust mechanisms for controlling network access and mitigating potential security threats. A clear understanding of these tools, combined with practical examples, allows system administrators to configure firewalls that align with their network security policies.

UFW is designed to simplify the process of managing a firewall. It abstracts many of the underlying complexities behind a straightforward command-line interface. This simplicity benefits both novice and experienced users who require a reliable method to restrict unauthorized access. The installation of UFW is typically straightforward on Debian systems. After ensuring that UFW is installed, enabling the firewall is accomplished with:

```
sudo ufw enable
```

By default, UFW denies incoming connections and allows outgoing traffic, creating a secure environment out-of-the-box. To verify the current UFW status and review existing rules, the command:

```
sudo ufw status verbose
```

provides a detailed listing of active rules. The output might include lines specifying permission for specific ports or IP addresses. Custom rules can be added by specifying the protocol and port number, such as:

```
sudo ufw allow 22/tcp
```

This rule permits incoming SSH connections on port 22, which is crucial for remote administration. Similarly, allowing HTTP traffic on

218

port 80 is achieved through:

```
sudo ufw allow 80/tcp
```

For added specificity, UFW supports rules for particular IP addresses. An example is allowing a specific IP address access to port 443:

```
sudo ufw allow from 192.168.1.100 to any port 443 proto tcp
```

These rules provide a granular approach to access control, ensuring that only trusted sources can communicate with critical services.

In contrast, iptables offers detailed control and is well-suited for administrators requiring in-depth customization of firewall rules. Iptables operates at the kernel level, providing fine-grained control over packet filtering, NAT (Network Address Translation), and logging. While iptables is more complex than UFW, its flexibility makes it invaluable for creating intricate security policies.

Iptables organizes rules into chains, which belong to various tables. The most common table is the `filter` table, which contains chains like INPUT, OUTPUT, and FORWARD. For example, a basic rule to drop all incoming connections can be implemented as:

```
sudo iptables -P INPUT DROP
sudo iptables -P FORWARD DROP
sudo iptables -P OUTPUT ACCEPT
```

In this configuration, incoming and forwarded packets are dropped by default while allowing outgoing packets. Specific rules can then be created to accept certain types of traffic. Allowing SSH access can be done with:

```
sudo iptables -A INPUT -p tcp --dport 22 -m conntrack --ctstate NEW,
    ESTABLISHED -j ACCEPT
sudo iptables -A OUTPUT -p tcp --sport 22 -m conntrack --ctstate
    ESTABLISHED -j ACCEPT
```

The above rules ensure that new and established SSH connections are permitted while leveraging connection tracking to manage ongoing sessions. Similarly, rules can be defined for web traffic. For HTTP and HTTPS, the iptables configuration might include:

```
sudo iptables -A INPUT -p tcp --dport 80 -m conntrack --ctstate NEW,
    ESTABLISHED -j ACCEPT
sudo iptables -A INPUT -p tcp --dport 443 -m conntrack --ctstate NEW,
    ESTABLISHED -j ACCEPT
```

To enhance logging and monitor dropped packets, a logging rule can be appended to the iptables configuration:

```
sudo iptables -N LOGGING
sudo iptables -A INPUT -j LOGGING
sudo iptables -A LOGGING -m limit --limit 2/min -j LOG --log-prefix "
    IPTables-Dropped: " --log-level 4
sudo iptables -A LOGGING -j DROP
```

This set of commands creates a custom chain named LOGGING that logs dropped packets with a specified prefix. The limit option ensures that excessive logging does not overwhelm system logs. Such detailed logs can help in diagnosing network attacks and identifying suspicious traffic patterns.

Management of iptables rules typically involves saving and restoring configurations across reboots. Debian provides utilities such as iptables-save and iptables-restore to facilitate this process. To save the current set of rules, use:

```
sudo iptables-save > /etc/iptables/rules.v4
```

Restoring the saved configuration after a reboot can be configured through init scripts or systemd units. This process ensures that the firewall configuration remains consistent across system restarts, preserving security policies.

Combining UFW and iptables may seem redundant; however, UFW operates as a front end to iptables. When UFW is enabled, it automatically creates iptables rules based on the user-defined configuration.

Users opting for UFW benefit from the simplicity of high-level commands while still leveraging the power of iptables behind the scenes. It is important to note that if custom iptables rules are required that extend beyond the capabilities of UFW, administrators might opt to disable UFW entirely to avoid rule conflicts.

In environments with dynamic network environments, automated scripts can be utilized to adjust firewall settings based on system conditions. For instance, creating a Bash script that adjusts rules when a new network interface is detected can significantly enhance security in environments with multiple network segments. An example script is shown below:

```bash
#!/bin/bash

# Reload firewall rules when a new interface is detected
INTERFACE="eth1"
if ip addr show $INTERFACE &>/dev/null; then
    echo "Interface $INTERFACE detected. Updating firewall rules."
    sudo iptables -A INPUT -i $INTERFACE -p tcp --dport 22 -m
    conntrack --ctstate NEW,ESTABLISHED -j ACCEPT
    sudo iptables -A INPUT -i $INTERFACE -p tcp --dport 80 -m
    conntrack --ctstate NEW,ESTABLISHED -j ACCEPT
fi
```

This script checks for the existence of a specific interface and updates the iptables rules accordingly. Incorporating such automated processes ensures that firewall policies remain relevant even as network configurations evolve.

Monitoring firewall performance and ensuring that the configuration is effective is as important as its initial setup. Tools such as ulogd and fail2ban work in tandem with iptables to provide enhanced logging and intrusion detection. Fail2ban, for example, can parse log files generated by iptables, automatically blocking IP addresses that show signs of malicious behavior. Installation and configuration of fail2ban on Debian can help mitigate brute-force attacks by temporarily banning offending IP addresses.

Examining real-time firewall logs can also reveal any unexpected behaviors. Tailoring system logs for firewall events, for instance by examining the output generated by the LOGGING chain, allows administrators to fine-tune their rules. An example command to monitor these logs is:

```
sudo tail -f /var/log/syslog | grep IPTables-Dropped
```

This command continuously displays new log entries that match the specified prefix, making it suitable for real-time monitoring during troubleshooting sessions.

While UFW and iptables serve distinct purposes, they share complementary roles in enforcing network security. UFW is particularly well-suited for straightforward use cases and environments where rapid deployment is essential. Iptables, conversely, offers the depth and flexibility required for complex configurations and advanced security measures. Selecting between these tools, or implementing a combination of both, depends on the specific requirements of the network and the preferences of the system administrators.

Understanding the structure and methodology of firewall configurations is critical to defending against network intrusions and ensuring that only authorized traffic is allowed. Whether configuring rules for trusted services like SSH, HTTP, and HTTPS or implementing logging measures to identify potential denial-of-service attacks, a well-configured firewall forms a foundational part of a broader security strategy. Each command and rule contributes to a layered defense mechanism that protects the system against unauthorized access while ensuring that legitimate connectivity is maintained.

This systematic approach to setting up a basic firewall in Debian reinforces the broader principles of secure network configuration discussed in earlier sections. Recognizing the balance between accessibility and security, the effective use of firewall tools like UFW and iptables ultimately empowers administrators to implement resilient systems capable of adapting to evolving network threats and operational demands.

6.5. Using SSH for Secure Remote Access

SSH (Secure Shell) is the primary tool used in Debian for secure remote command-line access and file transfers. Its robust encryption capabilities protect data in transit, making it an indispensable utility for system administrators and users alike. This section elaborates on configuring SSH, optimizing its security features, and employing it for both command-line operations and secure file transfers.

SSH is designed to replace older, less secure protocols such as Telnet and rlogin. It operates over a secure channel by authenticating connections and encrypting all transmitted data. The SSH server in Debian is typically provided by the `openssh-server` package. Ensuring that this package is installed is the first step in setting up secure remote access:

```
sudo apt update
sudo apt install openssh-server
```

After installation, the SSH server is configured via the `/etc/ssh/sshd_config` file. This file contains various settings that control authentication methods, encryption algorithms, and connection parameters. A common security practice is to disable root login. Editing the configuration file to set:

```
PermitRootLogin no
```

ensures that login attempts using the root account are denied. Additionally, it is advisable to specify allowed authentication methods. For instance, one might configure the SSH daemon to accept only public key authentication by setting:

```
PasswordAuthentication no
```

```
ChallengeResponseAuthentication no
PubkeyAuthentication yes
```

Such settings force users to rely on cryptographic keys for authentication, reducing the risk of brute-force attacks.

Key-based authentication involves generating a pair of cryptographic keys (a private key and a corresponding public key) on the client machine. This can be achieved with:

```
ssh-keygen -t rsa -b 4096
```

This command creates a 4096-bit RSA key pair. The public key is then copied to the remote server using the `ssh-copy-id` utility:

```
ssh-copy-id user@remotehost
```

Upon successful transfer, the SSH server acknowledges the public key during connection attempts, allowing the client to establish an encrypted session without transmitting a plaintext password. This method not only enhances security but also simplifies repeated connections.

Once connectivity is secured, command-line access can be utilized for various administrative tasks. For example, connecting to a remote server is straightforward:

```
ssh user@remotehost
```

Advanced users can leverage SSH tunneling and port forwarding to securely access services behind a firewall or to route traffic through an encrypted channel. For local port forwarding, the command structure is:

```
ssh -L local_port:destination_host:destination_port user@remotehost
```

This command binds a local port to destination services on the remote network. Conversely, remote port forwarding involves:

224

```
ssh -R remote_port:localhost:local_service_port user@remotehost
```

which permits remote clients to access a service running on the local machine. These port forwarding techniques are essential for secure access to internal network services and for bypassing network restrictions.

SSH also supports secure file transfers via SCP (Secure Copy) and SFTP (SSH File Transfer Protocol). SCP is a command-line utility that provides a straightforward mechanism for transferring files between local and remote systems. A typical file transfer using SCP is:

```
scp /path/to/local/file user@remotehost:/path/to/remote/directory
```

For recursive directory transfers, the -r option is utilized:

```
scp -r /path/to/local/directory user@remotehost:/path/to/remote/
    directory
```

SFTP offers an interactive interface for managing files on a remote host. Initiate an SFTP session with:

```
sftp user@remotehost
```

Once connected, standard file operation commands such as ls, cd, get, and put are available to navigate directories and transfer files. This duality in functionality ensures that users have both an interactive and a non-interactive tool at their disposal.

Securing an SSH connection does not solely involve configuring authentication. It is also important to implement connection settings that mitigate potential attacks. Configuring the maximum number of authentication attempts prevents prolonged brute-force attacks. For example, setting:

```
MaxAuthTries 3
```

in the sshd_config file limits the number of failed authentication at-

225

tempts allowed per connection. Moreover, setting a timeout for idle sessions helps prevent unauthorized access if a user leaves their session unattended:

```
ClientAliveInterval 300
ClientAliveCountMax 2
```

These settings cause the SSH server to close idle connections after a specified period, further reducing security risks.

In addition to these server-side settings, client-side configurations can further enhance the SSH experience. A configuration file located at ~/.ssh/config allows users to define shortcuts for frequently accessed hosts and specify default options. An example configuration is:

```
Host remotehost
    HostName remote.example.com
    User username
    Port 22
    IdentityFile ~/.ssh/id_rsa
    ForwardAgent yes
```

This file facilitates easier connection management by specifying default parameters for each host, thereby reducing the need to enter repeated options on the command line.

SSH also provides support for connection multiplexing, which allows multiple SSH sessions to share a single network connection. This feature reduces connection overhead and can be enabled in the client configuration using:

```
Host *
    ControlMaster auto
    ControlPath ~/.ssh/sockets/%r@%h-%p
    ControlPersist 600
```

With connection multiplexing, subsequent SSH sessions to the same host become nearly instantaneous, as they reuse the pre-existing connection, optimizing both caching and resource usage.

For advanced users, further hardening of SSH can be achieved by restricting which users or groups can access the system remotely. In the `sshd_config` file, directives such as:

```
AllowUsers user1 user2
AllowGroups sshusers
```

limit access to specified accounts, reducing the potential attack surface. Additionally, specifying permitted IP addresses using:

```
Match Address 192.168.1.0/24
    PasswordAuthentication no
```

ensures that only trusted network segments can attempt to authenticate, further reinforcing system security.

Monitoring and maintaining the SSH service is crucial for long-term system stability. Logging settings in the `sshd_config` file allow administrators to monitor connection attempts and other relevant activities:

```
LogLevel VERBOSE
```

A higher log verbosity facilitates audit trails that are instrumental during security reviews. Administrators can use system log files, often located in `/var/log/auth.log`, to analyze SSH-related activities and identify potential security incidents.

In environments that require high availability, configuring SSH failover and redundancy through load balancers or proxy servers is an effective strategy. Solutions such as HAProxy can distribute SSH connections across multiple backend servers. Although this configuration introduces additional complexity, it provides redundancy and scalability for enterprise-level deployments.

The inherent versatility of SSH makes it a critical component of secure, remote administration. Whether the objective is to manage servers in isolated data centers or maintain connectivity in distributed environments, SSH provides a secure channel for command execution and file

transfers. Its comprehensive configuration options empower administrators to tailor security and performance to the specific needs of their
infrastructure.

Prudent SSH configuration not only protects against unauthorized access but also facilitates efficient administrative operations. Integration with key-based authentication, dynamic port forwarding, and automated client configurations ensures that remote access remains both
secure and practical. This holistic approach to using SSH solidifies its
position as the cornerstone of secure remote connectivity in Debian
systems.

6.6. Configuring a Samba Server

Samba is an open-source suite that implements the Server Message
Block (SMB) protocol, allowing file and printer sharing between Linux
and Windows clients. Configuring a Samba server in Debian is a process that builds upon an understanding of network interfaces, connection management, and secure remote access. This section details the
installation, configuration, and management steps required to share
resources effectively across heterogeneous networks.

Samba is typically installed using the Debian package manager. The
following command retrieves and installs the required packages:

```
sudo apt update
sudo apt install samba samba-common
```

After installation, the primary configuration file for Samba is located
at /etc/samba/smb.conf. This file controls global settings as well as
resource-specific definitions. Editing this file requires administrative
privileges. A backup of the original configuration is recommended before making changes:

```
sudo cp /etc/samba/smb.conf /etc/samba/smb.conf.bak
```

228

The structure of smb.conf is divided into a global section and sections for individual shares. In the global section, settings include the workgroup, security mode, and logging options. A typical global configuration may resemble:

```
[global]
    workgroup = WORKGROUP
    server string = Samba Server on Debian
    netbios name = debian-srv
    security = user
    map to guest = Bad User
    dns proxy = no
    log file = /var/log/samba/%m.log
    max log size = 50
    load printers = yes
    cups options = raw
```

The workgroup directive must match the Windows workgroup used by clients. Setting security = user ensures that only users with valid credentials can access privileged shares. The directive map to guest = Bad User allows Samba to map unknown users to a guest account. Logging directives help in troubleshooting connectivity and permission issues by saving per-client logs.

Defining file shares involves adding sections that specify directories to share, the permissions associated with those shares, and any specific rules. An example of configuring a public file share that allows guest access is:

```
[Public]
    path = /srv/samba/public
    browseable = yes
    writable = yes
    guest ok = yes
    read only = no
    create mask = 0775
    directory mask = 0775
```

This share serves files from the /srv/samba/public directory. Allowing guest access by setting guest ok = yes permits users without an account to access the share. The file and directory masks ensure that permissions are set correctly on newly created files and directories, reflecting both security and accessibility requirements.

For environments where authentication is required and resource access needs to be restricted, Samba can be configured to share directories with specific user access. For example, to share a directory accessible only to members of a certain group, the configuration might be:

```
[Private]
    path = /srv/samba/private
    browseable = no
    writable = yes
    valid users = @sambashare
    create mask = 0770
    directory mask = 0770
```

Here, `valid users = @sambashare` specifies that only users who are members of the `sambashare` group can access the share. Setting `browseable = no` hides the share from users who do not have permission to view it, thus improving security.

User management is crucial when configuring a Samba server with restricted access. Samba maintains its own user database. Existing system users must be added to Samba using the following command:

```
sudo smbpasswd -a username
```

This command prompts for a password which will be used for Samba authentication. After adding the user, enabling the account is necessary to ensure that the password is active. Managing user access also involves fine-tuning permissions on the underlying Linux directories. The file system permissions must align with the intended access levels configured in `smb.conf`. For instance, setting group ownership and permissions on the shared directories can be achieved with:

```
sudo groupadd sambashare
sudo usermod -aG sambashare username
sudo chown -R :sambashare /srv/samba/private
sudo chmod -R 0770 /srv/samba/private
```

This sequence establishes a dedicated group, adds a user to that group, and applies appropriate permissions to the directory. Aligning file system permissions with Samba configuration is essential to prevent access conflicts and unintended privileges.

Samba also supports printer sharing. To share a printer with Windows and Linux clients, ensure that the `cups` and related packages are installed. In the `[global]` section of `smb.conf`, enabling printer sharing is done by setting:

```
load printers = yes
cups options = raw
```

Then, define a printer share with:

```
[printers]
    comment = All Printers
    path = /var/spool/samba
    browseable = no
    guest ok = no
    writable = no
    printable = yes
```

Configuring printer shares in this manner allows clients to discover and connect to available printers. Additional options can be set to restrict access or modify how printing is handled, ensuring compatibility across operating systems.

Once the configuration changes in `smb.conf` are complete, testing the validity of the configuration is crucial. Samba provides a built-in command to check the configuration file:

```
testparm
```

The `testparm` command parses the configuration file and outputs any errors or warnings, along with a summary of the active settings. Reviewing the output ensures that the server is correctly configured before restarting the Samba services.

After confirming the configuration, restart the Samba services to apply the changes:

```
sudo systemctl restart smbd
sudo systemctl restart nmbd
```

The smbd daemon handles file and printer sharing, whereas the nmbd daemon is responsible for network browsing functions and NetBIOS name resolution. Verifying that these daemons are active can be done using:

```
sudo systemctl status smbd
sudo systemctl status nmbd
```

Output similar to the following indicates that the services are functioning correctly:

```
smbd.service - Samba SMB Daemon
   Active: active (running) since ...

nmbd.service - Samba NMB Daemon
   Active: active (running) since ...
```

Troubleshooting Samba issues frequently requires examining log files. Samba logs can be found in /var/log/samba/; these logs provide detailed information on failed access attempts, connection issues, and other critical events. Adjusting the log level in smb.conf (using the log level directive) can provide additional diagnostic details during troubleshooting without overwhelming the system's primary logs.

Client configuration on both Windows and Linux is straightforward. In Windows, accessing a Samba share is accomplished by entering the UNC path in File Explorer, such as \\debian-srv\Public. The client is prompted for credentials if the share is restricted. On Linux, file managers such as Nautilus and Dolphin can access Samba shares using URIs like smb://debian-srv/Public. Alternatively, mounting a Samba share on the command-line can be done using the CIFS (Common Internet File System) utilities:

232

```
sudo apt install cifs-utils
sudo mount -t cifs //debian-srv/Private /mnt/private -o username=
    username,domain=WORKGROUP
```

This command mounts the share to the local directory /mnt/private, enabling file operations as if the share were part of the local file system.

Managing a Samba server also involves periodic maintenance tasks such as updating user credentials, managing share directories, and monitoring access logs to detect unauthorized attempts. Adjusting configuration settings to respond to evolving security policies can be performed by editing smb.conf and reloading the Samba services. For example, to remove a user from the Samba user database, use:

```
sudo smbpasswd -x username
```

This command ensures that the user no longer has access to any Samba shares, aligning with dynamic changes in administrative policies.

In environments with mixed operating systems, performance tuning may be required. Samba supports a range of advanced options for optimizing performance, such as socket options, read and write raw settings, and asynchronous I/O. These options can be appended to the global section to fine-tune latency and throughput, depending on the specific workloads and network conditions.

Samba's flexibility extends to domain integration and Active Directory compatibility. For organizations that require centralized authentication, integrating Samba with an Active Directory domain provides a unified approach to user management. This configuration involves joining the Debian Samba server to an Active Directory domain using tools like winbind and adjusting smb.conf accordingly. Such integration allows seamless sharing across multiple platforms with centralized credential management.

The comprehensive configuration and management of a Samba server contribute significantly to a secure and efficient network environment. By leveraging detailed configuration files, aligning file system permissions, and employing robust user management strategies, Samba enables seamless file and printer sharing across Windows and Linux clients.

6.7. Using VPN for Private Networking

Virtual Private Networks (VPNs) provide a secure method for connecting remote users or networks together over untrusted public networks. This section explains the configuration and usage of VPNs in a Debian environment, focusing on establishing secure tunnels that protect data in transit and enable confidential communication across geographically dispersed networks.

A common solution for implementing VPNs in Debian is OpenVPN, an open-source VPN solution that uses SSL/TLS for key exchange and supports a variety of authentication mechanisms. OpenVPN can operate in both client-server and peer-to-peer configurations. Installation on a Debian system is straightforward:

```
sudo apt update
sudo apt install openvpn
```

Once installed, configuring OpenVPN involves setting up a secure server and corresponding client configurations. The server configuration file is usually located in /etc/openvpn/server.conf. A sample configuration might include settings for port, protocol, and encryption parameters:

```
port 1194
proto udp
dev tun
ca /etc/openvpn/keys/ca.crt
cert /etc/openvpn/keys/server.crt
key /etc/openvpn/keys/server.key
```

```
dh /etc/openvpn/keys/dh.pem
server 10.8.0.0 255.255.255.0
ifconfig-pool-persist /var/log/openvpn/ipp.txt
push "redirect-gateway def1 bypass-dhcp"
push "dhcp-option DNS 8.8.8.8"
keepalive 10 120
cipher AES-256-CBC
user nobody
group nogroup
persist-key
persist-tun
status /var/log/openvpn/openvpn-status.log
verb 3
```

In this configuration, OpenVPN listens on port 1194 using the UDP protocol and creates a TUN device for routing traffic. The lines beginning with ca, cert, and key refer to the Certificate Authority, server certificate, and server key files, respectively. These files, along with the Diffie-Hellman parameters generated by the command:

```
openssl dhparam -out /etc/openvpn/keys/dh.pem 2048
```

ensure secure key exchange. The server directive defines the private subnet allocated to VPN clients. The directive push "redirect-gateway ..." instructs connected clients to route all their traffic through the VPN. Additionally, the DNS server is set to 8.8.8.8. The configuration further enhances security by lowering privileges through the user and group directives.

After creating the server configuration, generating the necessary keys and certificates is essential. One common approach is to use the EasyRSA suite, which simplifies the creation and management of a public key infrastructure (PKI). The process typically involves initializing a certificate authority, building server and client certificates, and revoking certificates if necessary. For example, initializing the PKI can be accomplished with:

```
cd /etc/openvpn/easy-rsa
./easyrsa init-pki
./easyrsa build-ca
```

235

```
./easyrsa gen-req server nopass
./easyrsa sign-req server server
./easyrsa gen-dh
```

Each step ensures that the VPN server will have robust cryptographic credentials. Clients require their own certificate and key to authenticate with the server. A client configuration file typically mirrors many of the server's settings but includes a reference to client-specific keys. A sample client configuration might be:

```
client
dev tun
proto udp
remote your-server-address 1194
resolv-retry infinite
nobind
persist-key
persist-tun
ca ca.crt
cert client.crt
key client.key
cipher AES-256-CBC
verb 3
```

In this setup, the client connects to the VPN server at your-server-address. The file references for `ca.crt`, `client.crt`, and `client.key` must be provided on the client machine, ensuring mutual authentication.

Proper firewall configuration is critical for VPN functionality. Since the VPN server listens on a specific port (1194 in the example), ensure that this port is open on the firewall. For systems using UFW, a rule can be added as follows:

```
sudo ufw allow 1194/udp
```

For iptables-based configurations, a rule equivalent is:

```
sudo iptables -A INPUT -p udp --dport 1194 -j ACCEPT
```

Ensuring that NAT (Network Address Translation) is configured appropriately is also necessary so that VPN clients can access the internet through the VPN server. This typically involves adding iptables rules to masquerade VPN client traffic. For example:

```
sudo iptables -t nat -A POSTROUTING -s 10.8.0.0/24 -o eth0 -j
    MASQUERADE
```

This rule ensures that all traffic originating from the VPN subnet is translated correctly to exit through the main network interface (eth0). Persisting such rules across reboots is recommended, either by saving the iptables configuration or by using a firewall management tool that reapplies rules dynamically.

Another emerging solution for VPNs is WireGuard, known for its simplicity and performance. WireGuard is integrated into the Linux kernel and is included in recent Debian releases. Its configuration process is more straightforward than OpenVPN's. Installation is achieved by executing:

```
sudo apt update
sudo apt install wireguard
```

WireGuard requires generating public and private keys. This can be performed with the wg command:

```
umask 077
wg genkey | tee privatekey | wg pubkey > publickey
```

A simple WireGuard server configuration file (/etc/wireguard/wg0.conf) may appear as:

```
[Interface]
Address = 10.0.0.1/24
ListenPort = 51820
PrivateKey = SERVER_PRIVATE_KEY

[Peer]
PublicKey = CLIENT_PUBLIC_KEY
AllowedIPs = 10.0.0.2/32
```

In this configuration, the server interface is given the IP address

237

10.0.0.1/24 and listens on port 51820. The [Peer] section defines the allowed IPs from the client and incorporates the client's public key. The same steps are repeated on the client side, with appropriate adjustment to IP addresses and keys. WireGuard's configuration is stored in a similar fashion, and the interface is activated using:

```
sudo systemctl start wg-quick@wg0
```

Both OpenVPN and WireGuard illustrate different approaches to securing VPN connections. OpenVPN offers extensive configurability and compatibility with diverse legacy environments. WireGuard, by contrast, emphasizes performance, ease of configuration, and lower overhead. Deciding between these technologies depends on the requirements for compatibility, throughput, and administrative simplicity.

VPN usage improves remote access security significantly by encrypting data transmitted over untrusted networks. VPNs not only secure traffic but also enable remote users to access internal network resources as if they were locally connected. Administrators often configure split tunneling to allow specific traffic to be routed through the VPN while letting other traffic use the local internet connection. In an OpenVPN client configuration, split tunneling can be implemented by removing or modifying the redirect-gateway directive and specifying routes that should go through the VPN. For example:

```
route 192.168.1.0 255.255.255.0
```

This command selectively routes traffic destined for the internal network through the VPN tunnel while other traffic bypasses it. Balancing security and performance is critical in environments with varied connectivity requirements.

Maintaining VPN services involves regular monitoring of connection logs and performance metrics. OpenVPN logs are typically found in /var/log/openvpn/ and provide data on connection attempts, disconnections, and potential issues during key exchange or decryption. Analyzing these logs helps in preempting potential security incidents and troubleshooting connectivity problems. Tools such as `grep` and `tail` are invaluable for real-time monitoring:

```
sudo tail -f /var/log/openvpn/openvpn-status.log
```

Logging in WireGuard can be achieved through standard system logs or by configuring additional logging mechanisms. Keeping an eye on these logs can provide early warnings about configuration errors or unauthorized access attempts.

VPNs provide additional layers of isolation and segmentation within larger network architectures. When combined with firewall rules and proper routing configurations, VPNs ensure that traffic from remote clients is securely segregated from general internet traffic. This segregation is essential in protecting sensitive data and ensuring that remote access does not inadvertently expose critical systems.

Integration with modern authentication methods, such as multi-factor authentication (MFA), further enhances VPN security. By requiring users to enter a time-sensitive code in addition to their private key or password, system administrators can thwart unauthorized access attempts even if credentials become compromised. Implementing MFA for VPN access may require interfacing with centralized authentication services or deploying specialized VPN solutions that support such features.

A well-designed VPN infrastructure also simplifies administrative tasks through centralized configuration and management. Using configuration management tools and version control systems for VPN configuration files promotes consistency across servers and expedites recovery in the event of configuration errors. Routine audits of VPN settings and periodic updates of cryptographic keys and certificates are practices that maintain the integrity of the VPN environment over time.

Whether using OpenVPN for its extensive feature set or WireGuard for its simplicity and high performance, configuring a VPN in Debian represents a critical aspect of modern network security. These technologies provide encrypted tunnels that safeguard data and ensure that remote connectivity operates under the same secure parameters as local networks. This protection is essential when connecting over public networks, where data interception and unauthorized access are significant risks.

Through careful configuration, continuous monitoring, and adherence to security best practices, VPNs serve as formidable barriers against unwanted intrusions. Administrators leveraging these tools are equipped to provide secure remote access, protect sensitive communications, and build resilient networks that adapt to the evolving cybersecurity landscape.

Chapter 7

File Systems and Storage Management

This chapter provides insights into Linux file systems, covering mounting, partitioning, and formatting procedures. It explores disk quotas, LVM for flexible storage management, and RAID configurations for redundancy. Essential techniques for file system checks and repairs are included, equipping users with the knowledge to effectively manage and maintain robust storage systems in Debian environments.

7.1. Understanding Linux File Systems

Linux supports a variety of file systems that have been optimized for different use cases, and understanding their internal structures, benefits, and limitations is crucial for effective system management. This section focuses on three widely used file systems in Linux environments:

241

ext4, Btrfs, and XFS. Building on the foundation established in earlier discussions on mounting, partitioning, and disk management, the following details provide an in-depth examination of each file system's design principles and operational characteristics.

The ext4 file system is the successor to ext3 and continues the tradition of reliability and performance improvement. It is a journaling file system that uses a method known as the journaling technique to log changes before they are committed to the main file system structure. This approach provides a quick recovery mechanism in the event of a system crash or power failure. The design of ext4 includes features like extents, delayed allocation, and multi-block allocation, which help avoid fragmentation and improve overall performance. The extent-based allocation, in particular, improves both read/write efficiency and metadata management by allocating contiguous blocks, thereby reducing the time required for data retrieval. Another notable benefit of ext4 is its wide compatibility and proven stability in production systems, making it a reliable option for general-purpose storage.

The practical benefits of ext4 become apparent when performing common administrative tasks. For example, creating an ext4 file system on a partition can be accomplished with the following command, which ensures that the partition is formatted with the correct block size and layout:

```
sudo mkfs.ext4 /dev/sda1
```

This command initializes the filesystem using default parameters, although advanced users may specify options for features such as reserved blocks and journaling modes to better suit specific workloads. In environments where consistency and robustness are paramount, ext4 offers a tested solution with a balance of performance and security.

Btrfs (B-tree file system) represents a more modern alternative de-

242

signed with scalability and flexibility in mind. Unlike traditional file systems, Btrfs integrates several advanced features directly into its design. One of the primary advantages of Btrfs is its support for snapshotting, which allows users to capture the state of the file system at specific points in time. This capability is especially useful for backup and recovery scenarios as well as for testing system changes without affecting the primary data. Built with a copy-on-write (COW) mechanism, Btrfs preserves the integrity of data by ensuring that any modification leads to new block allocations while maintaining older versions. As a result, users can easily revert to a previous state if necessary.

Btrfs also provides subvolume management, enabling the partitioning of the file system into distinct areas that can be managed separately. This approach not only simplifies administrative tasks but also enhances performance by isolating heavily used sections from less active areas. Furthermore, Btrfs includes support for online defragmentation, built-in RAID functionality, and transparent compression, making it suitable for both personal computing and enterprise storage solutions.

Administrators can create a Btrfs file system with a command analogous to that used for ext4, but with additional options to leverage its advanced features:

```
sudo mkfs.btrfs -L mybtrfs /dev/sdb1
```

This command assigns a label to the file system and initializes it with Btrfs defaults. Once created, the file system can be mounted and managed using Btrfs-specific tools that allow for subvolume and snapshot operations. The flexible design of Btrfs encourages experimentation and fine-tuning, which is invaluable in environments that demand dynamic storage solutions.

XFS is another powerful file system, particularly noted for its scalability and efficiency in handling large files and high-performance workloads. Developed initially in the 1990s, XFS has been extensively optimized for parallel I/O operations and is especially well-suited for systems dealing with very large storage arrays or data-intensive applications. A key strength of XFS is its ability to manage vast file systems with minimal overhead. Its architecture includes allocation groups, which allow concurrent operations on different parts of the disk, thereby maximizing throughput in systems with heavy concurrent access.

One of the critical design aspects of XFS is its metadata management system. By employing a robust journaling mechanism and an efficient B+ tree structure for indexing, XFS reduces the overhead associated with file allocation and metadata updates. This architecture minimizes fragmentation and ensures that both file access and system performance remain optimal even as the file system grows. Furthermore, XFS supports features such as delayed logging and real-time sub-volumes, which can be particularly beneficial for applications like video editing or database management that require high-speed access to large files.

Creating an XFS file system is straightforward. The initialization command is similar to other file systems but may include specific parameters to cater to the anticipated workload:

```
sudo mkfs.xfs -f /dev/sdc1
```

The -f option forces the creation of the file system if the target partition already contains data, which is useful during system setup phases where storage devices are repurposed. Once formulated, XFS is mounted in the standard way, with operational parameters that can be customized further to improve caching and I/O scheduling based on system requirements.

Each of the file systems discussed—ext4, Btrfs, and XFS—incorporates distinct architectural choices that cater to different practical needs.

Ext4's journaling and extent-based allocation make it an ideal general-purpose file system, balancing performance with reliability. In contrast, Btrfs offers a suite of integrated features such as snapshotting, subvoluming, and copy-on-write, which make it an excellent choice for environments where data integrity and the ability to revert to previous states are critical. Meanwhile, XFS excels in high-performance scenarios, particularly in systems that require the efficient handling of large files and heavy I/O loads.

A further point of differentiation lies in their management utilities. Administrative tools for ext4 and XFS are typically less complex, given their focused role in managing file storage on fixed partitions. However, Btrfs utilities encompass a broader range of functions that support advanced storage management tasks. For instance, Btrfs enables users to balance the file system by redistributing data across available devices, check for errors without taking the file system offline, and adjust performance parameters on the fly. These features are implemented through commands such as:

```
sudo btrfs balance start /mnt/mybtrfs
sudo btrfs scrub start /mnt/mybtrfs
```

These operations manage data distribution and integrity checking without requiring system downtime, which is essential for maintaining data availability in production systems.

The decision regarding which file system to deploy depends largely on requirements related to performance, data recovery capabilities, scalability, and administrative overhead. For many users, ext4 remains the default choice due to its simplicity and robustness. However, for scenarios where advanced data management features are advantageous, Btrfs presents a compelling option. In contrast, enterprise environments that demand high throughput and efficient handling of large files may prefer XFS. Evaluating these file systems in light of system-specific needs ensures that disk performance aligns with broader operational goals.

The integration of these file systems with existing system components must also be considered. The compatibility of each file system with system utilities, recovery tools, and monitoring systems can significantly influence overall system stability. For example, ext4's long history in Linux environments means that a wide range of recovery utilities and diagnostic tools are available, reducing the risk associated with data loss. In contrast, while Btrfs and XFS offer modern functionalities, they may require more specialized knowledge and tools for optimal configuration and maintenance.

Developing a comprehensive understanding of these file systems enhances the capacity to make informed decisions during both initial system deployment and ongoing system maintenance. As systems evolve and storage needs increase, the ability to transition between file systems or migrate data without extensive downtime becomes a crucial asset. By leveraging the strengths of ext4, Btrfs, and XFS, system administrators can tailor storage solutions that not only meet current performance demands but also anticipate future scalability challenges.

The benefits of a well-chosen file system extend beyond raw performance metrics. They encompass data safety, efficient resource utilization, and administrative simplicity. In-depth knowledge of file system architectures underpins effective system design, allowing administrators to mitigate common pitfalls such as fragmentation, inefficient metadata handling, and suboptimal disk utilization. The evolution of file system technology reflects a continuous effort to balance these competing demands, and the available choices today demonstrate significant advancements over earlier implementations.

The interplay of data management strategies—from journaling in ext4 to copy-on-write mechanisms in Btrfs and parallel I/O capabilities in XFS—illustrates the importance of aligning file system attributes with

246

specific application requirements. This alignment enhances overall system performance and can be particularly critical in environments that require high availability and rapid recovery capabilities. An informed selection process incorporates both performance benchmarks and the operational context, ensuring that the file system's characteristics directly support the intended workload.

System administrators are encouraged to experiment with these file systems in controlled environments before deploying them into production. Testing and validation are key to understanding the practical implications of design choices. Tools such as benchmarking utilities and monitoring applications can provide invaluable insights into how these file systems perform under different loads and configurations. An iterative approach to file system selection and management thus forms a core element of robust Linux system administration.

7.2. Mounting and Unmounting File Systems

A fundamental aspect of Linux system administration is the process of mounting and unmounting file systems, which allows the operating system to access data stored on different storage devices. Mastery of this process enables administrators to manually attach file systems to the directory tree and automate the mounting process for consistent behavior during system boot. The capabilities introduced in earlier sections regarding file system structures and disk management converge here, where understanding the interplay between hardware, file system types, and system configuration becomes essential.

At its core, the mount process involves associating a block device with a directory in the file system hierarchy, known as the mount point. The mount point serves as the gateway to access the contents of the attached file system. The `mount` command is central to the process, and its usage spans from simple one-time mounts to complex configurations involving multiple options for performance, security, and stability.

Manual mounting is performed by specifying the device and its designated mount point. For instance, mounting an ext4 file system might require the following command:

```
sudo mount -t ext4 /dev/sda1 /mnt/data
```

In this command, -t ext4 explicitly tells the system what file system type is used, though in many cases this specification is optional as Linux is capable of automatically detecting the file system. This command demonstrates a straightforward approach to manually making a file system accessible at /mnt/data. However, adding additional options can enhance the functionality. The -o flag permits specification of multiple options. For example, mounting a file system as read-only to safeguard against unintended changes can be performed by:

```
sudo mount -o ro /dev/sda1 /mnt/data
```

This ensures that the mounted file system is accessible without the risk of accidental modifications. Other mount options include setting file permissions, enabling user access, and specifying performance parameters such as noatime, which prevents the system from updating the access time for files, thereby reducing disk I/O overhead on frequently accessed file systems.

Beyond manual intervention, automating the mount process is crucial for systems that require persistent configurations across reboots. The primary mechanism for achieving this is the modifications to the /etc/fstab file. This configuration file contains a list of devices and their respective mount points, along with various options that dictate how and when the file system should be mounted. Each line in /etc/fstab typically follows a format similar to:

```
UUID=123e4567-e89b-12d3-a456-426614174000 /mnt/data ext4 defaults,
    noatime 0 2
```

In this configuration, the device is identified by its universally unique identifier (UUID), ensuring that the correct hardware is targeted regardless of order changes in device naming. The mount options are specified after the file system type: `defaults` applies a standard set of options, while `noatime` reduces disk write operations by not updating the file access times. The final two numbers define the dump and fsck options used during system boot.

It is essential to understand the implications of the options configured in `/etc/fstab`. For instance, options related to security might include `nodev`, `nosuid`, and `noexec` when mounting file systems that contain untrusted data. These options prevent device files from being interpreted, block operations that require elevated privilege, or stop the execution of binaries stored on the mounted partition, respectively:

```
UUID=987e6543-e89b-12d3-c456-426655441234 /mnt/secure ext4 defaults,
    nodev,nosuid,noexec 0 1
```

By incorporating these options, administrators can mitigate risks from potential exploits that might target improperly managed file systems.

The process of unmounting file systems is equally important, particularly before performing system maintenance, replacing storage devices, or shutting down systems properly. The `umount` command (note the omission of the letter n) detaches the file system from the mount point. A straightforward command is:

```
sudo umount /mnt/data
```

This command disconnects the file system mounted under `/mnt/data` from the Linux directory tree. Unmounting must be performed with care to ensure that no processes are actively using resources on the file system. In cases where a file system is busy, employing the `-l` (lazy unmount) option may be necessary, which allows the system to defer the unmount operation until the file system is no longer in use:

```
sudo umount -l /mnt/data
```

Lazy unmounting is particularly useful for network file systems or removable media that may otherwise remain locked due to lingering processes.

Management of mount points extends beyond static directories; dynamic mounting through the use of the autofs utility or systemd's automount feature further enhances system flexibility. These services enable on-demand mounting of file systems. With automounting, a file system is mounted only when it is accessed, reducing the amount of resources dedicated to idle storage and improving boot times. A typical entry in /etc/fstab for an automounted file system using systemd might take the form:

```
UUID=123e4567-e89b-12d3-a456-426614174000 /mnt/auto ext4 noauto,x-
    systemd.automount 0 2
```

The noauto option prevents the file system from mounting automatically at boot, while x-systemd.automount coordinates with systemd to mount the file system on first access. Testing an automounted file system, one may observe that accessing the directory triggers a mount. For instance, while listing the contents of /mnt/auto, systemd initiates the mount operation. Verification of this behavior can be done with:

```
ls /mnt/auto
```

```
[systemd] Mounted /mnt/auto
file1  file2  directory1
```

Such configurations ensure that resources are allocated efficiently and that file systems remain available only as needed.

Another aspect of managing mount points is the remounting of file systems with altered options without disconnecting them entirely. This process is useful when temporary changes in file access modes or performance characteristics are required. The mount command supports the -o remount option, enabling administrators to adjust parameters

250

on the fly. For instance, modifying a file system mounted as read-only to allow writing can be executed by:

```
sudo mount -o remount,rw /mnt/data
```

Conversely, converting a writable file system to read-only mode for purposes of maintenance or data preservation employs a similar command structure:

```
sudo mount -o remount,ro /mnt/data
```

Remounting is an efficient method to alter file system behavior dynamically, minimizing downtime while transitioning between different operational states.

Special attention must be given to file systems mounted over network protocols, such as NFS (Network File System) and CIFS (Common Internet File System). These types of mounts have unique requirements and options to consider, including network timeouts, caching strategies, and authentication methods. An example of mounting an NFS share involves:

```
sudo mount -t nfs -o rw,hard,intr nfs-server:/export/share /mnt/
    nfs_share
```

Here, options such as hard ensure that I/O operations remain persistent until the server recovers, while intr allows operations to be interrupted in the event of a server failure. Furthermore, for CIFS mounts, credentials can be managed via a credentials file to enhance security and simplify the mounting process:

```
sudo mount -t cifs -o credentials=/home/user/.smbcredentials,uid
    =1000,gid=1000 //server/share /mnt/cifs_share
```

The ability to mount remote file systems extends the flexibility of Linux systems beyond local storage, integrating disparate storage solutions into a coherent system architecture.

251

Handling errors and diagnostics is a critical component of mounting operations. System logs and outputs provided by commands are vital for troubleshooting. When a mount operation fails, inspecting dmesg or relevant log files in /var/log offers insights into the error. An error due to a file system inconsistency might produce a message indicating potential corruption or misconfiguration:

```
sudo dmesg | grep mount
```

Such diagnostic practices allow administrators to pinpoint issues quickly and undertake remedial actions. In some instances, file system repair tools, such as fsck for ext-based file systems, might need to be executed before a successful mounting can be achieved.

Interactions between mounting and system security further underscore the necessity for precise control over mount options. By effectively utilizing mount parameters that restrict capabilities (e.g., nosuid to disable set-user-identifier or nodev to block device files), administrators can mitigate risks associated with unauthorized privilege escalation and execution of untrusted code. This level of control is especially critical in multi-user systems or environments where data integrity is paramount.

Understanding the nuances of mounting and unmounting file systems fosters an appreciation for the balance between accessibility, performance, and security. The principles elucidated here integrate with the broader context of Linux file system management, reinforcing the interconnected nature of file system choice, mounting configurations, and overall system health. By carefully tailoring mount options and employing dynamic mounting techniques, administrators can optimize system behavior to meet specific operational and performance benchmarks while ensuring resilience in the face of faults or security threats.

7.3. Partitioning and Formatting Drives

Efficient storage management begins with the proper partitioning of physical drives, followed by formatting each partition with a suitable file system. This section explores the array of tools and techniques available in Linux for partitioning disks and formatting them with file systems tailored to specific operational requirements. Established concepts of mounting file systems and their internal structures naturally extend into the partitioning domain, where strategic allocation of storage contributes to system performance, data safety, and ease of management.

Disk partitioning subdivides a physical drive into isolated, manageable regions. Each partition can be formatted with a file system that best supports its intended usage. The conventional utility fdisk serves as one of the primary tools for managing Master Boot Record (MBR)-style partitions. Invoking fdisk in interactive mode allows administrators to create, delete, and modify partitions. A standard session using fdisk proceeds as shown below:

```
sudo fdisk /dev/sda
```

Within the fdisk interface, commands such as n to create a new partition, d to delete, and w to write changes are used. For example, creating a new primary partition that occupies the entirety of the available space involves invoking the n command followed by selecting the default partition number, first sector, and last sector. After writing the changes, the new partition appears ready to be formatted.

For drives utilizing the GUID Partition Table (GPT) scheme, gdisk or parted are often preferred. The gdisk utility functions similarly to fdisk with added support for GPT's features. An example command to initiate a gdisk session is:

```
sudo gdisk /dev/sdb
```

253

Alternatively, parted provides a non-interactive mode as well as support for scripting. Its utility becomes particularly useful for operations on larger drives and when working with both MBR and GPT partitioning schemes. A simple command to list partition details using parted is:

```
sudo parted /dev/sdc print
```

Partitioning schemes can be designed to cater to varying needs such as separating system files from user data, isolating swap partitions, or allocating areas for backup and recovery. Administrators must weigh the importance of flexibility, boot compatibility, and performance when deciding on the partitioning layout. For example, dedicated partitions for critical system directories enhance security by limiting access to files and reducing the potential impact of a full disk.

Once partitions have been successfully created, the next stage is to format these partitions with an appropriate file system. The selection of a file system should consider factors such as performance requirements, reliability, and the intended use of the partition. For general-purpose applications, ext4 remains a robust choice, while file systems such as XFS or Btrfs might be chosen for their unique strengths in handling large files or advanced storage features respectively.

Formatting a partition is performed using file system creation utilities, typically prefixed by mkfs. For instance, to format a new partition with ext4, the following command is used:

```
sudo mkfs.ext4 /dev/sda1
```

This command initializes the partition /dev/sda1 with the ext4 file system. Options can be added to define block size, inode size, and other parameters that affect performance and data management. Adjusting these options is particularly relevant in environments with unique performance or storage density requirements.

When choosing file systems, it is critical to understand the impact of various formatting options. For instance, creating an XFS file system on a partition designed for databases, where high throughput and parallel I/O are crucial, involves a format command such as:

```
sudo mkfs.xfs -f /dev/sdc1
```

The -f flag forces the creation of the file system even if the device appears to be in use or contains remnants of previous formatting. Similarly, formatting a partition with Btrfs to leverage advanced features like snapshotting and compression might be initiated with:

```
sudo mkfs.btrfs /dev/sdb1
```

Each file system also brings its own suite of tuning and maintenance tools designed to check and repair data integrity as well as optimize storage. Even though file systems such as ext4 can be tuned once formatted, it is the initial decisions made during the formatting process that set the stage for long-term performance and stability. Parameters such as reserved blocks in ext4 or the allocation strategies in XFS are determined at the time of formatting.

The role of partitioning extends beyond simple space division. Advanced partitioning strategies also cater to the unique requirements of modern computing environments, including dual-boot configurations, server virtualization, and high availability systems. In dual-boot scenarios, multiple operating systems may reside on the same physical drive with distinct partitions reserved for each system's root, swap, and home directories. This segmentation not only organizes data effectively but also enhances security by isolating the operational segments of each system.

On server-class hardware, disk partitions may be configured to optimize the performance of specific workloads. For example, a server hosting a database might benefit from separating the database files onto their own partitions, formatted with a robust file system that supports high levels of concurrent access, such as XFS. The separation of partitions ensures that a sudden surge in activity in one region does not negatively impact system performance across the board.

The automation of partitioning and formatting is particularly valuable in environments where large-scale deployment is required. Scripting tools, along with utilities like sgdisk, allow administrators to create, modify, and replicate partition tables across multiple drives. A typical scripted approach using parted might involve the following series of commands to create a new GPT partition table and a primary partition:

```
sudo parted /dev/sdd --script mklabel gpt
sudo parted /dev/sdd --script mkpart primary ext4 1MiB 100%
```

After partition creation, automating the formatting process ensures consistency across systems. For instance, a shell script that formats all new partitions with ext4 could be written as:

```
#!/bin/bash
for disk in /dev/sdd1 /dev/sde1; do
    sudo mkfs.ext4 -F "$disk"
done
```

Ensuring the script is executable and correctly configured for the target hardware leads to a reduced overhead in system preparation and deployment.

Attention to disk partitioning and formatting details also extends to considerations regarding error detection and correction. Tools such as badblocks can be employed prior to formatting to identify defective areas on a physical drive:

```
sudo badblocks -sv /dev/sdb1
```

Identifying and marking bad blocks ensures that subsequent formatting tasks do not allocate these sectors, thereby increasing system reliability. Advanced file system creation tools often integrate options that address these issues, providing administrators with the ability to enforce block-level checks during the formatting process.

Disk partitioning also interacts closely with the overall lifecycle management of storage. Creating dedicated partitions for system logs, temporary files, or swap space minimizes the risk that unregulated growth in one area affects the performance of critical services. These strategies are supported by formatting utilities that offer tailored options for various data types, thereby ensuring an efficient allocation of disk resources.

Another essential aspect of drive partitioning and formatting is the integration of modern storage technologies such as Solid State Drives (SSDs) and hybrid storage configurations. SSDs often require partition alignment adjustments to achieve optimal read/write performance. Tools such as `parted` or `fdisk` offer mechanisms to align partitions on boundaries that are multiples of the SSD's erase block size. An incorrect alignment can result in degraded performance and a reduction in the drive's lifespan. One may check the alignment using:

```
sudo fdisk -l /dev/sdf
```

The output provides details on the starting sectors of each partition, ensuring that they comply with the guidelines specified by the drive manufacturer. Furthermore, formatting an SSD with a file system such as ext4 may involve options that cater specifically to flash storage, like eliminating atime updates (via `noatime`) to reduce unnecessary write operations.

In modern enterprise environments, drives are often organized into logical volumes using tools like the Logical Volume Manager (LVM). Partitioning with LVM introduces an abstraction layer that facilitates dynamic resizing and the pooling of storage resources. Initial steps involve creating physical volumes with:

```
sudo pvcreate /dev/sdg1
```

These physical volumes are then aggregated into volume groups, which in turn can host multiple logical volumes. Each logical volume can be formatted with the appropriate file system, providing a flexible approach to managing storage that can adapt to evolving needs without requiring major system downtime.

The interplay between partitioning and formatting is critical not only during initial system configuration but also as systems scale and evolve over time. As data storage demands increase, re-partitioning and re-formatting may become necessary to optimize performance or increase capacity. Working within the Linux environment's robust suite of tools ensures that such operations can be executed with minimal disruption and maximum data integrity.

Understanding and mastering the tools for partitioning and formatting drives is integral to the overall strategy of Linux storage management. Decisions made during these processes have long-lasting effects on system stability, performance, and security. As administrators gain familiarity with utilities such as `fdisk`, `gdisk`, `parted`, and file system creation commands, they are better equipped to design storage layouts that are both efficient and resilient. The capacity to automate these tasks further increases operational efficiency, reducing both the time and potential errors associated with manual configurations.

7.4. Managing Disk Quotas

Disk quotas provide an essential mechanism for administrators to control and monitor the usage of disk space by individual users and groups. In environments with multi-user system access, managing quotas helps prevent any single user from monopolizing storage resources, thereby ensuring fairness and system stability. This section discusses the step-by-step process of setting up, administering, and troubleshooting disk quotas on Linux systems, expanding upon earlier concepts related to file systems, mounting, and partitioning.

The fundamental idea behind disk quotas is to enforce limits on the amount of disk space that can be consumed by users and groups. This is accomplished through a combination of kernel support and user-space utilities that track file system usage. Administrators typically designate specific mount points for quota enforcement. In most cases, quotas are activated on partitions where user data is stored and require modifications to the system's mount configuration file, /etc/fstab, to enable quota support at boot time.

To enable quota functionality, the partition of interest must be mounted with quota options. For instance, if a partition is mounted at /mnt/data, the corresponding line in /etc/fstab might be modified as follows:

```
UUID=123e4567-e89b-12d3-a456-426614174000 /mnt/data ext4 defaults,
    usrquota,grpquota 0 2
```

The inclusion of usrquota and grpquota flags in the mount options instructs the system to maintain separate quota records for individual users and groups, respectively. Once these options are specified, the file system must be remounted for the changes to take effect. This can be performed without a complete system reboot using the mount command:

```
sudo mount -o remount /mnt/data
```

After the partition is remounted with quota support, the next step is to create and initialize the quota database files. These files, commonly named aquota.user and aquota.group, are stored in the root directory of the mounted file system. The utility quotacheck scans the file system and generates these databases. The following command performs a quota check with options to create user and group quota files:

```
sudo quotacheck -cug /mnt/data
```

The -c flag instructs quotacheck to create new quota files, while -u and -g specify that both user and group quotas should be checked. Once the quota databases are created, they must be activated with the quotaon utility:

```
sudo quotaon -v /mnt/data
```

The -v flag enables verbose output, allowing administrators to verify that quota enforcement is active on the specified partition.

After quotas are activated, administrators can manage them using several utilities. One common tool is edquota, which provides an interface to edit quota limits for users or groups. Suppose an administrator wishes to set disk space limits for a user named alice. The command to edit alice's quota would be:

```
sudo edquota alice
```

When edquota opens a text editor, the quota record for alice might be presented as follows:

Disk quotas for user alice (uid 1001):

Filesystem	blocks	soft	
/dev/sda1	500000	550000	6

Here, the soft limit for disk blocks is a threshold which, when exceeded, will generate a warning. The hard limit represents an absolute maximum, beyond which the system will not allow further allocation. Similar steps can be followed to edit group quotas by replacing the username with the group name.

Administrators can obtain an overview of quota usage on a particular partition using the repquota utility. This command provides detailed reports on disk block and inode usage, comparing current usage against defined quotas:

```
sudo repquota /mnt/data
```

A sample output might be:

260

```
*** Report for user quotas on /dev/sda1
Block grace time: 7days; Inode grace time: 7days
                        Block limits              File limits
User           used    soft    hard  grace   used  soft  hard  grace
-------------------------------------------------------------------
alice        520000  550000  600000  5days   1210  1250  1300  none
bob          480000  500000  550000  none    1100  1150  1200  none
-------------------------------------------------------------------
*** End of report
```

This output clearly indicates any inconsistencies or potential overuse that might require administrative intervention.

In addition to setting fixed limits, administrators may need to enforce grace periods for soft limit violations. Grace periods provide users with a predefined window within which they can reduce their disk usage to fall within the allocated soft limits. The lengths of these grace periods are configured globally in system files related to quota management, ensuring consistency across the board. Proper administration of grace periods is crucial, as it balances strict quota enforcement with user flexibility.

The administration of disk quotas is not limited to manual editing alone. Scripting and automation can play a vital role in large-scale deployments, where quotas must be regularly monitored and adjusted. For example, a simple shell script could be developed to notify administrators when a user's quota usage exceeds 90% of their soft limit. A snippet of such a script might look as follows:

```bash
#!/bin/bash
THRESHOLD=90
for user in $(cut -f1 -d: /etc/passwd); do
    USAGE=$(repquota /mnt/data | grep "^$user" | awk '{print $2}')
    LIMIT=$(repquota /mnt/data | grep "^$user" | awk '{print $3}')
    if [ "$USAGE" -gt $((LIMIT * THRESHOLD / 100)) ]; then
        echo "Warning: User $user has used $(expr $USAGE \* 100 /
        $LIMIT)% of quota."
    fi
done
```

This script iterates through each user listed on the system, checks their quota usage, and generates a warning if the usage exceeds the defined threshold. Automating such monitoring tasks can significantly reduce administrative overhead and enable proactive quota management.

Occasionally, adjustments or removal of quotas may become necessary. For example, during maintenance periods, an administrator might need to temporarily disable quota enforcement to perform bulk operations or adjustments. This can be achieved using the `quotaoff` command:

```
sudo quotaoff /mnt/data
```

After performing the required maintenance, quotas can be re-enabled with the `quotaon` command as described previously. This ability to toggle quota enforcement offers flexibility in managing the file system without compromising overall data integrity.

Troubleshooting disk quota issues is an integral part of administration. Problems may arise due to inconsistent quota files, corrupted quota databases, or misconfigurations in the `/etc/fstab` file. In such situations, the first step is to perform a comprehensive quota check using `quotacheck` with appropriate options to rebuild the quota information:

```
sudo quotacheck -avug /mnt/data
```

The `-a` flag tells `quotacheck` to check all file systems listed in `/etc/fstab` that have quota options. Rebuilding the quota databases can resolve discrepancies and ensure that the disk usage statistics reflect actual usage.

Another practical consideration is the use of quota monitoring tools, which can be integrated into system monitoring frameworks to alert system administrators of potential issues before they escalate into critical problems. By incorporating regular quota reports into routine system audits, administrators can detect anomalies early and adjust user quotas as necessary.

The application of disk quotas is not limited solely to local file systems. In environments that utilize network file systems like NFS, quotas can be implemented to ensure equitable disk space distribution among multiple clients. However, the configuration and management of quotas on NFS shares can be more complex due to the client-server nature of the file system. Special considerations such as synchronizing quota files between the server and clients, as well as ensuring consistent package versions of quota management utilities, are necessary.

Configurational consistency across multiple file systems is crucial, particularly in a heterogeneous storage environment. When setting up quotas for both user and group accounts, it is important to define a clear policy that outlines the allocation, monitoring, and adjustment of quota limits. This policy must be communicated to all users to ensure awareness and prevent disputes over disk space usage. Documentation of these policies, along with periodic reviews of quota reports, maintains operational transparency and supports long-term system health.

The integration of quotas with logical volume management (LVM) further expands the flexibility of disk space allocation. LVM partitions enable dynamic adjustments of storage capacity, which can complement quota systems by ensuring that logical volumes are resized in accordance with overall usage trends. When combined, these technologies allow administrators to fine-tune resource allocation on a granular level, offering both immediate control over disk space and the ability to plan for future growth.

By understanding and applying the techniques outlined in this section, administrators can implement effective disk quota strategies that prevent disk space exhaustion and ensure fair usage policies across diverse user groups. The combination of manual commands, automated scripts, and diagnostic tools creates a robust framework for managing disk quotas in a Linux environment. As systems scale and user demands evolve, the continued application of these techniques will help maintain performance, security, and overall system reliability while balancing individual user needs with overarching resource constraints.

7.5. Using LVM for Storage Management

The Logical Volume Manager (LVM) provides an abstraction layer over physical storage devices that enables administrators to allocate, resize, and manage disk space with flexibility unmatched by traditional partitioning schemes. By decoupling the file system from physical media, LVM simplifies the resizing and movement of volumes, a capability that builds upon earlier discussions of partitioning and formatting drives. This section explores the inner workings of LVM, discusses its architectural components, and presents practical examples to illustrate its utility in a dynamic storage environment.

LVM organizes storage in a hierarchical manner. At the lowest level, physical storage devices or partitions are initialized as *physical volumes* (PVs). These PVs provide the raw storage blocks that LVM can aggregate. Combining one or more PVs forms a *volume group* (VG), which acts as a storage pool from which *logical volumes* (LVs) are allocated. Logical volumes serve as virtual partitions that can be formatted with any file system such as ext4, XFS, or Btrfs. The flexibility provided by LVM allows for the dynamic resizing of these logical volumes, making it possible to easily extend or reduce the allocated space as demands change.

The process of setting up LVM begins by identifying the disks or partitions intended for use. Consider a scenario where a new disk, `/dev/sdd`, is available for integration into a volume group. The first step is to convert the disk into a physical volume using the `pvcreate` command:

```
sudo pvcreate /dev/sdd
```

This command writes LVM metadata to the disk, preparing it for use within a VG. It is essential to verify that the PV has been properly created by using the pvdisplay utility:

```
sudo pvdisplay /dev/sdd
```

Once the physical volume is successfully initialized, it can be pooled with other PVs to form a volume group. The vgcreate command facilitates the creation of a VG. For example, a VG named vg_data can be created by executing:

```
sudo vgcreate vg_data /dev/sdd
```

If additional disks are available, they may be appended to the VG using the vgextend command. This dynamic addition of storage space ensures that the volume group can grow seamlessly as new hardware is incorporated.

After establishing the volume group, logical volumes are created within the VG to support various storage needs. Logical volumes provide a flexible space that can be dedicated to specific applications, directories, or data sets. To create an LV named lv_home with a size of 20 gigabytes within the vg_data volume group, the following command is used:

```
sudo lvcreate -n lv_home -L 20G vg_data
```

Verification of the logical volume creation is executable via the lvdisplay command:

```
sudo lvdisplay vg_data/lv_home
```

Once an LV is created, it must be formatted with a file system before mounting. The formatting process utilizes standard file system creation utilities. For instance, formatting the lv_home logical volume with ext4 is performed using:

```
sudo mkfs.ext4 /dev/vg_data/lv_home
```

After formatting, the logical volume can be mounted like any conventional partition. For example, mounting it to the directory /home is accomplished by:

```
sudo mount /dev/vg_data/lv_home /home
```

In addition to initial setup, LVM's real strength lies in the ease with which storage can be dynamically adjusted. As user requirements change, logical volumes may need to be resized. Extending an LV to accommodate increased storage demands is achieved with the lvextend command. Suppose the lv_home volume requires an additional 10 gigabytes; the command to effect this change is:

```
sudo lvextend -L +10G /dev/vg_data/lv_home
```

After extending the logical volume, the file system must be resized to utilize the additional space. For ext4, this can be accomplished using resize2fs:

```
sudo resize2fs /dev/vg_data/lv_home
```

This two-step process—extending the logical volume and then resizing the file system—demonstrates the layered approach LVM uses to separate the concerns of physical storage and file system structure.

Reducing the size of a logical volume is more complex and requires careful planning to avoid data loss. Before reducing the size, the file system must be shrunk to a size smaller than the target size of the LV. For example, to reduce lv_home by 5 gigabytes, one should first execute:

```
sudo resize2fs /dev/vg_data/lv_home 25G
```

Assuming the logical volume currently holds 30 gigabytes, resizing the file system to 25 gigabytes must be followed by reducing the LV itself:

266

```
sudo lvreduce -L 25G /dev/vg_data/lv_home
```

It is critical to ensure data integrity during this operation by performing file system backups and conducting thorough verifications before and after resizing operations.

LVM also supports snapshot functionality, which allows administrators to capture the state of a logical volume at a specific point in time. Snapshots are essential for creating backups and for testing system changes without impacting live data. To create a snapshot of lv_home, a new LV is created in the volume group using the -s flag. For example:

```
sudo lvcreate -L 2G -s -n lv_home_snap /dev/vg_data/lv_home
```

The snapshot volume, lv_home_snap, holds a consistent image of the logical volume as it existed at the time the snapshot was taken. It is important to monitor snapshots regularly and remove them when no longer needed, as they consume space in the VG and can affect performance.

A further benefit of LVM is its capability to migrate data between physical volumes without downtime, using the concept of pvmove. This feature is particularly useful in environments that require hardware maintenance or upgrades. To relocate data from one physical volume to another within the same volume group, the following command is used:

```
sudo pvmove /dev/sdd1
```

Monitoring and managing LVM configurations is supported by several utilities. Commands such as vgdisplay, lvdisplay, and pvdisplay provide in-depth information on current configurations, free space, and volumes' status. Administrators can integrate these tools with system monitoring solutions to automate alerts and maintenance tasks. For instance, a periodic script may check for low free space in a VG and notify the administrator if thresholds are reached.

Fault tolerance and recovery are additional considerations in LVM-managed environments. The flexibility of LVM simplifies backup procedures, as logical volumes can be snapshotted and then backed up using standard file system backup tools. Strategies that combine LVM snapshots with offsite storage or incremental backup solutions offer robust protection against data loss. The ability to roll back to a snapshot can also serve as a reliable recovery mechanism following erroneous updates or system failures.

The practical benefits of using LVM extend to scenarios involving virtualized environments and containerized applications. In many cases, virtual machines or containers require their own dedicated storage volumes that can be dynamically allocated. LVM's abstraction enables a single physical server to efficiently manage multiple storage pools, each tailored to the requirements of a specific virtualized instance. This adaptability contributes to higher resource utilization and simplifies storage management in complex server infrastructures.

In advanced configurations, LVM can be combined with RAID technologies to further enhance data redundancy, performance, and fault tolerance. By integrating RAID configurations at the physical layer prior to initializing PVs, or by using LVM's built-in mirroring capabilities, administrators can create storage solutions that are both highly available and scalable. The interplay between RAID and LVM requires careful planning, but the resulting systems can deliver superior performance in high-demand environments.

The strategic use of LVM represents a significant evolution from traditional static partitioning, providing administrators with a set of dynamic tools for managing disk space. Its ability to aggregate disparate storage devices into a unified pool and then carve logical volumes from that pool offers unprecedented flexibility. The commands and techniques discussed here exemplify the ease with which storage can be adjusted to meet changing demands, ensuring that systems remain responsive and efficient in the face of evolving data requirements.

The capabilities of LVM not only include resizing and snapshots but also extend to performance tuning through features like thin provisioning. Thin provisioning allows administrators to allocate storage on-demand, reducing the need for large upfront reserves of physical space. This concept of dynamic allocation is particularly useful in cloud environments, where efficient management of shared resources is paramount.

By integrating LVM into storage management practices, system administrators can optimize resource allocation, reduce downtime during maintenance, and improve overall system responsiveness. The flexibility, scalability, and robust feature set of LVM position it as an indispensable tool in modern Linux storage management.

7.6. RAID Configuration and Management

RAID (Redundant Array of Independent Disks) is a technology that aggregates multiple physical disks into a single logical unit to enhance performance, availability, or both. By combining disks in various configurations known as RAID levels, administrators can achieve redundancy, increased throughput, or a balance of the two. This section delves into configuring and managing RAID arrays in Linux using the mdadm utility, building on previous discussions regarding disk partitioning, LVM, and file system management.

RAID levels are defined by the way data is distributed across multiple disks. Each level offers unique advantages and trade-offs. RAID 0, for instance, stripes data across multiple disks, providing high data throughput and full usage of disk capacity, but it offers no redundancy.

Conversely, RAID 1 mirrors data between disks, ensuring that a failure of one drive does not lead to data loss. More advanced configurations such as RAID 5 and RAID 6 combine striping with parity checks to allow for failure of one or, in the case of RAID 6, two drives while preserving both performance and storage efficiency. RAID 10, a combination of mirroring and striping, is often used in high-performance environments where both fault tolerance and high throughput are required.

The software RAID implementation in Linux is most commonly managed via mdadm, a powerful tool that can create, assemble, and monitor RAID arrays. To begin using mdadm, ensure that the utility is installed on the system. On Debian-based systems, installation is achieved by running:

```
sudo apt-get install mdadm
```

A typical workflow for setting up a RAID array involves identifying the disks or partitions that will participate in the array. It is advisable that these disks are either dedicated or have been cleared of any existing data to prevent conflicts. For demonstration purposes, consider three disks: /dev/sdb, /dev/sdc, and /dev/sdd.

An example configuration for a RAID 5 array, which distributes parity information across all disks, is created with the following command:

```
sudo mdadm --create --verbose /dev/md0 --level=5 --raid-devices=3 /
    dev/sdb /dev/sdc /dev/sdd
```

In this command, /dev/md0 is designated as the RAID device, --level=5 specifies RAID 5, and --raid-devices=3 indicates that three disks will be used. The --verbose flag provides detailed output during the creation process. After issuing the command, mdadm begins initializing the array, and the status of the RAID creation can be monitored via:

```
cat /proc/mdstat
```

270

The output from `/proc/mdstat` displays the progress of the array initialization along with the current state of the RAID. For example, a partially assembled RAID array may show progress percentage until it reaches 100%, indicating that synchronization is complete.

Once the RAID array is created, it is often necessary to configure the system to automatically assemble the array on boot. This involves saving the RAID configuration. The following command updates the mdadm configuration file:

```
sudo mdadm --detail --scan | sudo tee -a /etc/mdadm/mdadm.conf
```

After updating mdadm's configuration file, the initramfs should be updated to include the new settings:

```
sudo update-initramfs -u
```

The RAID array is now persistent across system reboots. Following assembly, the RAID device must be formatted with a file system to be utilized by the system. For instance, formatting the newly created RAID 5 device with ext4 is done via:

```
sudo mkfs.ext4 /dev/md0
```

After formatting, the RAID array can be mounted like any standard partition:

```
sudo mkdir -p /mnt/raid5
sudo mount /dev/md0 /mnt/raid5
```

Management of RAID arrays involves monitoring array health, replacing failed disks, and ensuring that parity information is up-to-date. The `mdadm` utility offers comprehensive commands to query the status of an array. For example, to view the details of `/dev/md0`, the following command provides insights into the RAID level, active devices, and any degraded state:

```
sudo mdadm --detail /dev/md0
```

In instances where a disk in the array fails, `mdadm` helps to remove the failed device and substitute it with a new drive. To simulate a failure or remove a disk that is no longer operational, use:

```
sudo mdadm --manage /dev/md0 --fail /dev/sdb
sudo mdadm --manage /dev/md0 --remove /dev/sdb
```

Once a new drive is available, it can be added to the array to restore redundancy:

```
sudo mdadm --manage /dev/md0 --add /dev/sdb
```

After adding the disk, the array automatically begins a resynchronization process to integrate the new drive. Monitoring this process via `cat` `/proc/mdstat` is crucial until the synchronization completes.

Beyond RAID 5, configuring RAID 1 arrays serves environments where redundancy is prioritized over storage efficiency. A RAID 1 mirror is created with two or more disks that duplicate the same data. The command below sets up a RAID 1 array using /dev/sdb and /dev/sdc:

```
sudo mdadm --create --verbose /dev/md1 --level=1 --raid-devices=2 /
    dev/sdb /dev/sdc
```

This configuration ensures that if one disk fails, the mirror provides instant failover support without downtime. The performance is generally lower when compared to RAID 0 due to write duplication, but the enhanced reliability makes RAID 1 a common choice for critical data storage.

In performance-driven environments, RAID 0 can be employed to stripe data across multiple disks. This configuration is best used where data redundancy is not a primary concern, such as in temporary working directories or systems that can tolerate data loss. To create a RAID 0 array with two disks, the following command is used:

```
sudo mdadm --create --verbose /dev/md2 --level=0 --raid-devices=2 /
    dev/sdb /dev/sdc
```

While RAID 0 provides significant performance improvements by distributing I/O load across disks, its lack of redundancy means any disk failure results in complete data loss.

Administrators managing RAID arrays must also consider the monitoring and logging aspects of mdadm operations. Configuring mail notifications for RAID events can preemptively alert administrators to potential issues. Modifying the /etc/mdadm/mdadm.conf file to include the administrator's email and tuning the system to respond to array events can be achieved by adding parameters like:

```
MAILADDR admin@example.com
```

This setting ensures that any critical event, such as a degraded array or resynchronization failure, triggers an email alert, thereby facilitating prompt intervention.

Advanced RAID configurations may also include RAID 6, which tolerates the failure of two disks. Although RAID 6 has higher overhead due to additional parity calculations, it is ideal for large arrays where the risk of multiple simultaneous disk failures is more pronounced. The creation of a RAID 6 array with four devices is performed by:

```
sudo mdadm --create --verbose /dev/md3 --level=6 --raid-devices=4 /
    dev/sdb /dev/sdc /dev/sdd /dev/sde
```

The complexity of RAID 6 demands careful monitoring and regular integrity checks to ensure parity calculations remain accurate.

Routine maintenance of RAID arrays involves periodic checks, such as forced resynchronization or verification of parity data. For example, initiating a consistency check on a RAID 5 array can be done by writing to the appropriate sysfs file:

```
echo check | sudo tee /sys/block/md0/md/sync_action
```

This command prompts the array to verify the parity information, identifying inconsistencies that could indicate deteriorating disk conditions. Identifying potential issues before they result in data loss is a key advantage of proactive RAID management.

Understanding where RAID fits within the broader storage management strategy allows administrators to build systems that are both efficient and resilient. The interplay between RAID and LVM, for instance, enables the creation of logical volumes with built-in redundancy. By initializing physical volumes on RAID arrays, administrators can leverage the performance and fault tolerance of RAID while maintaining the flexibility of logical volumes. An example setup might involve creating a RAID 5 array and then using it as a physical volume in LVM:

```
sudo pvcreate /dev/md0
sudo vgcreate vg_raid /dev/md0
sudo lvcreate -n lv_data -L 100G vg_raid
```

The streamlined integration of RAID, LVM, and file systems creates storage solutions that can dynamically adapt to changing workload demands, scale with increasing capacity requirements, and maintain high levels of data integrity.

The comprehensive management of RAID arrays via mdadm is thus a cornerstone of effective Linux storage administration.

7.7. File System Checks and Repairs

Maintaining data integrity in Linux systems requires regular file system checks and timely repairs to address issues such as corruption, inconsistencies, or hardware-related anomalies. Building upon previous discussions on file system creation, mounting, and partitioning, this section explores the methodologies and tools used to verify and restore file system consistency. The primary utility in this domain is fsck, which is used across different file systems, while specialized tools such

274

as `xfs_repair` handle particular cases to ensure robust data management.

The `fsck` (file system check) tool serves as a front end to a variety of file system-specific checkers. When invoked, it examines the file system for errors, repairs structural inconsistencies, and updates metadata inconsistencies. In a typical scenario, an administrator might schedule periodic checks on file systems mounted on critical partitions. Executing `fsck` on an unmounted file system is the recommended approach to avoid conflicts and potential additional damage due to concurrent write operations.

Before performing any repair, it is advisable to mount the file system in a read-only mode or unmount it entirely. For example, to check a file system on `/dev/sda1`, the following command is suggested:

```
sudo fsck -n /dev/sda1
```

The option -n instructs `fsck` to perform a dry run without making any changes. This preliminary check helps administrators evaluate the extent of errors and determine whether a repair is necessary. Once issues are confirmed, a repair can be initiated without the dry run flag, often with an option such as -y to automatically accept fixes:

```
sudo fsck -y /dev/sda1
```

It is essential to ensure that the file system is not mounted during these operations. In scenarios where unmounting is not straightforward, such as with the root file system, booting into a maintenance mode or single-user mode becomes necessary.

Specialized file systems like XFS require distinct tools. While `fsck` is the standard for ext-family file systems, XFS employs `xfs_repair`. Prior to executing `xfs_repair`, the file system should always be unmounted. An example command to process an XFS file system is:

```
sudo umount /dev/sdb1
```

275

```
sudo xfs_repair /dev/sdb1
```

In cases where the file system is in use or mounted, system administrators might first need to force a remount in read-only mode. For example, remounting a file system as read-only can be accomplished by:

```
sudo mount -o remount,ro /dev/sdb1
```

Only after this precaution should the repair process be initiated.

Integral to the process of file system checks and repairs is the practice of monitoring system logs and diagnostic outputs. Utilities such as dmesg and journals in /var/log provide insights into hardware and software errors that could precipitate file system issues. A common diagnostic approach involves filtering log messages related to file system errors:

```
sudo dmesg | grep -i "ext4\|fsck\|error"
```

This command extracts error messages, helping administrators pinpoint devices requiring further investigation. In addition, modern file systems often support logging metadata that can be scrutinized using file system-specific tools, thereby identifying latent issues before they escalate.

Beyond immediate repairs, a proactive maintenance strategy involves periodic scheduling of file system checks. Administrators can utilize cron jobs or systemd timers to automate the invocation of fsck on non-critical partitions. An example cron entry for a daily check might involve:

```
0 3 * * * root /sbin/fsck -AR -T
```

In this example, the -A option directs fsck to check all file systems listed in /etc/fstab, while -R excludes the root file system from the automatic scan. The -T flag suppresses the printing of the title, making the output more concise for logging purposes.

In addition to standard repair routines, file system consistency may be threatened by sudden power losses or hardware failure. In these cases, journaling capabilities of file systems such as ext4 or XFS help mitigate data loss by maintaining a record of pending transactions. Upon reboot, the system often harnesses this journal to recover a consistent file system state automatically. However, if inconsistencies persist, manual invocation of fsck or xfs_repair becomes necessary to rectify deeper corruption.

Administrators should also be aware of less common issues that may require specialized tools. For instance, if a file system displays symptoms of bad sectors or hardware-level corruption, tools such as badblocks can be used to scan and identify problematic areas before running file system checks. A typical command for identifying bad blocks is:

```
sudo badblocks -sv /dev/sda1
```

Here, -s provides a progress indicator and -v enables verbose output. Once problematic sectors are identified, the file system can be marked to avoid them, depending on the file system's capabilities and repair tools.

Another critical consideration is the impact of file system checks on system performance. Running fsck on large partitions can be time-consuming and may require reserved maintenance windows, especially in production environments. In such cases, scheduling these operations during periods of low activity is essential. System administrators often use multi-threaded variants of file system checking tools or configure RAID systems with redundancy that allows for hot spares, reducing potential downtime during maintenance.

For systems utilizing Logical Volume Manager (LVM), file system checks are generally performed on the logical volume rather than directly on the underlying physical volume. The process is similar in terms of executing `fsck` but requires the proper device path corresponding to the logical volume, such as:

```
sudo fsck -y /dev/vg_data/lv_home
```

Ensuring that the logical volume is not active or only available in a safe mode is critical to prevent conflicts and to enable comprehensive checks.

Administrative resilience is further enhanced by adopting best practices around backup and recovery planning. Before performing extensive repairs, it is advisable to back up critical data so that any inadvertent repairs do not lead to further data loss. Integrating backup scripts with repair routines can ensure a fallback mechanism in case the repair process exposes deeper systemic issues. An ideal strategy is to perform incremental backups and integrate periodic file system snapshots with utilities that interface well with LVM or RAID arrays.

Moreover, maintaining an accurate inventory of file system states and repair logs contributes to predictive maintenance. Detailed logs of `fsck` outputs, along with automated monitoring for recurring errors, allow administrators to adjust system parameters or replace aging hardware before failures become catastrophic. In some cases, analysis of historical file system check data can elucidate patterns that point to systemic issues, guiding long-term infrastructure investments.

The importance of maintaining a consistent file system state cannot be overstated. Data integrity is not only a technical imperative but also a critical business requirement in environments where information loss can lead to operational disruptions or financial loss. Establishing a routine that incorporates periodic file system checks, proactive monitoring, and prompt repair action is essential for sustaining reliable system operations.

The tools and techniques covered in this section empower system administrators to safeguard data integrity. By understanding how to effectively use `fsck`, `xfs_repair`, and related utilities, administrators can diagnose and remedy file system inconsistencies before they escalate into significant issues. Thorough planning, proactive diagnostics, and integration with backup solutions ensure that file systems remain resilient, operational, and capable of meeting the demands of modern computing environments.

Chapter 8

Security and User Permissions

This chapter addresses Linux file permissions, user and group management, and configuring privileged access with sudo. It covers setting file permissions, ownership, and implementing security frameworks like SELinux or AppArmor. Techniques for securing network services and auditing system security are discussed, providing users with robust strategies to safeguard and manage access within Debian systems.

8.1. Understanding Linux File Permissions

Linux file permissions are a fundamental concept in Unix-like operating systems that provide a mechanism to control access to files and directories. Every file and directory is associated with a set of permission bits that determine which users can read, write, or execute the file. This system is integral to enforcing security policies and ensuring that only authorized users can operate on sensitive data. The permission model is applied to three distinct categories of users: the owner of the file, the group associated with the file, and others—users who are neither the owner nor members of the designated group.

The permission bits are expressed using three primary symbols: r for read, w for write, and x for execute. The read permission allows a user to view the contents of a file or list the contents of a directory. Write permission grants the ability to modify or delete a file, or to add, remove, or rename files within a directory. Execute permission is necessary to run a file as a program or script and, in the context of directories, to access files and subdirectories. These permissions are displayed in a symbolic notation, usually when the ls -l command is executed, and they appear as a string of characters, such as rwxr-xr--.

Understanding the layout of the symbolic notation is paramount. The first character in the permissions string indicates the file type; for example, - denotes a regular file, while d indicates a directory. The subsequent nine characters are divided into three groups of three. The first group represents the permissions for the file owner, the second for the group, and the third for others. In this context, a typical permissions string rwxr-xr-- indicates that the owner has read, write, and execute permissions, the group has read and execute permissions, and others have only read permission.

Permissions can also be represented numerically using the octal numbering system, which simplifies the process of setting permissions through commands like chmod. In octal notation, each permission is assigned a numerical value: read permission is equivalent to 4, write to 2, and execute to 1. These values are then summed for each user category. For example, if the owner has all three permissions, it is represented as 7 (4+2+1). Similarly, a permission string of rwxr-xr-- is translated to 754, where 7 corresponds to the owner's permissions, 5 to the group's permissions (read and execute: 4+1), and 4 to others' permissions (read only).

Practically, the chmod command is used to modify file permissions. A typical usage of the command involves specifying the desired numeric mode and the target file. For instance, the command below assigns read, write, and execute permissions to the owner, and only read and execute permissions to both the group and others.

```
chmod 755 myscript.sh
```

In this command, the number 7 for the owner indicates that the file permissions are set to allow reading, editing, and execution, while the group and others are limited to permissions 5 each, allowing reading and execution but not modification. This setup is common for scripts that need to be executed by multiple users but should only be modified by the owner. The careful assignment of these permissions is pivotal in preventing unauthorized modifications or executions that could lead to security breaches.

The significance of file permissions extends beyond individual files and plays an important role in system security, especially when applied to directories. For directories, the read permission allows a user to list the names of the files within the directory, while the write permission permits the creation, deletion, or renaming of files. Execute permission on a directory, however, is somewhat special: it does not allow listing of the directory contents but grants access to the directory's files and subdirectories. This distinction adds an additional layer of control, making it possible to restrict how users interact with directories even if they have read permissions.

In addition to the basic permissions, Linux file systems support additional attributes that modify default behavior. While the focus of this discussion is on the three primary permissions, it is important to note that special permission bits exist, such as the setuid, setgid, and sticky bits. The setuid bit, when set on an executable, causes the process to run with the permissions of the file's owner. Similarly, the setgid bit can ensure that files created within a directory inherit the group of the directory rather than the creating user's default group. Although these special permissions are an advanced topic, a firm grasp of the fundamental read, write, and execute permissions is essential for understanding the more sophisticated aspects of file system security.

Consider a typical directory structure where files are owned by different users and groups. Permissions help ensure that even if users have access to the same directory, they can only modify or execute files as permitted. For example, a collaborative project directory might be set so that all members of the project's group have the ability to execute project scripts, but only specific users have write access to critical configuration files. Such a configuration minimizes the risk of accidental or malicious changes while facilitating necessary collaboration.

A concrete example of this can be seen by examining the output of the `ls -l` command. The following listing displays file permissions, ownership, and group associations:

```
ls -l project_directory/
```

```
drwxr-xr-x 2 alice developers 4096 Apr 25 10:30 scripts
-rw-r--r-- 1 bob   developers 1024 Apr 25 10:30 config.txt
-rwxr-xr-x 1 alice developers 2048 Apr 25 10:30 run.sh
```

In this example, the directory `scripts` has read, write, and execute permissions for the owner (`alice`), and it is accessible to group members and others with read and execute permissions. The file `config.txt` is less permissive, allowing modifications only by the owner (`bob`), while `run.sh` is marked as executable, ensuring that it can be run as a script by authorized users. These permission schemes help control access at a granular level, ensuring that each file is accessible only to those with the appropriate trust level.

In addition to numerical assignments using chmod, symbolic representations offer a flexible alternative when modifying permissions. Symbolic notation uses operators such as +, -, and = to add, remove, or
explicitly set permissions for a file or directory. For example, if there
is a need to add write permission for the group on a file, the following
command can be used:

```
chmod g+w document.txt
```

Conversely, if write permission should be removed from the group, the
operator - is used:

```
chmod g-w document.txt
```

The symbolic methodology often makes modifications clearer, particularly when small changes are required, as opposed to resetting the
entire permissions set with an octal number. Moreover, it reduces the
likelihood of inadvertently altering unrelated permissions.

Linux permissions are not only applied at the time of file creation but
also interact with the process of file inheritance. Permissions that persist across operations, such as copying or moving files, are influenced
by factors like the default umask value. The umask is a system-level
setting that further restricts the default permissions granted to new
files and directories. By subtracting the umask values from the full
permission set, the system ensures that new files do not acquire overly
permissive access rights. For example, if the default umask is set to
022, new files typically receive permission 644, and new directories receive 755, ensuring that group members and others do not have write
permissions unless explicitly granted.

The nuances of Linux file permissions extend into system administration tasks as well. When managing multi-user environments, administrators must balance the need for accessibility with the imperative
of security. Files that require execution across different user accounts
must be carefully configured to ensure they run with the privileges in-

tended by the owner. In mixed environments where some users operate with limited privileges and others have elevated permissions, misconfigurations can lead to vulnerabilities that are exploitable by malicious actors. Therefore, a comprehensive understanding of read, write, and execute permissions, along with their practical application using tools like chmod and ls, is essential for maintaining a secure and stable operating environment.

A detailed comprehension of Linux file permissions aids not only in security but also in system troubleshooting and performance optimization. Misassigned permissions can result in unexpected behavior, such as applications failing to read configuration files or scripts failing to execute. Administrators and users alike must therefore verify that file permissions align with the intended access policies of the system. Systematic auditing of permission settings can help identify discrepancies that may otherwise lead to operational inefficiencies or security lapses.

The principles described here serve as building blocks for more advanced topics in Linux system security. As users progress to more complex configurations involving user and group management, sudo privileges, and security frameworks like SELinux or AppArmor, the foundational understanding of file permission semantics remains critical. Mastery of these basic concepts ensures that advanced configurations are both secure and effective.

Integrating Linux file permissions into an effective security policy involves continuous monitoring and adjustment. Regular reviews of file permissions across critical directories, combined with automated tools and scripts that enforce permission policies, are practices that enhance the overall resilience of the system. The ability to quickly diagnose and remedy permission-related issues is a testament to a robust understanding of the underlying Unix permission framework, ensuring that system integrity is maintained even in complex environments.

8.2. Managing Users and Groups

User and group management is a critical administrative task in Linux systems, ensuring that each user has proper access levels and that privileges are assigned to maintain system security and organization. Linux uses a combination of files in the /etc directory, such as /etc/passwd for user account information and /etc/group for group data, along with dedicated commands to create, modify, and delete accounts. Effectively managing these accounts is essential for enforcing access policies and delegating responsibilities appropriately.

The creation of user accounts is typically handled by the useradd command. This command initializes a new user entry in the system and creates a designated home directory if requested. The basic syntax for creating a user is:

```
useradd username
```

By default, this command creates an account with minimal settings. To specify a home directory, login shell, and additional parameters such as a comment field for full name or identification, administrators can use options such as -d for the home directory and -s for the shell. For example:

```
useradd -d /home/jdoe -s /bin/bash -c "John Doe" jdoe
```

This command creates a user account jdoe with a home directory located at /home/jdoe, using /bin/bash as the login shell, and an entry comment that identifies the user. After creating an account, it is necessary to set a password using the passwd command:

```
passwd jdoe
```

The passwd command interacts with the administrator (or the user) to input and confirm a secure password, which is then encrypted and stored in the system's shadow file for enhanced security.

287

Groups in Linux facilitate the organization of users, allowing the assignment of common privileges for collective management. The groupadd command is used to create new groups. For instance, to create a group named developers, one may use:

```
groupadd developers
```

Adding a user to a group enhances collaboration and can restrict or grant access to shared resources. A user can belong to several groups simultaneously. To add an existing user to an additional group, the usermod command with the -aG option is used:

```
usermod -aG developers jdoe
```

This command appends the group developers to the supplementary groups of the user jdoe without altering existing group memberships. Conversely, modifying a user's primary group is accomplished via the -g option. For example, changing the primary group of a user can be done as follows:

```
usermod -g developers jdoe
```

It is important to distinguish between primary and supplementary groups when assigning roles and privileges. The primary group is referenced by many applications and file ownership defaults, and thus needs careful attention during account creation and management.

Deleting user accounts is occasionally necessary when an employee leaves or when accounts are no longer needed. The userdel command removes a user from the system. It is essential to handle this with care since removal of a user might leave orphaned files or affect system services. The basic usage is:

```
userdel jdoe
```

To remove the user's home directory and mail spool along with the user account, the command can be extended with the -r option:

```
userdel -r jdoe
```

This command cleans up the user's files, ensuring that residual directories do not compromise future system security or waste storage space.

Group management similarly includes deletion and modification of groups. To remove a group, the `groupdel` command is utilized:

```
groupdel developers
```

Caution is advised when removing groups, as doing so might impact the permissions and accessibility of files that reference that group. Before deleting a group, administrators should ensure that no critical files are exclusively owned by that group or reassign such files to another appropriate group.

The modification of existing user accounts can involve changing user details, login shells, or adding and removing group memberships. The `usermod` command is quite versatile. One common modification is updating the login shell for an account to adhere to updated security policies or to provide an improved user experience. This is performed with the -s option:

```
usermod -s /usr/bin/zsh jdoe
```

The above command switches the user jdoe to use the zsh shell instead of the previously configured shell. This can be useful when certain shells provide enhanced features or better security controls. Additional modifications include updating the account's comment field, which is handled by the -c option. For example:

```
usermod -c "Johnathan Doe, System Analyst" jdoe
```

These changes help to maintain accurate records in the system and ensure that administrators have a clear picture of user roles.

Another aspect of managing users and groups is the migration of users between groups. This process might be necessary when a reorganization occurs or when role adjustments are implemented. To fully replace a user's groups, the -G option with a complete list of supplementary groups is used without the append mode:

```
usermod -G developers,admins jdoe
```

This command resets the supplementary groups for jdoe to include only developers and admins. Administrators must perform such operations with caution to ensure that users retain necessary privileges and that the principle of least privilege is observed.

Command-line tools such as getent are invaluable for auditing and verifying current account configurations. Running the following command queries the system's group database and lists the settings for a specific group:

```
getent group developers
```

The output is typically similar to that produced by grep on /etc/group, and it provides a quick way to confirm that updates have been applied as expected. Similarly, individual user account details can be inspected using:

```
getent passwd jdoe
```

This command displays all pertinent information about the user account, including user ID (UID), group ID (GID), home directory, and preferred shell.

The integration of user and group management into broader system operations reflects a layered security approach. Well-defined groups enable administrators to craft specific access rules that reflect organizational hierarchies, department divisions, or project teams. For instance, a system configured to allow only certain groups to access sensitive directories can rely on group-based permission settings established earlier in the discussion on file permissions. Group management, therefore, complements file permission schemes, ensuring that file access is tightly controlled within a multi-user environment.

In practice, many Linux distributions allow additional layers of control through configuration files such as /etc/sudoers. Although configuration of sudo privileges is a distinct topic, it benefits directly from proper user and group management by ensuring that only users or groups with designated responsibilities have access to elevated privileges. This hierarchical control model, where administrative responsibilities may be delegated to specific groups, builds on the fundamental concepts of user management and helps to minimize the risk of privilege escalation attacks.

Automation and scripting play an increasingly important role in managing large-scale deployments with hundreds or thousands of user accounts. Administrators often use shell scripts or configuration management tools like Ansible to automate the creation, modification, or deletion of user accounts. An example of a simple shell script for batch user creation might be:

```
#!/bin/bash
while IFS=',' read -r username homedir shell fullname; do
    useradd -d "$homedir" -s "$shell" -c "$fullname" "$username"
    passwd "$username"
done < users.csv
```

In this script, a comma-separated file users.csv is processed to create multiple user accounts with specified attributes. Such automation ensures consistency across user accounts and reduces the chance of human error during repetitive tasks.

Managing users and groups in Linux is a continuous process that involves verifying account integrity, ensuring proper group associations, and monitoring for unauthorized changes. Regular audits using commands like grep to search for modifications in the /etc/passwd and /etc/group files provide valuable oversight for system administrators.

291

Combining these administrative practices with secure backup procedures for system files ensures that any unintended modifications or deletions can be promptly rectified.

The comprehensive understanding of creating, modifying, and deleting user and group accounts forms the basis for an organized and secure Linux operating environment. Maintaining clear policies on user privileges and group membership aids in the enforcement of security measures and streamlines administrative operations. This cohesive strategy allows for transparent management of access rights, enabling systems to remain robust, adaptable, and secure in a dynamic operational landscape.

8.3. Configuring sudo for Privileged Access

The sudo command is a cornerstone in Linux systems, enabling controlled access to administrative commands without requiring users to operate under the root account. This utility supports the principle of least privilege by allowing system administrators to delegate a limited set of predefined commands to specific users or groups. By configuring sudo, administrators can ensure that elevated privileges are granted temporarily and in a controlled manner, reducing the risk of unintended system modifications.

The configuration of sudo is managed primarily through the /etc/sudoers file. This file specifies which users and groups are granted access to which commands and under what conditions. Due to the sensitivity of this configuration, it is advisable to edit the file using the visudo command. This command provides syntax checking and error prevention to mitigate the risk of configuration mistakes that could potentially lock out administrative access. A typical invocation is as follows:

```
visudo
```

Within the /etc/sudoers file, configurations are established using a specific syntax. For example, to grant user alice the ability to execute all commands, the following line is used:

```
alice    ALL=(ALL:ALL) ALL
```

This entry means that alice is permitted to execute any command on any host as any user or group. The structure of this configuration is such that the first field specifies the user, the second field identifies the host or set of hosts, and the expression within parentheses states the target users and groups for the command execution. The final argument lists the commands which are allowed, with ALL signifying that there is no restriction on the command.

For scenarios where a controlled subset of commands needs to be limited to a user or group, the sudoers file allows administrators to specify particular commands. For instance, to allow user bob to restart the Apache service without granting full administrative privileges, the following entry is necessary:

```
bob      ALL=(root) NOPASSWD: /usr/sbin/service apache2 restart
```

In this configuration, bob is allowed to execute the command to restart Apache as the root user without being prompted for a password. The inclusion of NOPASSWD: enhances usability in scenarios where frequent authentication is impractical while still limiting the potential security risks to a single command.

Groups provide another level of granularity in privilege management. By defining a group and including multiple users in that group, administrators can simplify the enforcement of permissions. For example, to allow all members of the admin group to execute administrative commands, one could insert the following line in the sudoers file:

```
%admin  ALL=(ALL) ALL
```

The percentage sign indicates that the entry applies to a group rather than an individual user. The effective result is that every user in the admin group is granted full sudo privileges. This approach promotes efficient management in environments where multiple trusted users require administrative access.

Security considerations are paramount when configuring sudo. In addition to specifying which users or groups have access, the sudoers file supports environmental filtering. The Defaults directive is used to enforce security policies across all sudo operations. An illustrative example is the configuration of logging for all sudo commands. By including the following line in /etc/sudoers, every command executed through sudo is logged for auditing:

```
Defaults        logfile="/var/log/sudo.log"
```

This directive ensures that traces of administrative commands are stored securely, facilitating audits and forensic analysis in the event of system anomalies. In addition to logging, other defaults such as requiretty can enforce that sudo operations only occur within terminal sessions. Such measures are critical to prevent potential misuse in automated or non-interactive situations.

A common requirement is to allow certain commands to be executed only after password authentication, while others are exempted through the use of the NOPASSWD option. Balancing usability with security, administrators must analyze the operational context serially. For example, a set of maintenance scripts might require frequent execution by a specific user. Instead of providing unrestricted access, the following line can limit elevated privileges to the maintenance scope:

```
maintenance_user    ALL=(root) NOPASSWD: /usr/local/bin/maintenance_*
```

This configuration uses a wildcard to match any command prefixed by maintenance_ in the specified directory. Such an approach minimizes the administrative overhead while enforcing tight control on the allowed operations.

The inclusion of the `/etc/sudoers.d` directory further enhances modularity and maintainability of sudo configurations. Files placed in this directory are automatically included in the sudo configuration, allowing administrators to separate concerns by application or department. This modular approach not only simplifies management but also reduces the risk of inadvertently altering unrelated sudo policies. For example, an administrator might create a dedicated file for database administrators:

```
/etc/sudoers.d/dbadmins
```

Its content could include specific entries that grant members of the `dbadmin` group the capability to manage database services. Combining such configurations with group-based entries ensures a structured and maintainable administrative environment.

Another important aspect of sudo configuration is error handling and testing. Syntax errors in the `/etc/sudoers` file can render sudo unusable, which might lock out administrative users from performing critical tasks. The `visudo` command mitigates this risk by locking the file during editing and performing syntax checks before saving changes. It is a best practice to validate sudoers file modifications on a test system before deploying changes in a production environment to ensure that mistakes do not compromise system stability.

For users, the sudo command simplifies the process of executing administrative commands. Instead of logging into the root account, a user can prefix commands with `sudo` to invoke specific privileged operations. For example, updating system packages on a Debian-based system is accomplished through the following command:

```
sudo apt update && sudo apt upgrade
```

This command sequence allows a non-root user to perform package updates while ensuring that each command is authenticated according to the sudoers configuration. When users execute such commands, they are prompted to input their own password unless configured otherwise using NOPASSWD. This personal authentication reinforces accountability by ensuring that each administrative action is traceable to an individual user.

The security model of sudo also supports the concept of session-based caching. Once a user authenticates successfully, sudo caches the credentials for a short period, typically 15 minutes, thereby reducing the need for repeated password entries during short administrative tasks. Administrators can adjust this timeout period using the timestamp_timeout option in the Defaults directive:

```
Defaults timestamp_timeout=10
```

In this example, the authentication cache is reduced to ten minutes, thereby enhancing security by limiting the window during which unauthorized access might be exploited on a system left unattended.

Monitoring and auditing sudo usage further increases the security posture of a Linux system. System logs capture details of every sudo operation, facilitating accountability and enabling proactive detection of unusual activities. Administrators can combine these logs with automated monitoring tools to generate alerts in the event of suspicious command usage. This capability is critical in environments where adherence to strict security policies is required.

The flexibility of sudo extends to its integration with external authentication systems, such as LDAP or Active Directory, thereby centralizing control over privileged access across large organizations. Such integrations allow for centralized management of user credentials and group memberships, ensuring that permissions are consistent across multiple systems. When combined with configuration management tools, administrators are able to enforce a uniform sudo policy, minimizing

296

discrepancies that could otherwise lead to security vulnerabilities.

Critical to the philosophy behind sudo is the emphasis on accountability. By logging every command executed with elevated privileges, sudo establishes a clear audit trail. This logging capability not only aids in troubleshooting but also serves as a deterrent against misuse of privileged access. When administrators have access to detailed logs, it becomes easier to pinpoint potential security lapses and address them before they evolve into larger issues.

The process of configuring sudo is iterative and requires continuous review. As system roles and responsibilities evolve, the sudoers file must be updated to reflect new organizational requirements and security standards. Regular audits of the configuration, combined with user feedback, ensure that the privileges granted remain appropriate to the user's role. Once a configuration is deemed stable, it forms one component of the overall system security architecture, complementing user and group management practices and reinforcing the foundational principles of system security.

Thorough understanding of sudo configuration is vital for anyone responsible for maintaining Linux systems. The precise control over administrative privileges afforded by sudo empowers administrators to delegate sensitive operations confidently without compromising the integrity of the system. Maintaining best practices in configuring, auditing, and tightening sudo policies is a key responsibility in ensuring that elevated access remains both efficient and secure.

8.4. Setting up File Permissions and Ownership

Linux file security extends beyond simple permission bits to encompass file ownership. Mastery of commands such as `chmod` and `chown` is essential for effective system administration. This section provides a detailed examination of how to manipulate file and directory permissions as well as ownership, facilitating a secure and organized file system structure.

The chmod command is employed to change the permission mode of a file or directory. Permissions in Linux are divided into three basic sets: read (r), write (w), and execute (x). These may be set for the file's owner, group, and others. There are two principal methods to modify permissions using chmod—symbolic mode and octal mode. The symbolic method uses characters to represent the changes being made; for example, the operator + adds permissions, - removes them, and = sets the permissions exactly. A symbolic example to add execute permission for all users is:

```
chmod a+x filename
```

Here, a signifies all applicable user categories (owner, group, and others) and +x indicates that execute permission is added. Conversely, if one wishes to remove the write permission for others, the command is:

```
chmod o-w filename
```

This command removes the write permission from the "others" category. In contrast, the octal method employs numerical representations for permissions. In this scheme, read, write, and execute correspond to the numbers 4, 2, and 1, respectively, with values for each set summed to produce a single digit per category. For instance, to assign full permissions (read, write, execute) for the owner, and read and execute permissions for both group and others, one would use:

```
chmod 755 filename
```

This number is parsed as 7 for the owner (4+2+1), and 5 for both the group and others (4+1 each). Using octal notation not only promotes brevity but also reduces errors when setting complex permissions.

Special permission bits, such as setuid, setgid, and the sticky bit, offer additional layers of security and functionality. The setuid bit, indicated by the octal value 4000, allows an executable to run with the privileges of its owner rather than that of the executing user. The setgid bit (2000) ensures that files created within a directory inherit the group ownership of that directory. The sticky bit (1000) is often applied to directories to restrict file deletion. When a directory such as /tmp is set with the sticky bit, only the file owner, directory owner, or root can delete files within it. To set these special permissions, the octal notation is extended. For example, to set the setgid bit along with read, write, and execute permissions for the owner and read and execute for everyone else, one might use:

```
chmod 2755 directory
```

Understanding the implications of these bits is critical when configuring multi-user environments where elevated privileges must be restricted and monitored.

File ownership is modified using the `chown` command, which stands for "change owner." Every file in Linux has two main attributes: the owner (user) and the group. The general syntax for `chown` is as shown below:

```
chown user:group filename
```

For example, to change both the owner and the group of a file called `project.txt` to `alice` and `developers` respectively, the following command is issued:

```
chown alice:developers project.txt
```

It is equally possible to alter only the owner or only the group by specifying the parameter accordingly. Excluding the group value, you could change just the owner:

```
chown alice project.txt
```

Similarly, to modify only the group ownership, one can use the colon without a preceding username:

```
chown :developers project.txt
```

For directories, it is often necessary to change ownership recursively so that all contained files and subdirectories inherit the new owner or group. The -R option enables this feature:

```
chown -R alice:developers /path/to/directory
```

Recursive operations are particularly useful in environments where large hierarchies of data are organized under a single project or department. The ability to update ownership attributes for the entire directory tree simplifies administrative overhead and ensures consistency.

While using chmod and chown, it is critical to be aware of the default permissions set by the user's umask. The umask value is a system-level default that subtracts permissions from newly created files or directories. For example, a umask of 022 permits new files to have permissions of 644 (owner read and write, group and others read) and directories to have 755 (owner full access and group, others read and execute). Temporary adjustments to the umask may be necessary when the desired permissions differ from the defaults. The umask can be set in the shell as follows:

```
umask 027
```

Here, 027 ensures new files are created with permissions 640 (read and write for the owner, read for the group, and no permissions for others), thereby tightening security for sensitive files.

Attention should also be directed to system files and directories that require careful management. Files in directories like /etc or /var often have permissions set according to the system's security policies. For example, proper handling of configuration files can prevent unauthorized access or modifications, which might otherwise compromise system stability or security. As such, administrators must verify that changes

300

with chmod or chown do not inadvertently weaken protection.

Tools such as ls -l provide a detailed listing of files, including their permissions and ownership, which is invaluable for verifying that changes have been applied as intended. A typical output might appear as follows:

```
ls -l /home/alice/project
```

```
drwxr-xr-x  5 alice developers 4096 Jul 10 15:23 src
-rw-r-----  1 alice developers 2048 Jul 10 15:24 README.md
-rwxr-xr-x  1 alice developers 1024 Jul 10 15:25 run.sh
```

This output confirms that the directory src is accessible, and that file permissions and owner/group associations are maintained in accordance with the intended configuration. Consistent use of these verification commands facilitates ongoing audits and ensures adherence to security policies.

Changing permissions and ownership through chmod and chown is not isolated from overall system administration practices. When integrating these commands into scripts or automated deployment procedures, it is essential to include error handling and logging. A well-structured script that modifies permissions across a range of files might look like the following:

```bash
#!/bin/bash
TARGET_DIR="/var/www/html"
# Set permissions for directories and files separately
find "$TARGET_DIR" -type d -exec chmod 755 {} \;
find "$TARGET_DIR" -type f -exec chmod 644 {} \;
# Change owner and group for the target directory recursively
chown -R www-data:www-data "$TARGET_DIR"
```

In this example, directories are assigned execute permissions to allow traversal, while files receive read and write permissions for the owner, and only read permissions for the group and others. Additionally, recursive ownership alteration ensures that all elements comply with the

301

web server's user and group requirements. Such automation enhances consistency across deployments and reduces the risk of manual errors.

A comprehensive strategy for file permission and ownership management also involves regular review and audit. Administrators can schedule periodic checks using cron jobs and custom scripts to detect any deviations from the established security baseline. For instance, comparing output from `ls -lR` with a known good snapshot can highlight discrepancies that may require intervention. Automated monitoring not only safeguards the integrity of the file system but also provides early warning signs for potential security breaches or misconfigurations.

Established best practices also suggest documenting changes in permission and ownership settings. Maintaining logs of administrative modifications is particularly useful when troubleshooting unexpected behavior in applications or services. This traceability ensures that any alterations introduced as part of system updates or maintenance operations can be reconciled with overall security policies.

Understanding the interaction between `chmod`, `chown`, and the underlying file system permissions is critical for designing robust security and access controls. In environments where multiple users share resources, careful planning and execution of permission changes help prevent privilege escalation and unauthorized data access. Coordination with user and group management practices ensures that the logical boundaries established through ownership and permission settings are enforced consistently across the system.

The application of these concepts extends beyond small-scale configurations and is integral to the management of enterprise-level systems. Multi-user systems with complex departmental structures benefit from standardized policies regarding file ownership and permissions. Automated tools, combined with the manual expertise of system administrators, enable a dynamic balance between usability and security—a necessity for modern operating environments.

Fundamentally, the commands `chmod` and `chown` serve as the primary mechanisms by which administrators shape the access landscape of a Linux system. Their correct usage is paramount in ensuring that files and directories are not only accessible to authorized users but also protected from accidental or malicious tampering. Proficient management of file permissions and ownership lays a solid foundation for advanced topics such as access control lists (ACLs) and further security hardening measures.

8.5. Implementing SELinux or AppArmor

Security-Enhanced Linux (SELinux) and AppArmor are mandatory access control (MAC) systems designed to supplement the traditional discretionary access controls in Linux. They add an additional layer of security by enforcing fine-grained policies that restrict what processes can do regardless of the ownership or permissions of files. Both frameworks aim to reduce the potential damage of compromised processes by defining explicit rules for process behavior and resource access. While SELinux relies on a complex policy language and extensive labeling of files and objects, AppArmor offers a more straightforward path through path-based security profiles. Understanding and implementing these frameworks is critical to maintaining robust system security, particularly in environments where the principle of least privilege must be strictly enforced.

SELinux implements a security policy based on labels assigned to files, processes, and sessions. Each resource is tagged with a security context, and policies determine which interactions are permitted between different contexts. Administrators can view the current status of SELinux with the command:

```
sestatus
```

This command outputs the mode of SELinux (enforcing, permissive, or disabled), along with other details such as policy version and loaded modules. Transitioning SELinux from a permissive mode, where violations are logged but not enforced, to an enforcing mode is a critical step in hardening the system. For immediate enforcement, one may use:

```
setenforce 1
```

Conversely, for troubleshooting purposes, it might be necessary to temporarily shift to permissive mode:

```
setenforce 0
```

The configuration is maintained in the file /etc/selinux/config, where the desired mode can be set to either enforcing, permissive, or disabled. Careful planning is advised before transitioning to enforcing mode to ensure that the security policies align with the system requirements.

A principal component of SELinux is its policies. The targeted policy is the prevailing model in many distributions, where a significant portion of the system is protected by SELinux, yet specific processes such as system daemons are confined. Administrators are often required to create custom policy modules to address unique access requirements. A simple example of creating a custom SELinux policy involves first writing a policy file, such as local.te, with contents similar to:

```
module local 1.0;

require {
    type httpd_t;
    type httpd_sys_content_t;
};

# Allow httpd to execute custom script
allow httpd_t httpd_sys_content_t:file execute;
```

Once the file is written, the policy module can be compiled and loaded
using the commands:

```
checkmodule -M -m -o local.mod local.te
semodule_package -o local.pp -m local.mod
semodule -i local.pp
```

This process compiles the policy, builds the package, and installs it into
the running SELinux policy. These steps illustrate the granular control
SELinux offers, imposing restrictions that go beyond Unix file permissions and limiting specific interactions between domains.

AppArmor, in contrast, operates through a set of profiles that are associated with executable paths. Each profile defines a set of permissions for the associated program, including file access, network connections, and interaction with other resources. Profiles are stored in
/etc/apparmor.d/ and can be either in a complain mode, where violations are logged, or in enforce mode, where violations are actively
blocked. The status of AppArmor can be checked using:

```
apparmor_status
```

This command lists all the loaded profiles along with their current
modes. To switch a profile from complain to enforce mode, the administrator can use:

```
sudo aa-enforce /etc/apparmor.d/usr.sbin.mysqld
```

This command ensures that the profile for the MySQL daemon is in
enforcement mode, restricting access as defined by the profile. Similarly, to set a profile to complain mode for monitoring purposes, the
command is:

```
sudo aa-complain /etc/apparmor.d/usr.sbin.mysqld
```

Such flexibility is vital for iterative policy development, allowing
changes to be safely tested before being permanently enforced.

305

AppArmor profiles are typically less complex than SELinux policies, which makes them more approachable for administrators new to MAC systems. A sample AppArmor profile might appear as follows:

```
#include <tunables/global>

/usr/sbin/mysqld {
    # Allow read and write access to database files
    /var/lib/mysql/ r,
    /var/lib/mysql/** rwk,

    # Allow network connections on designated ports
    network inet stream,

    # Deny all access to sensitive files
    /etc/shadow r,

    # Allow execution of necessary binaries
    /usr/bin/mysql* ix,

    # Capability restrictions
    capability net_bind_service,
}
```

This profile demonstrates how AppArmor limits MySQL's access to only necessary directories and files while expressly denying access to sensitive files such as /etc/shadow. Using the #include directive, administrators can reference common settings stored in the global tunables file, promoting consistency across multiple profiles.

The installation and configuration of either framework are typically supported natively by distributions such as Fedora, CentOS (for SELinux), and Ubuntu (for AppArmor). For SELinux, distributions often include a set of policies that cover most system services, which can be extended or refined to match specific operational needs. Regular system updates may modify these policies; therefore, administrators should review policy changes following an update to ensure that custom settings remain valid and that security is not inadvertently reduced.

306

Both SELinux and AppArmor require that administrators understand how to interpret audit logs and troubleshoot access denials. For SELinux, the ausearch tool allows administrators to search through the audit logs for specific denials, a crucial step in refining policies. A typical command to review denied accesses might be:

```
ausearch -m avc -ts recent
```

This command extracts messages related to Access Vector Cache (AVC) denials and helps pinpoint which policy might be causing a problem. Similarly, AppArmor logs denials in system logs that can be monitored through tools such as dmesg or by inspecting the /var/log/syslog or /var/log/kern.log files. Careful analysis of these logs provides guidance on whether a profile should be adjusted or if legitimate access requests are being blocked.

While the learning curve for SELinux is steeper than that for AppArmor, the decision between the two might depend on the specific security needs and the level of control required by the organization. SELinux offers a more detailed and fine-grained approach, beneficial for environments where precise control over each interaction is paramount. AppArmor, being simpler to configure and manage, may be more appropriate in cases where ease of use and rapid profile development are prioritized over exhaustive access control configuration.

In practical deployment scenarios, both frameworks permit significant customization and integration with system automation. For example, integrating SELinux policy management into configuration management tools such as Ansible can standardize security policy enforcement across many servers. An Ansible task might look like:

```
- name: Ensure SELinux is in enforcing mode
  selinux:
    state: enforcing
```

Likewise, AppArmor profiles can be managed using scripts that auto-

307

mate the switching between enforce and complain modes based on system roles or during periods of system maintenance. This level of automation ensures that security policies are consistently applied, greatly reducing the chance of misconfiguration during manual changes.

As both SELinux and AppArmor evolve, it is essential for administrators to stay informed about best practices and changes in default policies. Vendor documentation, community forums, and specialized training sessions are valuable resources for keeping up-to-date with these dynamic security frameworks. Knowledge of these tools not only bolsters overall system security but also prepares the administrator for emerging security threats that may require more nuanced responses.

The strategic implementation of MAC systems complemented with traditional file permissions, user and group management, and sudo configurations provides a comprehensive approach to system security. By layering these controls, systems are better protected against both external and internal threats. The use of SELinux or AppArmor thus represents a proactive step in reducing the attack surface of a Linux environment. Fortifying systems in this manner underscores the importance of precise access controls, ultimately resulting in a more robust and resilient operational framework.

Implementing and maintaining SELinux or AppArmor requires a blend of theoretical understanding and practical skills. Administrators must commit to regular policy reviews, adhere to established security guidelines, and continuously monitor system behavior using the integrated logging and auditing features provided by these frameworks. Such diligence minimizes the likelihood of security lapses and ensures that even if one layer of defense is compromised, additional controls provide the necessary barriers to prevent widespread system breaches.

8.6. Securing Network Services

Securing network services is fundamental to maintaining a robust Linux environment. As network services often serve as the primary interface between external connections and internal resources, they present attractive targets for unauthorized access. This section examines methods for securing these services by configuring firewalls, implementing secure protocols, and minimizing the number of open ports. These practices complement earlier discussions on file permissions, user management, and access control mechanisms, contributing to an overall defense-in-depth strategy.

Firewalls provide the first layer of defense by controlling the flow of network traffic. Tools such as `iptables` and `nftables` are widely used to define rules that govern incoming and outgoing traffic. A basic configuration might involve denying all unsolicited incoming connections while allowing necessary communications. For example, the following `iptables` commands illustrate a simple firewall setup that blocks all inbound traffic by default, then selectively permits essential services:

```
# Flush existing rules to start with a clean slate
iptables -F
iptables -X

# Default policy: drop incoming traffic
iptables -P INPUT DROP
iptables -P FORWARD DROP
iptables -P OUTPUT ACCEPT

# Allow all loopback (lo0) traffic
iptables -A INPUT -i lo -j ACCEPT

# Allow existing connections and associated traffic
iptables -A INPUT -m state --state ESTABLISHED,RELATED -j ACCEPT

# Allow SSH connections on port 22
iptables -A INPUT -p tcp --dport 22 -j ACCEPT

# Allow HTTP and HTTPS traffic
iptables -A INPUT -p tcp --dport 80 -j ACCEPT
```

```
iptables -A INPUT -p tcp --dport 443 -j ACCEPT

# Save the configuration (this command may vary by distribution)
service iptables save
```

The commands above create a controlled environment where only traffic intended for known services is permitted. Similar configurations can be implemented using nftables, which offers a modern, efficient means of managing firewall rules. The choice between these tools depends on system requirements and familiarity. Both approaches enforce a strict policy that minimizes exposure to unwanted network traffic.

Securing network services also requires the use of secure protocols, which ensure that data transmitted over the network is encrypted and authenticated. Protocols such as Secure Shell (SSH), Transport Layer Security (TLS), and Secure Sockets Layer (SSL) are widely employed in various service contexts. For instance, using SSH for remote administration keeps command-line communications confidential. The SSH service is typically configured in the /etc/ssh/sshd_config file. Recommended settings might include disabling password authentication and relying exclusively on key-based authentication:

```
# Disable password-based authentication
PasswordAuthentication no

# Limit user logins to only specified users or groups
AllowUsers adminuser

# Enforce key-based login security
PubkeyAuthentication yes

# Use a nonstandard port (optional, but can reduce automated attacks)
Port 2222
```

After adjusting these settings, it is essential to restart the SSH service:

```
systemctl restart sshd
```

For web services, the use of HTTPS (via TLS/SSL) not only encrypts data exchanged between clients and the server but also authenticates the server's identity. The process of obtaining a digital certificate from a trusted Certificate Authority (CA) and configuring the web server ensures that connections are secure. In Apache, this might involve editing the SSL configuration file:

```
<VirtualHost *:443>
    ServerName example.com
    DocumentRoot /var/www/html

    SSLEngine on
    SSLCertificateFile /etc/ssl/certs/example_com.crt
    SSLCertificateKeyFile /etc/ssl/private/example_com.key
    SSLCertificateChainFile /etc/ssl/certs/chain.pem

    <Directory /var/www/html>
        Options Indexes FollowSymLinks
        AllowOverride All
        Require all granted
    </Directory>
</VirtualHost>
```

This configuration enforces encrypted connections for web clients and discourages the use of insecure HTTP. Likewise, other services such as mail servers or file transfer protocols benefit from secure protocol usage, with alternatives like SMTPS, IMAPS, and FTPS replacing their unencrypted counterparts.

In addition to encryption, minimizing the number of open ports reduces the exposure of a system to potential threats. Unused ports provide opportunities for attackers to exploit vulnerabilities. Routine audits of open ports are therefore essential. Administrators commonly use tools such as netstat, ss, or nmap to list and verify active services. A command such as the following provides a snapshot of active ports and associated services:

```
ss -tulpn
```

The output of this command enables administrators to identify which services are actively listening for connections. An example output might be:

```
Netid   State    Recv-Q   Send-Q   Local Address:Port      Peer Address:Port
        Process
tcp     LISTEN   0        128      0.0.0.0:2222            0.0.0.0:*
        users:(("sshd",pid=1234,fd=3))
tcp     LISTEN   0        128      0.0.0.0:80              0.0.0.0:*
        users:(("apache2",pid=2345,fd=4))
tcp     LISTEN   0        128      0.0.0.0:443             0.0.0.0:*
        users:(("apache2",pid=2345,fd=5))
```

This information directs attention to active services and assists in identifying any unexpected or unnecessary open ports. Following identification, configuration files can be adjusted, or corresponding services disabled, to tighten security.

Another important strategy in network service security is to enforce strict access controls. Limiting service access to known, trusted hosts via firewall rules or TCP wrappers reduces the risk of unauthorized access. For example, TCP wrappers can restrict services by modifying the /etc/hosts.allow and /etc/hosts.deny files. An example configuration might be:

```
# /etc/hosts.allow
sshd: 192.168.1.0/24

# /etc/hosts.deny
sshd: ALL
```

In this configuration, only hosts on the 192.168.1.0/24 subnet are permitted to connect via SSH, with all other hosts denied access. This layered approach complements firewall settings by providing a secondary level of access control based on host IP addresses.

In environments where network services are exposed to the Internet, implementing intrusion detection systems (IDS) and intrusion prevention systems (IPS) can further enhance security. Tools such as Snort or Suricata monitor network traffic for patterns associated with malicious

312

activity. When integrated with firewall rules and secure protocols, IDS/IPS systems provide real-time alerts and automated responses to potential threats, preventing unauthorized access before damage occurs.

Another effective method to minimize attack vectors is service hardening. This process involves disabling unnecessary service features, limiting the resources available to a service, and using `chroot` environments or containerization techniques to isolate a service from the rest of the system. For instance, a service running within a chroot jail has its file system interactions limited to a specified directory tree, thereby reducing potential system-wide impact in the event of a compromise. Such isolation can be implemented using tools like `chroot` or lightweight containerization solutions like Docker, which inherently restrict processes to controlled environments.

Service hardening also includes periodic software updates and the application of security patches. Vulnerabilities are continuously discovered in network software, and keeping systems current is vital for mitigating known exploits. Automated update tools and package management systems help ensure that security patches are applied promptly. Cooperation with vulnerability scanning tools to periodically assess the system can reveal outdated packages or misconfigured services that might otherwise present security risks.

Combining these strategies—firewall configuration, secure protocol implementation, port minimization, and access controls—forms a multi-layered approach to network service security. Configuring each layer correctly is essential for safeguarding a Linux system against both external and internal threats. This approach ensures that even if one component or layer is attacked, additional measures are in place to protect critical systems and data.

The techniques discussed in this section integrate directly with earlier chapters concerning permissions and user management. By systematically applying controlled access through firewalls and secure protocols, administrators enforce the principle of least privilege and reduce the surface for potential attacks. Each measure reinforces the other: secure protocols guarantee that only authenticated data is exchanged, while firewalls and access controls ensure that only authorized traffic reaches sensitive services.

Routine audits of firewall settings, open ports, and service configurations are essential practices. Administrators should schedule regular reviews using scripts or automated tools to check for compliance with the organization's security policy. For example, a periodic script might verify that only required ports are open and that firewall rules have not been inadvertently modified:

```bash
#!/bin/bash
# List all open ports and compare with expected list
open_ports=$(ss -tulpn | awk '{print $5}' | cut -d: -f2 | sort | uniq
    )
echo "Open ports: $open_ports"
```

Integrating such scripts with a monitoring system ensures that any deviation from the established security baseline is promptly detected and corrected.

A comprehensive strategy for securing network services demands continuous vigilance, proactive configuration management, and the application of best practices in network security. By effectively managing firewalls, enforcing secure protocols, and minimizing open ports, system administrators create a resilient environment that is capable of defending against the evolving landscape of cyber threats.

8.7.   Auditing and Monitoring Security

Auditing and monitoring security are critical components of a comprehensive defense strategy in Linux systems. These practices enable ad-

ministrators to verify that security policies are enforced, detect suspicious activities, and respond promptly to potential security incidents.
Building on earlier discussions of file permissions, user management,
and access control, auditing and monitoring provide the oversight required to maintain long-term system integrity. This section presents
an in-depth exploration of tools, techniques, and best practices for auditing system security, monitoring logs, and detecting anomalous behavior.

Central to auditing security is the concept of logging, which creates a
historical record of system activity. Standard logging facilities, such as
syslog and rsyslog, capture events from various system daemons and
applications. Logs typically include system messages, authentication
attempts, service startups and shutdowns, and kernel alerts. These
logs are stored in files found under directories such as /var/log/ and
serve as a primary resource for retrospective analysis. In many Linux
distributions, the centralized logging mechanism has been extended
to incorporate journald, which provides a binary log format accessible with the journalctl command. For example, a basic command to
display recent system messages with journalctl is:

```
journalctl -r
```

This command retrieves log entries in reverse chronological order, facilitating quick access to the most recent events. Complementary to
centralized logging, dedicated audit frameworks such as auditd offer
more granular insight into system events. auditd is designed to track
system calls and file accesses, providing an audit trail that supports
compliance requirements and forensic investigations.

The auditd service is configured via the file /etc/audit/auditd.conf
and monitored using rules defined in /etc/audit/audit.rules or supplementary files within /etc/audit/rules.d/. A sample rule to monitor changes to critical configuration files, such as /etc/passwd, might

be expressed as:

```
-w /etc/passwd -p wa -k passwd_changes
```

In this rule, -w sets a watch on the specified file, -p ensures that write (w) and attribute (a) changes are logged, and the -k option assigns a tag for easy identification in reports. Administrators may query audit logs using the tool ausearch. For example, to search for records tagged with passwd_changes, the following command is useful:

```
ausearch -k passwd_changes
```

Such targeted queries help identify anomalous alterations and facilitate rapid incident response.

Log analysis and correlation are vital to detect suspicious behavior. Tools such as Logwatch and GoAccess can summarize log data and generate reports that highlight unusual trends. These automated summaries not only reduce the manual burden of sifting through log files but also provide actionable insights. A typical Logwatch command to generate a daily security report might be:

```
logwatch --detail High --range yesterday
```

This command produces a detailed report of events from the previous day, focusing on high-priority alerts and anomalies. Regular review of such reports enables administrators to detect potential breaches, such as repeated failed login attempts or unexpected changes in system files.

Supplementing traditional logging, intrusion detection systems (IDS) and intrusion prevention systems (IPS) add real-time monitoring capabilities. Tools like Snort, Suricata, and OSSEC continuously analyze network traffic and system logs for signatures of known attacks or abnormal behavior. OSSEC, for instance, is a host-based IDS that integrates file integrity monitoring, log analysis, and rootkit detection. An OSSEC configuration typically involves defining rules and decoders to interpret log entries and network activities. A simplified excerpt of an

316

OSSEC rule might appear as follows:

```
<rule id="100001" level="10">
  <if_sid>550</if_sid>
  <match>sudo</match>
  <description>Sudo command usage detected</description>
</rule>
```

Such rules can trigger alerts if certain commands are executed in an unexpected context or if they deviate from established usage patterns. Integrating these systems with notification services, such as email alerting or integration into a Security Information and Event Management (SIEM) platform, further enhances the ability to respond in real time.

Monitoring tools are also critical for the detection of suspicious activities on network services. Solutions like Fail2ban monitor log files in real time, detecting patterns indicative of brute-force attacks or repeated connection failures. When such patterns are identified, Fail2ban automatically updates firewall rules to block offending IP addresses for a specified period. A typical Fail2ban configuration involves specifying patterns to look for in log files and defining actions to mitigate the detected threat. An example of a jail configuration for SSH in /etc/fail2ban/jail_local is:

```
[sshd]
enabled   = true
port      = 2222
filter    = sshd
logpath   = /var/log/auth.log
maxretry  = 5
```

This configuration monitors SSH attempts on port 2222, triggering a ban if more than five failed login attempts are detected. The resulting automated response significantly reduces the window of opportunity for attackers.

Another approach to auditing and monitoring involves using file integrity monitoring (FIM) tools. FIM tools, such as Tripwire and AIDE (Advanced Intrusion Detection Environment), compute cryptographic checksums of critical system files and compare them with known-good baselines. Any alteration to these files, whether due to unauthorized modifications or accidental changes, is promptly reported. Configuring AIDE typically involves initializing a database that captures the current state of critical files, followed by periodic checks to detect changes. An example command to initialize the AIDE database is:

```
aide --init
mv /var/lib/aide/aide.db.new /var/lib/aide/aide.db
```

Subsequent integrity checks are then performed with:

```
aide --check
```

The output supplies a detailed report of any discrepancies, enabling administrators to reconcile legitimate updates with potential security breaches.

The effective monitoring of security is not limited to tools and configurations; it also involves establishing clear policies and procedures for incident response. Guidelines should be documented and regularly reviewed to ensure alignment with evolving security requirements. Regular drills and simulated attacks can test the effectiveness of the monitoring infrastructure and the responsiveness of the security team. In environments with regulatory requirements, a well-documented auditing process can also support compliance efforts by demonstrating adherence to established security frameworks.

Automation plays a vital role in modern auditing practices. Scheduling regular log analysis and system audits through cron jobs or systemd timers ensures that the process is both continuous and consistent. A sample cron job for running a daily audit script might be:

```
0 2 * * * /usr/local/bin/daily_audit.sh >> /var/log/daily_audit.log
    2>&1
```

This entry schedules an audit to run every day at 2 AM, logging its output to a designated file. The script itself can include commands to check open ports, validate file permissions, and review recent log entries for anomalies. Such automation reduces the risk of human oversight and ensures that any deviations from baseline security configurations are detected promptly.

Moreover, centralized log management is essential in environments with multiple systems. Solutions such as the Elastic Stack (ELK), Graylog, or Splunk facilitate the aggregation, indexing, and visualization of logs from across the network. Centralized log management not only simplifies the monitoring process but also enables cross-correlation of events between systems, making it easier to detect coordinated attacks. For example, an ELK configuration involves setting up Filebeat on endpoints to ship logs to a centralized Logstash instance, which then stores the data in Elasticsearch. Kibana dashboards built atop Elasticsearch indices provide visual insights into trends and anomalies.

Integrating these centralized monitoring systems with alerting mechanisms transforms raw data into actionable intelligence. Alerts can be configured to trigger when anomalous patterns emerge—such as an unusual spike in failed login attempts, unexpected changes in file integrity, or network traffic anomalies—alerting administrators instantly so that countermeasures can be deployed.

Finally, continuous professional development and staying abreast of emerging trends is crucial in the realm of security monitoring. The threat landscape evolves rapidly, and new vulnerabilities surface regularly. Participation in security forums, subscribing to threat intelligence feeds, and attending industry conferences are all part of maintaining a robust security posture. Through these channels, administrators can gain insights into best practices, learn from the experiences of others, and adopt cutting-edge tools and techniques as they become available.

Auditing and monitoring form the backbone of proactive security management in Linux systems. By implementing robust logging, employing advanced detection tools, and establishing a culture of continuous review and improvement, administrators can significantly enhance the resilience of their systems. The careful orchestration of audit trails, real-time monitoring, and automated responses creates a dynamic security environment capable of withstanding evolving threats, ensuring that both current and future security challenges are met with appropriate and effective countermeasures.

Chapter 9

Shell Scripting and Automation

This chapter introduces shell scripting fundamentals, covering variables, data types, and control flow structures. It explains input/output management, function use in scripts, and debugging techniques. The focus extends to automating tasks with shell scripts and scheduling them using cron, equipping users with skills to streamline and automate their workflows within Debian environments.

9.1. Getting Started with Shell Scripting

Shell scripting in Unix-like environments, particularly within Debian systems, serves as an essential tool for automating tasks and simplifying complex workflows. A shell script is a text file containing a sequence of commands that the shell interpreter executes in order. This approach not only facilitates rapid execution of repetitive tasks but also promotes clarity in system operations through modular, self-contained programs.

One of the fundamental elements of a shell script is its structure. Every script typically begins with a shebang line, which specifies the interpreter that processes the script. The shebang line should be the very first entry in the file, as it instructs the operating system on which interpreter to invoke. For instance, the following example indicates that the script is to be run using the Bash shell:

```
#!/bin/bash
```

Following the shebang, a shell script may include comments, variable declarations, function definitions, and command sequences. Comments are marked with a hash symbol (#) and provide context or explanations for the commands that follow without affecting the script's behavior. A well-documented script aids in maintainability and collaborative development. It is advisable to include comments that detail the purpose, usage instructions, and any prerequisites for running the script.

Shell scripts can be structured with sequential commands, control flow constructs, and loops to handle iterative processes. For instance, a simple script that prints a message to the terminal can be created as illustrated below:

```
#!/bin/bash
# This script prints a welcome message to the user
echo "Welcome to your shell scripting tutorial!"
```

Once the script is written, it must have the appropriate permissions to be executed. Setting executable permissions is done using the chmod command. The command below assigns execution permissions to the script myscript.sh:

```
chmod +x myscript.sh
```

322

Executing the script can be accomplished by referencing its relative or absolute path, as shown here:

```
./myscript.sh
```

Understanding script execution modes is critical. Scripts may be executed in a subshell or sourced into the current shell environment. Sourcing a script using the dot command or source keyword executes its contents in the current shell, preserving environment changes such as variable assignments. This distinction is important when the script is intended to modify the existing shell environment.

Shell scripting best practices are integral to creating reliable, efficient code. First, always validate inputs when the script requires external data. This validation ensures that any required parameters are provided and that they are within expected value ranges. Embedding conditional checks early in the script can help avoid errors during execution. Furthermore, using consistent indentation and naming conventions enhances code clarity and overall readability.

Maintaining robust logging within a script can prove invaluable during debugging and for future reference. A simple approach is to append outputs or errors to log files. For instance, if a script performs backup operations, any encountered errors can be logged to track the source of issues:

```bash
#!/bin/bash
# Backup script with error logging
backup_dir="/backup"
source_dir="/data"
timestamp=$(date +%Y%m%d%H%M%S)
log_file="/var/log/backup_$timestamp.log"

if [ ! -d "$backup_dir" ]; then
    echo "Backup directory does not exist. Creating now..."
    mkdir -p "$backup_dir"
fi

rsync -av "$source_dir" "$backup_dir" 2>> "$log_file"
if [ $? -eq 0 ]; then
```

```
    echo "Backup completed successfully at $timestamp."
else
    echo "Backup encountered errors. Refer to $log_file for details."
fi
```

Attention to error handling is another best practice. It is advisable to check the return status of commands and handle error cases appropriately. The return status of the last executed command is held in the special variable $?. By analyzing this value, scripts can determine whether a command executed successfully and take remedial action or log an error if necessary. Encapsulating frequently executed tasks in functions simplifies error handling across the script.

Modularization through functions is beneficial when a script performs complex or repetitive tasks. Functions encapsulate specific actions and reduce redundancy by allowing reuse of code blocks. A simple example is shown below:

```
#!/bin/bash
# Function to display a greeting message
greet_user() {
    local user_name=$1
    echo "Hello, $user_name! Welcome to your Debian system."
}

# Main script execution starts here
if [ $# -eq 0 ]; then
    echo "Usage: $0 <username>"
    exit 1
fi

greet_user "$1"
```

When writing a script intended for wider use or distribution, it is essential to make it as portable and readable as possible. This involves avoiding Bash-specific extensions if the script is meant to be run in different shell environments, using clear variable names, and structuring code to facilitate easy modifications or extensions. Moreover, scripts should ideally include a usage description or help message that guides the user on how to execute the script properly. This can be implemented by checking command-line arguments and providing default help options when necessary.

Managing environmental variables within a script is another important aspect. Many scripts depend on variable settings that affect command behavior. It is a common practice to check for the existence of required environmental variables and, if they are not defined, assign them default values or prompt the user for input. This minimizes user errors and guarantees that the script operates under expected conditions.

It is also advisable to incorporate version information and usage instructions within the script itself. Embedding version control information allows users and administrators to track changes and ensure compatibility with system updates. A typical approach is to define a version variable near the top of the script and output it upon request:

```bash
#!/bin/bash
# Script version and usage information
VERSION="1.0.0"

if [ "$1" = "--version" ]; then
    echo "Shell Scripting Tutorial Script Version: $VERSION"
    exit 0
fi

if [ "$1" = "--help" ]; then
    echo "Usage: $0 [options] <arguments>"
    echo "Options:"
    echo "  --help      Show this help message"
    echo "  --version   Show script version"
    exit 0
fi
```

Adopting a systematic approach to debugging is critical. Testing scripts line-by-line and using tools like set -x can aid in tracking variable values and command execution. Activating verbose mode by inserting the command set -x at the start of a script displays each command along with its arguments as they are executed. Once debugging is complete, this mode should be disabled using set +x to avoid cluttering the output during normal operations. Code instrumentation at strategic points can also provide insights into script performance and help isolate problematic sections efficiently.

Effective maintenance of shell scripts also relies on best practices regarding version control. Managing scripts in a repository not only tracks changes over time but also facilitates collaborative debugging endeavors. Version control systems such as Git allow developers to branch, merge, and revert changes systematically. In collaborative environments, document changes in the commit history to provide context for modifications, especially when the script is being used to automate critical system functions.

The flexibility of shell scripting enables integration with other system utilities and programming languages. Often, scripts call upon utilities such as awk, sed, or language-specific interpreters to extend their functionality. Incorporating these utilities within scripts must be done while ensuring that the external commands are available on the system and that their versions are compatible with the script requirements. Where dependencies exist, it is advisable to document such prerequisites clearly at the beginning of the script for future reference.

Another aspect deserving attention is the encoding and formatting of shell scripts. Scripts saved in UNIX format without the Byte Order Mark (BOM) and using Unix-style line endings ensure compatibility across various text editors and execution environments. Editors such as Vim or Nano should be configured appropriately to maintain these standards, thereby avoiding potential pitfalls when transferring scripts between different operating systems.

Attention must also be given to security implications when writing and executing shell scripts. Scripts that execute commands with elevated privileges or handle sensitive data should implement stringent access control. Avoid embedding sensitive information directly within the script and use symbolic links or configuration files with restricted permissions where applicable. Ensuring that input data is sanitized and using well-tested libraries or utilities further minimizes the risk of security vulnerabilities.

The creation of robust, dependable shell scripts requires not only understanding the fundamental syntax and structure but also adhering to a set of best practices aimed at clarity, modularity, and security. Steps taken to validate user input, handle errors gracefully, and document code can greatly reduce maintenance overhead and enhance long-term usability. Adopting techniques such as modular design through functions and employing robust debugging practices constitute a foundation that can be built upon as scripts grow in complexity.

The consolidation of shell scripting practices outlined provides a framework for crafting scripts that are both powerful and easy to maintain. Emphasis on clarity and precise instructions, backed by concrete code examples and execution guidelines, establishes a reference for both novice and experienced users. This foundation equips users with the necessary skills to develop shell scripts that adhere to the conventions required for a stable and secure Debian environment.

9.2. Variables and Data Types

Shell scripting permits the use of variables to store data and enables performing operations on these data values. Variables in shell scripts are essential constructs that allow dynamic assignment and manipulation of values during runtime. While shell scripting does not enforce data type declarations as seen in statically typed languages, understanding how to effectively use variables, and the implicit nature of data types in shells such as Bash, is crucial for creating robust scripts.

In a shell script, variables are typically defined by assigning a value to a name without any intervening spaces. The syntax follows the form `variable=value`. It is important to note that by default all variables are treated as strings. For example, assigning a simple string value is as straightforward as:

```
#!/bin/bash
greeting="Hello, Debian user!"
echo "$greeting"
```

When a variable is referenced, it is preceded by a dollar sign (\$). The use of double quotes around variable references is recommended to preserve whitespace and avoid unexpected word splitting, particularly when variable values contain spaces or special characters.

Although shell variables are inherently untyped, operations on these variables may assume numeric context when needed. Arithmetic operations can be performed using the `expr` command or by utilizing built-in arithmetic expansion. Arithmetic expansion is executed within the `$((...))` construct. An illustrative example:

```
#!/bin/bash
num1=10
num2=5
sum=$((num1 + num2))
echo "The sum is: $sum"
```

It is essential to note that arithmetic expansion only supports integer arithmetic. When fractional arithmetic is required, utilities such as bc or external programming languages should be integrated into the script. This limitation underscores the significance of understanding the nature of data types in shell scripting, where the conversion between a string and a numerical context is implicit and determined by the operation being performed.

The shell provides several built-in variable types. One such type is the read-only variable which is established using the `readonly` command. Declaring a variable as read-only prevents further modifications during the script's execution. For example:

```
#!/bin/bash
readonly PI=3.14159
echo "The value of PI is: $PI"
# Attempting to reassign PI will result in an error.
# PI=3.14
```

Another important feature is the use of environment variables that can be exported to be available in subprocesses. The export command accomplishes this:

```
#!/bin/bash
export PATH="/usr/local/bin:$PATH"
echo "The updated PATH is: $PATH"
```

An additional category of variables in Bash is arrays. Arrays allow storage of ordered collections of values, and they are referenced using an index. The syntax for declaring an array uses parentheses. Consider the following example:

```
#!/bin/bash
colors=("red" "green" "blue")
echo "The first color is: ${colors[0]}"
echo "All colors: ${colors[@]}"
```

Manipulating array elements follows similar principles to scalar variables. Looping over arrays using constructs such as for provides a mechanism to process multiple items efficiently. A code snippet demonstrating iteration over an array:

```
#!/bin/bash
colors=("red" "green" "blue")
for color in "${colors[@]}"; do
    echo "Processing color: $color"
done
```

Advanced usage may include associative arrays, which enable referencing data by string keys rather than numerical indexes. Associative arrays must be explicitly declared before usage. An example is presented as follows:

```
#!/bin/bash
declare -A capitals
capitals=( ["France"]="Paris" ["Germany"]="Berlin" ["Italy"]="Rome" )
echo "The capital of Italy is: ${capitals["Italy"]}"
```

While working with variables, proper quoting is a best practice. Incorrect quoting can result in errors such as word splitting or globbing issues. Double quotes should encapsulate variable expansions to preserve literal strings. If a variable's value is permitted to contain spaces, quoting prevents these issues. For instance:

```
#!/bin/bash
message="This message contains spaces and special characters !@#"
echo "$message"
```

Another important aspect of variable handling in shell scripting is parameter expansion. This mechanism provides additional functionality to manipulate variable values without the use of external commands. Common parameter expansions include default values, substring extraction, and pattern substitution. For example, specifying a default value if a variable is unset can be done as follows:

```
#!/bin/bash
echo "The value is: ${variable:-default_value}"
```

Substring extraction allows part of a variable's content to be isolated. The syntax $variable:offset:length is used for this purpose. This is particularly useful when only a portion of a stored string is needed. An example:

```
#!/bin/bash
text="DebianLinux"
sub=${text:6:5}
echo "Extracted substring: $sub"
```

In addition to these, removing patterns from variables is another parameter expansion feature. The syntax $variable#pattern or $variable##pattern for removing a prefix, and $variable%pattern or $variable%%pattern for removing a suffix, can streamline string

330

manipulation tasks. For example:

```
#!/bin/bash
file="report.final.doc"
base=${file%%.*}
echo "Base file name: $base"
```

Testing for a variable's existence is also important for creating resilient scripts. The conditional expression using -z or -n checks if a variable is empty or non-empty respectively. Validation steps prevent issues arising from missing or improper values. A common conditional structure is illustrated below:

```
#!/bin/bash
if [ -z "$username" ]; then
    echo "Username is not set. Please assign a username."
    exit 1
fi
```

Shell operations often require modifying case, formatting strings, or performing pattern matches. Utilizing built-in shell string manipulation functions reduces reliance on additional utilities and simplifies debugging. For example, converting a string to uppercase can be achieved in various ways, including the use of the tr command:

```
#!/bin/bash
lowercase="debian"
uppercase=$(echo "$lowercase" | tr '[:lower:]' '[:upper:]')
echo "Uppercase version: $uppercase"
```

In certain scenarios, variable transformations may also be performed directly using Bash's built-in features. For instance, substring removal as described previously can be used to modify file names or extract parts of configuration parameters without resorting to external tools.

It is imperative to address that, in shell scripts, all data begins as string representations. The shell's ability to interpret these strings as numbers or commands depends on context and the operations applied. As such, ensuring that a string that represents a number does not inadvertently contain non-numeric characters is crucial before performing

331

arithmetic operations. This validation can be integrated using regular expression checks or by invoking arithmetic expansion in a controlled section of the script.

In complex scripts, environment consistency and performance considerations lead developers to favor explicit data type usage even though Bash does not natively support robust data type declarations. Therefore, it is advisable to document expected data types within comments and maintain a clear structure. Using descriptive variable names and providing inline documentation for purpose and expected format ensures that others can modify and extend the script without introducing errors. Furthermore, careful error handling when casting or formatting data fortifies the script against unexpected input or behavior, given the limitations of implicit typing in shell scripting.

Finally, it is essential to consider the implications of variable scope. Variables defined at the script's top level are global by default. However, inside functions, local variables can be created using the `local` keyword. Limiting the scope of variables reduces unintended side effects and prevents collisions between variable names. An example of proper usage within a function is shown below:

```
#!/bin/bash
calculate_sum() {
    local a=$1
    local b=$2
    echo $((a + b))
}

result=$(calculate_sum 8 12)
echo "The calculated sum is: $result"
```

The dynamic nature of variable handling in shell scripts allows for rapid prototyping and straightforward implementation of automation tasks. However, the trade-off between flexibility and error-proneness demands careful attention to detail; appropriate input validation, quoting, and scope definition are all integral to mitigating common pitfalls.

This deliberate approach not only improves script reliability but also contributes to maintainability and ease of collaboration in multi-user environments.

By embracing these practices, scripts can operate more predictably across a variety of systems and user scenarios. The effective use of variables and a clear understanding of data types form a foundation upon which more sophisticated scripting techniques can be built. This depth of understanding is essential for developing scripts that are both efficient and resilient in managing system tasks within a Debian environment.

9.3. Control Flow Structures

Control flow structures in shell scripting are pivotal for developing dynamic and adaptable scripts. By incorporating constructs such as conditional statements, loops, and case statements, developers can control the execution path of scripts based on variable values and user inputs. These structures allow scripts to respond to different scenarios and inputs, making them more robust and flexible.

Conditional statements, most notably the if-else construct, are used for decision making. The basic syntax for an if-else statement initiates with a conditional expression enclosed within square brackets. The statement evaluates the expression and executes the corresponding block of commands if the condition is met. An optional elif clause allows for multiple conditions to be checked sequentially. For example:

```
#!/bin/bash
# Check if a file exists
filename="example.txt"

if [ -f "$filename" ]; then
    echo "The file '$filename' exists."
elif [ -d "$filename" ]; then
```

333

```
      echo "'$filename' is a directory."
else
      echo "The file '$filename' does not exist."
fi
```

In the above snippet, the conditional expression uses the -f operator to check for a regular file and the -d operator to determine if the path is a directory. These tests are essential for ensuring that the script handles file system objects appropriately. The use of quoting and proper spacing around brackets is critical to avoid syntax errors and ensure accurate evaluation.

Loops are essential for repeating tasks and processing multiple data elements efficiently. The shell offers several types of loops, including for, while, and until loops. Each of these loops suits different scenarios based on iterative control requirements.

A for loop is commonly used to iterate over a list of items, such as files, user inputs, or array elements. The following example demonstrates a for loop that processes a list of filenames:

```
#!/bin/bash
# Iterate over a list of files in the current directory
for file in *; do
    if [ -f "$file" ]; then
        echo "File: $file"
    fi
done
```

The wildcard * expands to all files and directories in the current directory. Within the loop, the if statement checks if each item is a file before proceeding with further actions. This combination of loop and condition exemplifies how control flow constructs are integrated for precise file processing.

While loops are used when the number of iterations is unknown and the continuation condition is evaluated before each iteration. A common use case is reading from a file line by line:

```
#!/bin/bash
# Read a file and process each line
input_file="data.txt"
while IFS= read -r line; do
    echo "Processing: $line"
done < "$input_file"
```

In the snippet above, the while loop uses the read command to iterate over each line of the file. The special variable IFS (Internal Field Separator) is set to avoid unexpected word splitting, and the -r flag prevents backslash escapes from being interpreted.

The until loop is similar to the while loop but continues execution until the test condition becomes true. Its structure is essentially the inverse of the while loop. Consider an example where a script waits for a particular file to appear:

```
#!/bin/bash
# Wait until a file exists
target_file="trigger.txt"
until [ -f "$target_file" ]; do
    echo "Waiting for $target_file to be created..."
    sleep 2
done
echo "$target_file has been created."
```

This loop evaluates the condition at the beginning of each iteration. The script continues to sleep and check until the specified file exists, demonstrating how until loops offer a natural way to wait for external events or conditions.

Another control structure that enhances script flexibility is the case statement. This structure provides a more concise alternative to multiple if-elif-else chains, particularly when the script must select actions based on the value of a variable. The syntax involves specifying patterns that match potential values and executing the corresponding command block. An illustrative example is provided below:

```
#!/bin/bash
# Use a case statement to handle user input
```

335

```
read -p "Enter a command (start/stop/status): " user_command

case "$user_command" in
    start)
        echo "Starting the service..."
        # Insert command to start the service
        ;;
    stop)
        echo "Stopping the service..."
        # Insert command to stop the service
        ;;
    status)
        echo "Checking the service status..."
        # Insert command to check status
        ;;
    *)
        echo "Invalid command. Options are: start, stop, status."
        ;;
esac
```

In this structure, the input from the user is matched against predefined patterns. The asterisk (*) serves as the default case, ensuring that any unrecognized input is handled appropriately. The use of ; ; terminates each block of commands within the case construct.

Control flow constructs can be enhanced further with compound commands and logical operators. Operators such as && and || enable the combination of commands to create succinct conditionals. The && operator executes the second command only if the first command succeeds, while the || operator executes the second command only if the first command fails. Consider the following example:

```
#!/bin/bash
# Combined commands using logical operators
mkdir new_directory && echo "Directory created successfully." || echo
    "Failed to create directory."
```

This example shows how a single line of code can carry out conditional execution based on the success or failure of the mkdir command. Logical operators are useful for writing concise scripts that remain readable while performing multiple checks simultaneously.

336

Nested control structures are another facet of shell scripting that allow complex decision-making processes. Combining loops with conditional statements, or even embedding one control structure within another, aids in managing multi-layered logic. A nested example might involve iterating over a list of files and applying different processing routines based on file extensions:

```
#!/bin/bash
# Process files based on file extensions using nested conditionals
for file in *; do
    if [ -f "$file" ]; then
        case "$file" in
            *.txt)
                echo "Text file detected: $file"
                # Process text file
                ;;
            *.log)
                echo "Log file detected: $file"
                # Process log file
                ;;
            *)
                echo "Unrecognized file type: $file"
                ;;
        esac
    fi
done
```

This script iterates over each file in the directory, checks if it is a regular file, and then chooses an appropriate action based on its extension using a nested case statement. The layered control flow ensures that each file is processed according to its specific type, demonstrating modularity and precision in handling diverse data.

Loop controls such as `break` and `continue` further refine the behavior of iterative structures. The `break` command terminates the nearest enclosing loop immediately, while `continue` skips the remainder of the current iteration and proceeds with the next iteration. The utility of these commands is evident, for instance, when searching for a target value in a sequence:

```
#!/bin/bash
```

```
# Searching for a target value in an array and terminating once found
numbers=(10 20 30 40 50)
target=30

for num in "${numbers[@]}"; do
    if [ "$num" -eq "$target" ]; then
        echo "Target $target found."
        break
    fi
    echo "Checked number: $num"
done
```

In this example, the loop iterates over an array of numbers. When the target value is found, the break statement halts further iterations, preventing unnecessary processing. Such controls are indispensable in optimizing script performance and ensuring precise execution flow.

Error handling within control structures is an additional layer of script robustness. Incorporating checks for unexpected conditions or erroneous user inputs within the branches of conditional statements can preempt script failures. It is advisable to include appropriate messages and exit conditions when errors arise. For instance, validating user input in a loop or a case statement can prevent misconfigurations and guide the user toward correct usage.

The combination of these control flow structures provides a rich set of tools for scripting. By understanding and effectively utilizing if-else statements, loops, case syntax, and loop controls such as break and continue, developers can build complex, efficient, and readable scripts. These constructs form the backbone of dynamic script behavior, ensuring that scripts respond correctly under varying conditions and inputs.

The careful integration of control flow constructs with variable management and command execution permits developers to write scripts that not only automate tasks but also adapt to changes and errors gracefully. Focusing on writing clear, maintainable, and modular code through proper usage of these structures will lead to scripts that are easier to

338

debug and extend over time, enhancing their overall reliability in a Debian environment.

9.4. Handling Input and Output

Managing input and output in shell scripts is fundamental for creating interactive applications and automating tasks involving data exchange. The ability to capture user input, process data, and direct output to various locations such as the terminal or files enhances the flexibility and utility of scripts. This section delves into the various techniques for handling input and output, building on the variable manipulation and control flow concepts discussed earlier.

One of the simplest forms of user interaction in shell scripting is reading input from the terminal. The read command is central to this functionality, enabling scripts to accept data from users during execution. The basic usage of read involves specifying a variable that should store the input value. For instance:

```
#!/bin/bash
echo "Enter your name: "
read user_name
echo "Hello, $user_name. Welcome to the script."
```

In this example, the script prompts the user to enter their name. The read command captures the input, which is then stored in the variable user_name. Printing the variable with appropriate quoting ensures that any whitespace or special characters are preserved.

Enhancements to basic input can be achieved by using the -p option with read. This option allows the script to display a prompt inline without requiring a separate echo command. For example:

```
#!/bin/bash
read -p "Enter your name: " user_name
echo "Hello, $user_name. Welcome to the script."
```

The -s flag is useful for sensitive inputs, such as passwords, where echoing the input to the terminal is not desirable. When used in conjunction with -p, it prompts the user while keeping the input confidential:

```
#!/bin/bash
read -s -p "Enter your password: " user_password
echo
echo "Password has been securely recorded."
```

Handling multiple inputs in a single command can be executed by listing multiple variable names after read. Input fields, separated by spaces, are assigned sequentially. An example is as follows:

```
#!/bin/bash
read -p "Enter your first and last name: " first_name last_name
echo "Your full name is: $first_name $last_name"
```

Redirecting input from files is also an essential capability. While the above examples capture input from a user interactively, input redirection allows a script to process data stored in files. The redirection operator < sends a file's content as input to the script or a specific command. Consider the code snippet below, which reads from a file line by line:

```
#!/bin/bash
input_file="data.txt"
while IFS= read -r line; do
    echo "Processing: $line"
done < "$input_file"
```

The use of IFS= and the -r option preserves leading/trailing whitespace and backslashes within each line. By iterating over the file, the script can perform operations on each line individually, facilitating text processing tasks.

In addition to standard input, managing output is equally crucial. The primary command for output is echo, which writes text to the standard output, typically the terminal. Careful use of quotes around variables ensures that output is formatted correctly. For instance:

```
#!/bin/bash
name="Debian User"
echo "Welcome, $name!"
```

Output can be formatted further by using `printf`, which provides more control over layout, spacing, and data type formatting. The syntax of `printf` resembles that found in languages such as C. An example is presented below:

```
#!/bin/bash
value=42
printf "The answer to life, the universe, and everything is %d.\n" "
    $value"
```

Redirection of output to files is a powerful feature for logging and data storage. The redirection operators > and >> allow output to be written to or appended to a file, respectively. The following example demonstrates redirecting output to a file:

```
#!/bin/bash
output_file="output.log"
echo "Script execution started at $(date)" > "$output_file"
echo "Processing data..." >> "$output_file"
```

This example creates or overwrites `output.log` with the first line and then appends further information. Managing log files in this manner aids in troubleshooting and creates an audit trail for the script's execution. Additionally, error outputs can be redirected to a separate file using 2>, which channels the standard error stream. For example:

```
#!/bin/bash
command_that_may_fail 2> error.log
```

The redirection of both standard output and standard error can be combined to create a comprehensive log. Consider the following command that consolidates both streams into a single file:

```
#!/bin/bash
./run_script.sh > combined.log 2>&1
```

Here, 2>&1 directs the standard error to the same target as standard output. The ordering of these operators is important to achieve the desired redirection.

A useful technique in handling both input and output in scripts is the use of pipelines. The pipeline operator | passes the standard output from one command as the standard input to another command. Pipelines facilitate the chaining of commands and can simplify complex data transformations. An example of using a pipeline is shown below:

```bash
#!/bin/bash
ps aux | grep sshd | awk '{print $2}'
```

This pipeline lists active processes, filters those related to the SSH daemon, and then extracts the process IDs. Pipelines reduce the need for intermediate files and enable real-time data processing.

Interacting with files also includes the creation of temporary files and ensuring proper file handling. The construction of temporary files can be achieved using the mktemp command, which creates a uniquely named file in a secure manner. An example is provided below:

```bash
#!/bin/bash
temp_file=$(mktemp /tmp/script_output.XXXXXX)
echo "Intermediate data stored in: $temp_file"
echo "Processing..." > "$temp_file"
# Process the temporary file as needed
rm "$temp_file"
```

The use of mktemp ensures that file names do not conflict, particularly when scripts run concurrently. Clean-up of temporary files is a best practice to prevent cluttering the filesystem.

Handling multi-line input and output is another aspect that developers must consider. When dealing with multi-line data, ensuring that each line is processed correctly requires careful use of quoting and control loops. The readarray (or mapfile) command is specifically designed

342

for reading all lines of a file into an array. This facilitates operations that require random access to line data. For example:

```
#!/bin/bash
readarray -t lines < data.txt
for line in "${lines[@]}"; do
    echo "Read line: $line"
done
```

In this context, the -t option trims the trailing newline characters from each line in the array, ensuring cleaner output when the data is later processed.

When performing file input and output, it is imperative to consider error handling. Verifying the existence of a file before attempting to read it prevents runtime errors. Similarly, ensuring that the target directory for an output file exists can preempt failures during write operations. A defensive programming approach might include checking these conditions:

```
#!/bin/bash
input_file="data.txt"
if [ ! -f "$input_file" ]; then
    echo "Error: Input file $input_file not found." >&2
    exit 1
fi

output_dir="logs"
if [ ! -d "$output_dir" ]; then
    mkdir -p "$output_dir"
fi
output_file="$output_dir/$(basename "$input_file").out"
```

By incorporating these checks, the script ensures that it does not proceed under erroneous conditions. Writing error messages to the standard error stream using >&2 clearly delineates them from normal output.

Another method for capturing command output is command substitution, which allows the output of a command to be used as part of a variable assignment. This is accomplished using backticks or the preferred

343

$()$ syntax. For example:

```
#!/bin/bash
current_date=$(date +%Y-%m-%d)
echo "The current date is: $current_date"
```

Command substitution is particularly useful for embedding dynamically generated data directly within script logic.

When designing scripts that both read input and produce output, it is beneficial to implement options that permit customization of behavior. For instance, a script may accept command-line arguments to specify input sources or output destinations. Utilizing built-in utilities like getopts streamlines the parsing of such options. An example is as follows:

```
#!/bin/bash
while getopts "i:o:" opt; do
    case "$opt" in
        i) input_file=$OPTARG ;;
        o) output_file=$OPTARG ;;
        *) echo "Usage: $0 -i input_file -o output_file" >&2; exit 1
        ;;
    esac
done

if [ -z "$input_file" ] || [ -z "$output_file" ]; then
    echo "Error: Both input and output files must be specified." >&2
    exit 1
fi

echo "Processing input from $input_file and writing to $output_file"
```

This snippet demonstrates how getopts can handle options for specifying input and output files. Ensuring that mandatory options are provided prevents the script from executing in an undefined state. Combining these techniques with robust error and usability messages creates a user-friendly and maintainable script.

The redirection, substitution, and option parsing methods described above form a comprehensive toolkit for managing input and output

344

in shell scripts. Mastery of these techniques is essential for developing interactive and automated solutions that can adapt to various environments, particularly within Debian systems. By emphasizing robust error handling, secure file management, and clear data processing logic, scripts become both reliable and maintainable, facilitating effective system administration and user interaction.

9.5. Working with Functions in Scripts

In shell scripting, functions provide a means to encapsulate blocks of code, allowing scripts to be modular, maintainable, and reusable. By defining functions, developers can separate complex tasks into smaller units, abstract repetitive operations, and improve script readability. Functions in Bash and other shell environments are declared with a specific syntax and can manage local variables, return status codes, and accept parameters, much like subroutines in other programming languages.

A function in a shell script is typically defined using the following syntax:

```
function_name() {
    # Commands perform the function's tasks
}
```

Alternatively, the keyword `function` can be explicitly used to define a function:

```
function function_name {
    # Commands perform the function's tasks
}
```

The body of a function comprises any valid shell commands, including control flow structures, variable assignments, and input/output operations. Functions provide the advantage of consolidating logic that may be executed multiple times throughout a script. For example, if

345

a script needs to perform error logging in several different contexts, a dedicated logging function can centralize the implementation:

```bash
#!/bin/bash
log_message() {
    local message="$1"
    local log_file="/var/log/script.log"
    echo "$(date '+%Y-%m-%d %H:%M:%S') - $message" >> "$log_file"
}
```

In this example, the function `log_message` takes a single argument and appends the message with a timestamp to a designated log file. The use of `local` for the variable `message` ensures that the variable scope is confined to the function itself, preventing unintended side effects in the global script environment.

Passing arguments to functions is straightforward. Parameters are referenced in the function body using positional parameters $1, $2, etc. The special parameter $@ or $* represents all arguments passed to the function. Consider the following example, which illustrates parameter handling and arithmetic operation:

```bash
#!/bin/bash
sum_two_numbers() {
    local num1=$1
    local num2=$2
    local sum=$((num1 + num2))
    echo "$sum"
}

result=$(sum_two_numbers 15 27)
echo "The sum is: $result"
```

Here, the function `sum_two_numbers` accepts two parameters, performs an arithmetic addition, and outputs the result. Capturing the output of the function through command substitution ($()) enables the script to further manipulate or display the computed value.

Functions also enable structured error handling in scripts. A function can return an exit status using the `return` command. The exit status,

346

typically an integer between 0 and 255, signals success or failure. A return value of 0 conventionally represents success, while nonzero values indicate various error conditions. For instance, consider a function designed to check the existence of a file:

```bash
#!/bin/bash
check_file_existence() {
    local file_path="$1"
    if [ -f "$file_path" ]; then
        return 0
    else
        return 1
    fi
}

file="important.conf"
if check_file_existence "$file"; then
    echo "File $file exists."
else
    echo "File $file does not exist."
fi
```

In this case, the function `check_file_existence` encapsulates the file existence check. The script then uses the return status to determine the subsequent action. This approach enhances script clarity by separating verification logic from higher-level workflow control.

A key consideration in function design is the management of variable scope. Defining variables with the `local` keyword within a function limits their lifetime to that function, avoiding name collisions with global variables. Without `local`, modifications to a variable inside a function could inadvertently alter the global environment. For example:

```bash
#!/bin/bash
counter=0

increment_counter() {
    local increment=$1
    counter=$((counter + increment))
    echo "Inside function, counter: $counter"
}
```

347

```
increment_counter 5
echo "Outside function, counter: $counter"
```

The example demonstrates that even though `counter` is a global variable, managing intermediate variables within the function using `local` helps prevent accidental overwrites. Developers should carefully assess whether a variable should be global or local to maintain proper encapsulation.

Functions can be nested within scripts to enhance modularity. When a script grows in complexity, it is common to divide it into a set of utility functions, each responsible for a specific task, such as input validation, logging, data processing, and cleanup. This division not only reduces code duplication but also facilitates debugging and testing. Breaking down a complex operation into smaller functions allows each component to be tested independently, thereby isolating the source of errors more efficiently. As an illustrative example, a script that processes user data might use functions for parsing, sanitizing, and processing the input:

```
#!/bin/bash
sanitize_input() {
    local raw_input="$1"
    # Remove potentially dangerous characters
    local sanitized=$(echo "$raw_input" | tr -d ';|&')
    echo "$sanitized"
}

process_data() {
    local data="$1"
    echo "Data processed: $data"
}

main() {
    read -p "Enter your data: " user_input
    local safe_input=$(sanitize_input "$user_input")
    process_data "$safe_input"
}

main
```

In this modular approach, the `sanitize_input` function removes unwanted characters from the user input, and `process_data` handles the primary task associated with the input. The `main` function coordinates user interaction and subsequent processing. This clear separation of duties facilitates enhancements and future modifications.

Moreover, functions in shell scripts can be employed recursively, although caution must be exercised with recursion in scripts due to potential performance limitations and stack depth restrictions. When recursion is necessary for a task like traversing a directory structure, it is important to incorporate base cases to prevent infinite recursion. For example, a recursive function that prints directory contents might be structured as follows:

```bash
#!/bin/bash
traverse_directory() {
    local dir="$1"
    # Base case: if the directory does not exist, exit the function
    if [ ! -d "$dir" ]; then
        echo "Directory $dir does not exist."
        return 1
    fi
    for file in "$dir"/*; do
        if [ -d "$file" ]; then
            echo "Entering directory: $file"
            traverse_directory "$file"
        else
            echo "File: $file"
        fi
    done
}

traverse_directory "/path/to/directory"
```

This recursive function demonstrates how to navigate directories using function calls. Security and performance considerations must be taken into account when deploying recursive functions in production environments.

Proper documentation within functions is also essential. Adopting a consistent commenting style that explains the purpose, parameters, and expected behavior of a function assists future maintainers and collaborators. Comments preceding a function definition or inline within the function body act as a guide for understanding the logic encapsulated in the function. For example:

```bash
#!/bin/bash
# Function: calculate_area
# Description: Computes the area of a rectangle given its width and
    height.
# Parameters:
#    $1 - width of the rectangle
#    $2 - height of the rectangle
# Returns:
#    Echoes the computed area
calculate_area() {
    local width=$1
    local height=$2
    local area=$((width * height))
    echo "$area"
}
```

Well-documented functions not only clarify the code for others but also serve as internal documentation for the current developer, especially when revisiting the script after an extended period.

Enhanced functionality in functions can be achieved by using advanced features such as arrays and parameter expansion. Functions can return multiple values by echoing results that are subsequently captured into arrays, or they can modify global arrays directly if required. Additionally, advanced parameter expansion techniques, such as default values and substring extraction, can be integrated within functions to handle various input scenarios robustly.

When designing functions, it is also advisable to consider potential side effects and ensure that a function performs a specific, well-defined task. Functions with side effects, such as modifying global state or writing to files, should be clearly documented, and their use should be minimized to avoid unexpected interactions. Adopting a functional programming mindset in shell scripting, where functions are used as pure or nearly pure operations, can substantially improve the maintainability and testability of the script.

Incorporating these practices, functions become a central pillar of effective shell scripting. They allow scripts to be structured in a modular manner, separating concerns and streamlining complex workflows. As scripts evolve, refactoring code into well-defined functions facilitates easier debugging, testing, and future enhancements. The use of functions also promotes reusability; libraries of shell functions can be shared across multiple scripts to standardize common operations, supporting a more maintainable codebase in a Debian environment.

9.6. Debugging and Error Handling

Ensuring that a shell script behaves as expected under varying conditions is critical for creating robust and efficient automation solutions. Debugging and error handling techniques are two intertwined aspects that help a script manage unexpected situations and provide insight into its execution. The process of debugging involves identifying, isolating, and correcting errors, while error handling focuses on detecting problems at runtime and responding to them in a controlled manner.

One of the simplest methods to gain insight into a script's behavior is to use debugging mode. By inserting the command set -x at the beginning of a script, the shell prints each command and its arguments as they are executed. This verbose output provides a step-by-step trace of command execution that is particularly useful for diagnosing logical or syntax errors. Once debugging is complete, running set +x disables this feature. Consider the following snippet:

```
#!/bin/bash
set -x
echo "Starting script execution."
# Perform a series of operations
```

351

```
result=$((5 + 3))
echo "Result of arithmetic operation: $result"
set +x
echo "Script execution finished."
```

This approach is especially valuable when a script contains complex control flow structures or multiple function calls. In addition to tracing the execution, inserting diagnostic echo statements at strategic points assists in confirming the state of variables and the progression of logic.

Error handling in shell scripts centers around the use of exit codes, conditional checks, and traps. Every command invoked in a script returns an exit status that indicates whether the command succeeded or failed. Commonly, a status of 0 signifies success, while nonzero values indicate an error. The special variable $? holds the exit status of the most recently executed command. By testing this variable immediately after a command, a script can determine whether to proceed or handle an error situation. For example, checking the result of a file copy operation might be performed as follows:

```
#!/bin/bash
cp source.txt destination.txt
if [ $? -ne 0 ]; then
    echo "Error: Failed to copy file." >&2
    exit 1
fi
echo "File copied successfully."
```

This snippet demonstrates the practice of testing the exit status and redirecting error messages to stderr using >2. This distinction between normal and error output makes the output more meaningful when logged or redirected.

Another powerful error handling tool is the trap command. The trap command allows a script to specify actions that should be executed when it receives a specific signal or when an error or exit condition occurs. By trapping signals such as EXIT, INT, or ERR, a script can ensure that cleanup actions are taken or that detailed error messages are generated before exiting. The following example uses `trap` to catch an exit signal and perform cleanup operations:

```bash
#!/bin/bash
cleanup() {
    echo "Performing cleanup before exit."
    # Remove temporary files or close open resources here
    rm -f /tmp/temp_file.txt
}
trap cleanup EXIT

# Simulate script operation
echo "Script is running."
# Introducing an error by attempting to write to a non-existent
    directory
echo "Some data" > /non_existent_directory/file.txt
```

By setting a trap on EXIT, the script ensures that the cleanup function is invoked regardless of whether the script terminates normally or due to an error. This guarantees that resources are released and that the system state remains consistent.

Many scripts benefit from using the -e option in conjunction with error handling. The `set -e` command instructs the shell to exit immediately if any command returns a nonzero exit status. This technique enforces strict error handling, preventing a script from continuing in an unpredictable state after a failure. However, using `set -e` requires careful control because some commands are expected to fail or are used in conditional statements. A typical script leveraging this option appears as follows:

```bash
#!/bin/bash
set -e
echo "Starting critical operations."
# The script will exit if the following command fails
mkdir /some/protected/directory
echo "Directory created successfully."
```

When integrated into scripts, `set -e` reinforces error detection while necessitating that each critical command is either checked or expected to succeed. In addition to immediate termination, custom error mes-

353

sages and logging can be implemented by combining error checking with conditional tests.

Error handling can be further enhanced by writing custom functions that encapsulate common error handling routines. For example, creating an error reporting function allows for consistent formatting of error messages across the script. Such a function might log errors to a file while also writing to the terminal:

```
#!/bin/bash
log_error() {
    local error_message="$1"
    echo "$(date '+%Y-%m-%d %H:%M:%S') - ERROR: $error_message" >> /
    var/log/myscript_error.log
    echo "ERROR: $error_message" >&2
}

# Example usage
cp /path/to/source /path/to/destination
if [ $? -ne 0 ]; then
    log_error "Failed to copy file from /path/to/source to /path/to/
    destination."
    exit 1
fi
```

This function not only standardizes error output but also creates a persistent record of issues, benefiting long-term maintenance and troubleshooting efforts.

Differentiating between recoverable and unrecoverable errors is another significant aspect of error handling. For recoverable errors, a script might choose to retry the operation or prompt the user for corrective input. In contrast, unrecoverable errors should cause the script to exit cleanly, closing any open resources and providing a useful error message. A retry mechanism might be implemented using a loop that checks the exit status of a command and reattempts the operation with a delay:

```
#!/bin/bash
max_attempts=3
attempt=1
```

```
retry_command() {
    local success=0
    while [ $attempt -le $max_attempts ]; do
        echo "Attempt $attempt:"
        some_command && success=1 && break
        echo "Command failed. Retrying in 2 seconds..."
        sleep 2
        attempt=$((attempt + 1))
    done

    if [ $success -ne 1 ]; then
        echo "Command failed after $max_attempts attempts."
        exit 1
    fi
    echo "Command succeeded."
}

retry_command
```

This structure uses a loop to retry the failing command, increasing the robustness of the script in environments where transient failures may occur. Adjustable parameters, such as the maximum number of attempts and delay duration, provide flexibility in dealing with different error conditions.

When integrating debugging techniques with error handling, combining verbose logging with failure detection enables developers to pinpoint precise moments of failure. This is particularly useful in production environments where direct observation of the script's execution is impractical. By redirecting output to log files and invoking the trap command, a script can capture sufficient context to diagnose issues after the fact. An example that combines these techniques is shown below:

```
#!/bin/bash
set -e
log_file="/var/log/myscript_debug.log"

log_message() {
    local message="$1"
    echo "$(date '+%Y-%m-%d %H:%M:%S') - $message" >> "$log_file"
```

```
}

cleanup() {
    log_message "Script terminated. Cleaning up resources."
    rm -f /tmp/temp_data.txt
}
trap cleanup EXIT

log_message "Script started."
echo "Performing a series of operations..."
# Simulate a command that might fail
false
log_message "This message will not be logged if the command above
    fails."
```

The integration of verbose logging and cleanup protocols ensures that even if a command fails, the state of the system is recorded and remedial actions are taken. This comprehensive strategy supports both immediate troubleshooting and long-term analysis of issues.

In addition to these techniques, developers can make use of external debugging tools and shell options. Tools like bashdb provide interactive debugging functionality similar to traditional debuggers used for compiled languages. This tool allows for setting breakpoints, stepping through scripts, and inspecting variable values interactively. Although this approach requires additional setup, it is invaluable for complex scripts where pinpointing errors in nested functions and loops is challenging.

Adopting best practices is essential to maintain reliable scripts. This includes writing modular code with clear error handling pathways, thorough logging, and cautious use of commands that may fail in unpredictable ways. It is beneficial to test scripts in controlled environments and simulate error conditions to verify that error handling behaves as expected. Incorporating peer reviews and static analysis tools can further aid in identifying potential flaws before deployment.

The dual approach of debugging and error handling forms the backbone of resilient shell scripts. By employing a combination of verbose execution tracing, strategic use of `trap` and `set -e`, as well as structured error reporting functions, developers can create scripts that not only fail gracefully but also provide actionable information to correct issues. Emphasizing robust error detection and cleanup routines during script development significantly improves system reliability and minimizes downtime caused by unforeseen issues.

9.7. Automation with Scripts and Cron Jobs

Automation in Unix-like systems is a powerful technique to simplify routine administrative tasks and maintain consistent system behavior. One of the most prevalent methods for automating shell script execution is by using `cron`, a time-based job scheduler that allows tasks to be executed at specified intervals. The integration of shell scripts with cron enables administrators and users alike to create a robust automation framework for backups, updates, monitoring, and other repetitive tasks.

The `cron` daemon reads its configuration from files known as crontabs. Each user, including the system administrator, can have a dedicated crontab file that specifies tasks along with their scheduling syntax. A typical crontab entry consists of five fields representing minute, hour, day of month, month, and day of week, followed by the command to be executed. The syntax takes the following form:

```
# m h  dom mon dow   command
30 2 * * * /home/user/backup.sh
```

In this example, the script `backup.sh` is scheduled to run daily at 2:30 AM. Each field allows values or ranges, and the asterisk (*) is used as a wildcard that denotes any valid value in the corresponding position. The flexible scheduling format supports expressions such as comma-

357

separated lists, hyphenated ranges, and step values (using the slash operator).

Before integrating a shell script with cron, it is imperative to ensure that the script is both executable and robust. Scripts intended for scheduled tasks must have proper error handling, logging, and minimal user interaction. For instance, consider a script that performs system backups. The script should log its operations, verify that critical files are available, and handle unexpected errors gracefully. An example script might look as follows:

```bash
#!/bin/bash
# backup.sh: A script to perform system backup

LOG_FILE="/var/log/backup.log"
BACKUP_SOURCE="/home/user/data"
BACKUP_DEST="/mnt/backup_drive/data_backup_$(date +%Y%m%d).tar.gz"

echo "$(date '+%Y-%m-%d %H:%M:%S') - Starting backup." >> "$LOG_FILE"

if [ ! -d "$BACKUP_SOURCE" ]; then
    echo "$(date '+%Y-%m-%d %H:%M:%S') - ERROR: Source directory
    $BACKUP_SOURCE does not exist." >> "$LOG_FILE"
    exit 1
fi

tar -czf "$BACKUP_DEST" "$BACKUP_SOURCE" >> "$LOG_FILE" 2>&1

if [ $? -eq 0 ]; then
    echo "$(date '+%Y-%m-%d %H:%M:%S') - Backup completed
    successfully." >> "$LOG_FILE"
else
    echo "$(date '+%Y-%m-%d %H:%M:%S') - ERROR: Backup failed." >> "
    $LOG_FILE"
    exit 1
fi
```

This backup script demonstrates the integration of essential practices such as logging, error checking, and the use of dynamic filenames that incorporate the current date. Such practices are critical when tasks are automated, as the lack of direct interaction requires robust logging and recovery measures.

Once the script is thoroughly tested and confirmed to work in isolation, scheduling the task with cron is the next step. Adding a new entry to the crontab file is typically done using the `crontab -e` command. Within the crontab editor, a suitable entry might be added as follows:

```
0 3 * * * /home/user/backup.sh
```

This entry schedules the backup script to run daily at 3:00 AM. To validate that the crontab entry is correctly configured, administrators can list current cron jobs with the command `crontab -l`. Additionally, ensuring that the cron daemon is running and that log files indicate proper execution is vital for maintaining confidence in the automation system.

Cron jobs operate in a different environment than interactive shell sessions. Therefore, scripts executed by cron should not assume the presence of common environment variables or a pre-configured environment. It is best practice to explicitly define environment settings within the cron entry or within the script itself. For example, specifying the PATH variable is a common precaution:

```
PATH=/usr/local/sbin:/usr/local/bin:/usr/sbin:/usr/bin:/sbin:/bin
0 3 * * * /home/user/backup.sh
```

Incorporating environmental definitions ensures that commands within the script are located and executed as expected. It is also advisable to leverage full path names for commands used within the script, such as `/bin/tar` or `/usr/bin/echo`, to avoid issues stemming from non-standard PATH definitions.

Beyond basic scheduling, cron's flexibility allows administrators to set up more advanced workflows. For instance, tasks can be configured to run on specific days of the week or month by adjusting the appropriate cron fields. To schedule a script on every Monday at 4:15 AM, the entry would be:

```
15 4 * * 1 /home/user/weekly_report.sh
```

Similarly, step values in the schedule can be useful. For example, if a script must run every 10 minutes, the minute field can be configured as:

```
*/10 * * * * /home/user/monitor.sh
```

The dynamic scheduling capabilities of cron extend to handling tasks based on specific conditions as well. Although cron does not support conditional execution directly, scripts can embed conditional logic to modify behavior. For example, a script that checks for specific system events or usage thresholds before taking action may look like this:

```
#!/bin/bash
# monitor.sh: A script that monitors disk space and sends alerts

ALERT_THRESHOLD=90
DISK_USAGE=$(df / | tail -1 | awk '{print $5}' | sed 's/%//')

if [ "$DISK_USAGE" -ge "$ALERT_THRESHOLD" ]; then
    echo "$(date '+%Y-%m-%d %H:%M:%S') - WARNING: Disk usage above
      threshold: $DISK_USAGE%" | mail -s "Disk Alert" admin@example.com
fi
```

In this example, the script extracts the disk usage percentage and sends an email alert if the usage exceeds a predefined threshold. When scheduled via cron, such a script provides ongoing monitoring without manual intervention. Ensuring that necessary utilities such as mail are installed and properly configured is an important precondition for such tasks.

Using cron for automation is not limited to user-defined scripts; system-level maintenance tasks are often configured during installation. Understanding the cron system's structure and permissions is essential. Several directories exist, such as /etc/cron.daily, /etc/cron.weekly, and /etc/cron.monthly, which are used by the system to execute scripts at predefined intervals. Placing a script in one of these directories enables automation without explicit crontab entries. System administrators should ensure that scripts placed in these directories are executable and follow the designed naming and logging conventions.

Security is a critical consideration when automating tasks with cron. Scripts that run with elevated privileges, particularly those executed by the root user, must be rigorously audited for vulnerabilities. Scripts should avoid exposing sensitive information, and logging should not inadvertently output confidential data. Using secure file permissions and limiting access to crontab files helps maintain a secure automation environment. Moreover, validating all inputs and ensuring that commands are safely constructed reduces the risk of unintended operations when scripts are run automatically.

Troubleshooting cron jobs necessitates a systematic approach. Since cron jobs lack interactive output, examining log files is crucial. Many systems log cron job executions to /var/log/syslog or a dedicated cron log file. Administrators can use tools such as grep to search for cron-related entries and validate that jobs are executing as scheduled. For example:

```
grep CRON /var/log/syslog
```

Additionally, redirecting output from a cron job to dedicated log files, as illustrated in backup and monitoring script examples, provides a persistent record of job execution. This logging structure is instrumental in diagnosing failures, performance issues, or unexpected behavior within automated tasks.

A best practice for complex automation schedules is to maintain a separate log management strategy. Combining cron log output with application-specific logs can yield a comprehensive view of system behavior. Automated log rotation, using utilities such as logrotate, ensures that log files do not grow indefinitely and that historical data is archived appropriately. Such strategies contribute to long-term system stability and simplify auditing and compliance processes.

Cron jobs offer a range of advanced options, including the use of environment variables and the addition of special strings such as @reboot. The @reboot directive schedules a job to run once at system startup. For example:

```
@reboot /home/user/startup_tasks.sh
```

This entry can be particularly useful for initializing system services or running user-specific tasks immediately after boot. However, care must be taken to ensure that all dependencies and environment conditions are met when tasks run at reboot.

Integrating shell scripts with cron greatly improves efficiency and reliability. By designing scripts with robust error handling, logging, and explicit environment settings, administrators can create an automated framework that requires minimal human intervention and adapts to changing system needs. The modularity of shell scripting, combined with the scheduling flexibility of cron, forms a foundation for an effective automation strategy in Debian and other Unix-like environments.

Effective automation not only reduces administrative overhead but also minimizes the risk of human error. Through comprehensive testing, detailed logging, and systematic scheduling, cron jobs can transform routine tasks into predictable, manageable processes that enhance overall system performance and reliability.

Chapter 10

Troubleshooting and System Recovery

This chapter offers strategies for diagnosing system issues, recovering from boot failures, and managing services. It addresses disk and file system recovery, software package repair, and troubleshooting network connectivity. Tools for monitoring and auditing are discussed, along with creating and using rescue disks, providing comprehensive guidance for maintaining system integrity and ensuring effective recovery in Debian environments.

10.1. Identifying and Diagnosing System Issues

Diagnosing system issues in a Debian environment requires a systematic approach that leverages a variety of logs, diagnostic utilities, and error messages. This section delineates practical techniques for identifying problems in services, processes, and system components by interpreting logs and using command-line tools effectively.

At the core of system diagnostics are log files that capture events, warnings, and error messages generated by both the kernel and user-space applications. In Debian systems, important logs reside in the directory /var/log. The file syslog or messages (depending on the configuration) records system-wide events and is a primary resource for troubleshooting. The kernel's output is often captured by dmesg, which provides insight into hardware issues, driver errors, and low-level system events. Analyzing these logs can reveal the timing and frequency of faults, which is critical for understanding systemic problems.

The first step in diagnosing issues is to review recent events. Commands such as tail, less, or specialized log viewers are useful when scanning large log files. For example, the following command views the last 50 lines of the syslog:

```
tail -n 50 /var/log/syslog
```

This command helps isolate recent errors, warnings, or unusual activities. In addition to static log files, the journal managed by systemd provides a comprehensive mechanism for event logging. The tool journalctl allows filtering by service, time, or severity. To inspect the most severe recent messages, one may execute:

```
journalctl -p 3 -xb
```

which retrieves all emergency, alert, critical, and error level messages since the last boot.

When investigating issues, the meaning of error codes and messages should be cross-referenced with official documentation or community resources. Understanding common error codes, like exit statuses from scripts or daemons, facilitates rapid identification of misconfigurations. It is useful to recognize recurring patterns; for instance, repeated failures in network connectivity might indicate a hardware issue, misconfigured routing, or DNS errors.

A more granular approach is often necessary when error messages are cryptic. Tools such as dmesg provide kernel ring buffer outputs that are especially helpful when hardware errors are suspected. An example command is:

```
dmesg | grep -i error
```

This command filters messages to show lines containing the keyword "error". Since kernel logs are verbose, filtering for relevant keywords can isolate the root cause efficiently.

Another layer of diagnostics involves examining process-specific logs. Many services maintain their logs separately under directories like /var/log/apache2 for web server logs or /var/log/mysql for database errors. These logs often include detailed error messages, stack traces, and time-stamped events that indicate operational failures. When logs indicate that a service has failed repeatedly, the administrator might need to inspect configuration files for syntax errors or dependency issues.

The use of diagnostic utilities extends beyond log scanning. Utilities such as strace enable tracing of system calls made by failing processes. By intercepting system calls, strace helps diagnose issues related to file access, networking, or resource allocation. A typical invocation to trace a process might be:

```
strace -o trace.log -p <pid>
```

where <pid> is replaced by the process identifier of the running service. Reviewing the output file trace.log allows the administrator to see a detailed account of the calls made by the process, providing insight into its operational failures.

Interpreting diagnostics outputs often requires correlating information from multiple sources. For instance, a service crashing might log an error message in its own log file while simultaneously generating kernel errors in dmesg. In such cases, compiling data from both sources helps determine if the issue originates in user-space configuration or from a deeper system-level conflict.

Advanced diagnostic techniques also involve the use of scripting to automate the extraction and analysis of logs. A simple Python script can be written to parse log files for repeated error patterns. Consider the following example:

```python
#!/usr/bin/env python3
import re

logfile = '/var/log/syslog'
pattern = re.compile(r'error', re.IGNORECASE)
error_count = 0

with open(logfile, 'r') as f:
    for line in f:
        if pattern.search(line):
            error_count += 1
            print(line.strip())

print("Total errors found:", error_count)
```

This script opens the syslog, searches each line for the occurrence of the word "error", and prints lines that contain the pattern. Such automation is valuable when dealing with large log files and can be extended to generate reports or trigger alerts when error counts exceed predefined thresholds.

Moreover, cross-referencing log timestamps with scheduled tasks or automated maintenance activities can illuminate the cause of seemingly random failures. Tools like cron logs and application-specific schedule records often reveal conflicts or resource overloading during peak times. A thorough review of log files from processes such as backup operations or periodic updates may reveal failures that indirectly affect system performance.

Diagnostic tools provided by Debian also include utilities for monitoring system performance. Tools like top, htop, and vmstat provide real-time statistics on CPU usage, memory availability, and I/O wait times. Monitoring these metrics during a degradation of service can help correlate performance bottlenecks with specific errors captured in the logs. A snapshot command using htop might be invoked to observe process behavior:

```
htop
```

While these commands do not directly output error messages, they supply valuable context that aids in diagnosing performance-related issues that manifest as system errors.

Another utility of interest is systemctl, which not only manages systemd services but also provides detailed status information for these services. For example, running:

```
systemctl status apache2
```

displays the service's current state, recent log entries, and any errors associated with the last attempted startups. Such information is indispensable when troubleshooting service-specific issues.

Interpreting the contents of log files should be approached with a clear understanding of log formats. Many log files use a common structure: a timestamp indicating when the event occurred, an identifier that typically includes the source of the log entry (such as the daemon or process name), and a descriptive message. Familiarity with this structure helps in scripting and manual analysis alike, as it enables splitting log entries into parsable components. Tools like awk or sed are often employed to manipulate logs. An example command that extracts timestamps from a log might be:

```
awk '{print $1, $2}' /var/log/syslog | sort | uniq -c
```

This command pipeline extracts the first two fields from each log line,

367

sorts them, and aggregates duplicate occurrences, providing insights into periods of high error frequencies.

The analytical process is iterative. After isolating a suspicious event in the logs, it is necessary to correlate information across multiple sources to validate the diagnosis. For instance, if a network service error is recorded, both the specific application logs and the network-monitoring logs (such as those gathered by utilities like ss or netstat) should be examined. This cross-correlation is essential to confirm that an error was not triggered by external factors such as a temporary network outage.

Additionally, administrators must be aware of the context within which errors occur. Consider a scenario where a configuration change is implemented; system logs immediately following the change may exhibit errors related to syntax or permissions. Detecting the correlation requires an understanding of recent administrative actions. Maintaining a change log or tracker can streamline the diagnostic process, as it creates a temporal mapping of configuration adjustments to system behavior.

Methodically reviewing error messages also involves verifying the integrity of the system's software packages. Package management utilities like dpkg and apt log installation details that can indicate if a package is missing dependencies, corrupted, or partially installed. Reviewing output logs from these utilities can preemptively indicate issues before they manifest as runtime errors. For instance, checking the status of a package can be performed with:

```
dpkg -l | grep <package-name>
```

This diagnostic check confirms whether a package is determined to be correctly installed or if it is flagged by the package manager as problematic.

As diagnosing system issues extends over multiple layers of the system stack, administrators must combine information from kernel messages, service logs, performance metrics, and package management outputs. This holistic view is critical in discerning the underlying causes of problems and facilitates the implementation of targeted remediation strategies without redundancy or oversight.

Integrating these practices into regular system monitoring routines promotes operational stability and responsiveness to unexpected issues. With a systematic approach based on reliable diagnostic tools, log analysis, and automated techniques, system administrators can efficiently isolate and resolve common issues, thereby ensuring the robust performance of the Debian system.

10.2. Recovering from Boot Failures

When a Debian system fails to boot, a systematic recovery process is required to diagnose and resolve underlying issues. The boot process in Linux involves multiple components such as the bootloader (commonly GRUB), the kernel, and the init system. Errors in any of these components can impede the startup sequence. Techniques for troubleshooting and recovering from boot failures include using recovery mode, repairing GRUB configurations, and employing boot repair tools. These methods serve as essential tools in the administrator's repertoire for restoring operational status after encountering boot anomalies.

Boot failures occur for various reasons. A misconfigured GRUB, corrupted kernel images, or issues in the initramfs can result in a failure to load system services. Hardware changes, such as altered disk identifiers, can also cause boot problems if the bootloader configuration references outdated parameters. Consequently, diagnostic steps begin with isolating the fault. The initial approach is to identify whether the problem occurs before or after GRUB loads. If the bootloader menu is inaccessible or misconfigured, then the error likely originates in the bootloader. Conversely, if GRUB loads correctly but the kernel or init system fails, further inspection of kernel parameters and driver configurations is required.

Recovery mode, also known as single-user mode, provides a controlled environment intended for maintenance and troubleshooting. Booting into recovery mode typically presents a minimal system with limited functionality, allowing access to the filesystem and logs without interfering background services. In Debian systems that employ GRUB, recovery mode is accessible from the boot menu. Administrators can select a recovery mode option that typically appends a parameter such as |single| or |rescue| to the kernel boot command line. This alternative boot mode provides an opportunity to perform administrative tasks such as repairing filesystem errors, reconfiguring bootloader settings, or reinstalling corrupted packages.

In cases where boot failures result from a corrupted or misconfigured bootloader, it is necessary to repair GRUB configurations. The GRUB bootloader reads settings from configuration files typically located in /boot/grub/grub.cfg. However, direct editing of this file is discouraged because it is automatically generated. Instead, changes should be made in /etc/default/grub and scripts located in /etc/grub.d/. An incorrect setting, such as an invalid kernel parameter, can result in a boot failure that prevents the system from progressing past GRUB. To reconfigure GRUB, one can reboot into recovery mode or use a live CD to gain system access and then edit the configuration files.

For example, if the system fails to recognize the correct root partition, correcting the configuration in /etc/default/grub to reflect the proper UUID may resolve the problem. An excerpt of a corrected entry might appear as follows:

```
GRUB_CMDLINE_LINUX_DEFAULT="root=UUID=xxxxxxxx-xxxx-xxxx-xxxx-
```

```
        xxxxxxxxxxxx quiet splash"
```

Following modifications to the GRUB configuration, regenerating the GRUB configuration file is crucial. The command to update the GRUB menu on Debian is:

```
update-grub
```

Boot repair tools offer another avenue for addressing boot failures. Tools such as `boot-repair` provide an automated method to detect and fix common bootloader issues. Although originally popularized in Ubuntu environments, `boot-repair` is available for Debian as well. When the system is accessed via a live CD or a recovery mode shell, `boot-repair` can be installed and executed to analyze the boot configuration and make necessary adjustments. Installing `boot-repair` might involve commands such as:

```
sudo add-apt-repository ppa:yannubuntu/boot-repair
sudo apt-get update
sudo apt-get install -y boot-repair
```

Once installed, invoking the tool with administrative privileges launches an interface that guides the recovery process. Although the automated mode is effective in many scenarios, experienced administrators may prefer to review the proposed changes and adjust the settings manually.

The diagnostic process in recovering from boot failures also emphasizes the review of system logs and kernel messages. Boot failures often leave residual data in log files such as `/var/log/syslog`, `boot.log`, or through the kernel message buffer accessed via |dmesg|. A careful examination of these logs can reveal which stage of the boot process encountered problems. For example, kernel panics or segmentation faults that occur during initialization will be captured in these logs. A sample command to review kernel messages might be:

```
dmesg | less
```

371

Analyzing these logs in conjunction with changes made to GRUB or kernel configuration files assists in confirming whether the applied fixes have resolved the issues. In scenarios where diagnostic logs reveal corruption in the initramfs, rebuilding it can be an effective remedy. Generating a new initramfs is accomplished with a command such as:

```
update-initramfs -u
```

This command detects installed kernel images and rebuilds the associated initramfs archive. A properly configured initramfs is essential for mounting the root filesystem and loading necessary drivers during boot.

Recovery mode not only facilitates system repairs but also provides access to a minimal command-line interface where filesystem integrity can be verified. Filesystem errors often contribute to boot failures, particularly if a disk contains bad sectors or if a recent improper shutdown led to corruption. The utility fsck (file system consistency check) is commonly used to detect and repair filesystem errors. In a recovery shell, an administrator might unmount the affected filesystem or remount it read-only and then run:

```
fsck -f /dev/sda1
```

where /dev/sda1 represents the partition that failed the filesystem check. It is critical to perform these actions in a recovery or single-user context to prevent further damage caused by concurrent writes.

Another scenario involving boot failures arises when kernel updates or package upgrades result in compatibility issues. In such circumstances, the recovery mode offers an avenue to rollback to a previous kernel version. The GRUB menu typically provides an "Advanced options" selection, which lists prior kernel versions. Booting with an older kernel can restore functionality and provide time to further investigate compatibility issues with newer kernels. Once the system is booted with a stable kernel, the administrator can review the changelogs and error reports associated with the recent updates to determine if a complete recovery or a patch is necessary.

In addition to the manual repair techniques, some administrators prefer using dedicated scripts to assist in the recovery process. A custom recovery script might verify critical system files, check GRUB configurations, and perform disk integrity checks sequentially. The following example demonstrates a simple script that conducts several of these checks:

```
#!/bin/bash
echo "Checking GRUB configuration..."
grep -E "menuentry|linux" /boot/grub/grub.cfg

echo "Verifying filesystem integrity..."
fsck -n /dev/sda1

echo "Displaying kernel messages related to boot errors..."
dmesg | grep -i "error\|fail"

echo "Recovery checks completed. Review above output for potential
    issues."
```

This script does not make permanent modifications to the system but rather aggregates various diagnostic outputs to aid a manual review. Such scripts can be expanded with additional checks or integrated into automated recovery workflows.

Successful recovery from boot failures depends on a methodical approach that begins with identifying the stage of failure, evaluating configuration files, and validating system logs. Whether the issue originates from a misconfigured bootloader, corrupted filesystem, or faulty kernel images, initiating the recovery process in a controlled environment such as recovery mode minimizes the risk of exacerbating the problem. In addition, employing boot repair tools and automated scripts enhances the administrator's ability to swiftly diagnose and repair boot-related issues.

Collaboration between diagnostic observations and corrective actions

373

is critical. Changes such as updating the GRUB configuration or re-building the initramfs should be followed by a re-test of the boot process. In many cases, running the system in recovery mode temporarily to confirm that changes have the intended effect can prevent prolonged downtime. Once a solution is implemented, documenting the modifications and the sequence of diagnostic steps taken is valuable for future reference and for informing system maintenance practices.

Employing these recovery techniques supports the notion that boot failures, though disruptive, are generally resolvable with a systematic approach. Awareness of the boot process and an understanding of the tools available in Debian contribute directly to effective troubleshooting. Maintaining a clear perspective on the dependencies between the bootloader, kernel, and filesystem enhances the precision of recovery measures, thereby reinforcing system reliability and operational continuity.

10.3. Managing Services and Processes

Issues related to services and processes are common in Debian systems, and proper management is essential for maintaining overall system stability. A process-oriented approach involves understanding service dependencies, leveraging systemd for control, and applying configuration adjustments that persist between reboots. Managing services includes restarting, stopping, and reconfiguring them to handle failures and avoid potential conflicts.

Service management in Debian is predominantly handled by `systemd`, which provides commands for controlling services, querying their status, and diagnosing failures. The `systemctl` command serves as the primary interface for managing systemd units. For example, to check the status of a service, such as the SSH daemon, the following command is used:

```
systemctl status ssh
```

This command not only displays whether the service is active, inactive, or failed, but also provides recent log entries and relevant metadata. Understanding the output is critical. Status messages often indicate if a service has failed because of misconfigurations, missing dependencies, or resource constraints. The precise timestamps and error messages can direct the administrator to the root cause of the issue.

When a service is unresponsive or misbehaving, restarting it can restore its normal operation. The command to restart a service is:

```
systemctl restart <service-name>
```

Replacing `<service-name>` with the appropriate service identifier initiates a controlled shutdown and subsequent reinitialization. It is advisable to restart services in a sequence that respects service dependencies, ensuring that dependent processes are stopped before restarting their parent services.

Stopping a service that is causing conflicts or consuming excessive resources is another important management strategy. The command to stop a service is:

```
systemctl stop <service-name>
```

A formal shutdown of a misbehaving service prevents orphaned processes and resource leaks. In cases where a process remains active despite attempts to stop it gracefully, administrators may resort to forceful termination. Although systemd provides options to kill lingering processes using `systemctl kill`, tools like `kill` or `pkill` may be employed for fine-tuned control, especially when pinpointing individual processes by their process identifiers (PIDs).

To ensure stability, configuring services to start automatically during boot is important. Service enablement is accomplished with:

```
systemctl enable <service-name>
```

Conversely, if a service should not start on boot due to instability or incompatibility issues, it can be disabled:

```
systemctl disable <service-name>
```

In addition to these commands, systemd allows for reloading service configuration files without requiring a full restart. This is particularly useful when minor configuration tweaks have been made. The command used is:

```
systemctl reload <service-name>
```

This command signals the service to reread its configuration, ideally without interrupting active connections. However, whether a service supports reloading depends on its implementation.

Beyond basic service management, diagnosing issues with processes involves examining resource usage and performance metrics. Tools like top or htop allow administrators to monitor CPU, memory, and I/O utilization in real time. These tools can identify runaway processes that may lead to system instability. The following command launches htop:

```
htop
```

Within htop, processes can be sorted by resource consumption, which often uncovers misbehaving services whose high CPU usage or memory leaks contribute to broader performance degradation.

When processes crash or exhibit abnormal behavior, their log files offer valuable insights. Service-specific logs are typically located in directories such as /var/log/, and can include error messages, warnings, or stack traces. For instance, the Apache web server maintains its error logs in /var/log/apache2/error.log. A typical review of log entries involves scanning the file with:

```
tail -n 50 /var/log/apache2/error.log
```

Combining log analysis with performance monitoring yields a comprehensive picture of service health. When integrated with tools like journalctl, administrators can filter log messages by service or priority. For example, to retrieve error-level log entries specifically for the database service, the command might be:

```
journalctl -u mysql -p err --since "1 hour ago"
```

By limiting the output to recent errors, administrators can pinpoint the onset of issues and correlate these with configuration changes or resource depletion.

Configuration management plays a significant role in preventing recurring issues with services and processes. Well-documented configuration files simplify troubleshooting and serve as a reference when reverting problematic changes. For instance, editing the configuration of a critical service like the NGINX web server should follow a systematic workflow: backup the current configuration, make incremental modifications, and validate changes using built-in testing utilities. NGINX provides a command to check the syntax of its configuration files:

```
nginx -t
```

This command verifies the integrity of configuration files and reports errors before the service is restarted. Similar testing capabilities exist for other services, reinforcing the practice of validating configurations prior to applying them in a production environment.

In complex environments where multiple services interact, dependencies and race conditions can lead to subtle failures. Systemd offers mechanisms to define dependencies using unit files. In the unit file for a custom service, directives such as After= and Requires= manage startup order and dependency relationships. For example, a unit file

377

snippet for a service that must start after the network is available would include:

```
[Unit]
Description=Custom Service
After=network.target
Requires=network.target
```

Understanding and appropriately configuring these directives ensures that services are brought up in a stable sequence, limiting the possibility of race conditions during the boot process. Administrators are encouraged to review the unit files located in /etc/systemd/system/ or /lib/systemd/system/ to better understand the interdependencies of bundled services.

When services are repeatedly failing, it is beneficial to enable automatic recovery features. Systemd's restart policies can be specified within unit files to automatically attempt a service restart following an unexpected termination. By setting parameters such as Restart=on-failure and RestartSec=5, administrators can instruct systemd to pause briefly before attempting to restart a failed service. An example unit file entry is:

```
[Service]
Restart=on-failure
RestartSec=5
```

These configurations provide resilience against transient errors and system hiccups by reducing manual intervention requirements and minimizing downtime.

In addition to system-level tools, administrators often employ scripting to streamline routine service management tasks. A well-crafted script can check the status of multiple services and perform corrective actions automatically. The following example is a shell script that checks whether critical services are inactive and restarts them if needed:

```
#!/bin/bash

SERVICES=("ssh" "apache2" "mysql")
for service in "${SERVICES[@]}"
do
    status=$(systemctl is-active $service)
    if [ "$status" != "active" ]; then
        echo "Service $service is $status. Restarting..."
        systemctl restart $service
    else
        echo "Service $service is active."
    fi
done
```

Such scripts are invaluable in environments with a large number of essential services, allowing administrators to enforce stability through regular checks and automated recovery actions.

Monitoring the state of services over time is a proactive strategy to identify and mitigate intermittent issues. Integration with system monitoring tools and alerting frameworks provides real-time feedback on service health. For instance, using systemd's built-in logging and third-party monitoring systems, an administrator can set thresholds for service restarts or prolonged downtime, triggering alerts that prompt immediate review.

Efficient management of services also involves understanding process isolation. Systemd creates control groups (cgroups) for managing resources allocated to processes. Administrators can investigate resource usage at the cgroup level to identify services that are consuming disproportionate amounts of CPU or memory. The systemd-cgls command provides a hierarchical view of these groups:

```
systemd-cgls
```

This view aids in isolating resource bottlenecks and ensuring that services do not overrun their resource allocations, thereby enhancing overall system stability.

For services that require frequent configuration changes, version control of configuration files is recommended. Maintaining a repository for these files not only tracks changes but also facilitates rapid rollback in the event of misconfiguration. This practice is part of a broader configuration management strategy that integrates tools such as etckeeper with system updates and maintenance operations.

The combined use of command-line tools, diagnostic utilities, configuration management practices, and automation scripts constitutes a comprehensive approach to managing services and processes. Administrators who invest time in understanding these tools are better equipped to quickly resolve issues, reduce downtime, and maintain system performance. By considering dependencies and establishing robust recovery policies within systemd unit files, it is possible to build a resilient environment where services consistently perform as expected.

Through careful monitoring, proper logging, and disciplined configuration management, the maintenance of services and processes becomes a proactive effort rather than a reactive repair job. Such management ensures that operational issues are promptly identified and remedied, preserving system stability and integrity across diverse workloads and usage patterns.

10.4. Disk and File System Recovery

Ensuring the integrity of file systems is critical for system stability, and disk corruption can lead to data loss and system downtime. Techniques for disk and file system recovery in Debian involve both preventive measures and reactive recovery procedures. This section outlines methods for diagnosing and recovering corrupted file systems and recovering lost data using tools like fsck and testdisk, along with practical command-line examples and detailed analysis.

Corruption in file systems can result from power outages, hardware failures, unexpected shutdowns, or even software bugs. When corruption occurs, the file system may become inaccessible or display erratic behavior when attempting to read or write data. The first step in recovery is to identify the affected disk or partition. Administrators can use tools like lsblk and fdisk to list available disks and partitions, ensuring the correct target is selected for recovery tasks. For example, the following command lists block devices along with their mount points:

```
lsblk -f
```

Once the affected partition is identified, verifying the file system's integrity is crucial. The fsck (file system consistency check) utility is designed to detect and repair inconsistencies. It is important to note that fsck should be run on unmounted partitions to prevent data loss from concurrent writes. In emergencies where unmounting is not possible, booting into a recovery or single-user mode is recommended.

A basic diagnostic check using fsck is performed as follows:

```
sudo fsck /dev/sda1
```

In this example, /dev/sda1 represents the target partition. The utility scans the file system and reports potential inconsistencies. Administrators can use interactive options or specify parameters to automate the repair process. For instance, the -y flag instructs fsck to answer "yes" to all prompts, automating repairs:

```
sudo fsck -y /dev/sda1
```

While automation is useful, it is critical to analyze the output for indicators of recurring problems or hardware failures that may require additional intervention.

At times, file system corruption is severe, and fsck may not suffice to recover lost data. In such cases, testdisk is a powerful tool capable of recovering lost partitions and data from severely damaged disks.

Testdisk can analyze disk sectors, detect lost partitions, and rebuild partition tables when necessary. The recovery process with testdisk is typically performed from a live environment or recovery mode to avoid further disturbances on the disk.

To begin with testdisk, the administrator launches the utility with root privileges:

```
sudo testdisk
```

Once testdisk is executed, it presents a text-based user interface that guides the user through selecting the disk, specifying the partition table type, and performing a scan for lost partitions. The tool automatically detects the appropriate partition table (such as MBR or GPT) in most cases. A detailed analysis is recommended during the scanning process, and users should follow the instructions to recover identified partitions.

Testdisk not only recovers lost partitions but also facilitates copying files from damaged file systems to safer storage media. In scenarios where partitions are intact but certain files are missing, testdisk can be used to navigate the file system structure and retrieve individual files or directories. For example, after the scan, selecting the option to list files allows users to browse through the file system hierarchy:

```
[In Testdisk interface]
Select 'Advanced' > Choose your partition > 'List'
```

This functionality is particularly valuable when only a subset of data is corrupted and a complete reinstallation of the file system is unnecessary.

It is important to emphasize that while recovery tools like fsck and testdisk are powerful, each recovery scenario demands a careful evaluation of risks. Before initiating any repair action, backing up critical data, if accessible, is recommended. This principle applies even in controlled recovery environments because repair utilities may sometimes lead to further data degradation if anomalies are misinterpreted.

In addition to these tools, knowledge of underlying file system structures such as ext4, XFS, or Btrfs is advantageous when interpreting diagnostic outputs. For instance, ext4 file systems can suffer from issues related to orphaned inodes, journal inconsistencies, or block allocation errors. Administrators should refer to file system logs located in /var/log/ for clues and to verify that repair actions have been effective. A command to inspect the system log for ext4-related messages might be:

```
grep -i ext4 /var/log/syslog
```

If repeated errors are detected during fsck operations on an ext4 file system, it may be necessary to consider advanced recovery options, such as mounting the file system in a read-only mode to extract data prior to reformatting the partition.

Apart from testdisk, the companion tool photorec is available for recovering individual files from damaged disks. Although photorec ignores the file system structure, it locates files based on header information. This approach can recover data that is otherwise inaccessible when the partition table is not salvageable. Invoking photorec is similar to testdisk:

```
sudo photorec
```

It then guides the user through selecting the target disk, file system type, and destination for recovered files. While the recovered files may lack original filenames and directory structures, photorec remains a robust fallback when conventional repair strategies fail.

A practical scenario involves encountering unreadable sectors in a disk that contains essential user data. In such cases, an administrator might first run fsck to determine if simple repairs are possible. If fsck reports irreparable errors, switching to `testdisk` or `photorec` to extract data is advisable. It is also beneficial to monitor the disk's hardware status using tools like `smartctl`, which provides insights into disk health through SMART (Self-Monitoring, Analysis, and Reporting Technology) parameters:

```
sudo smartctl -a /dev/sda
```

Interpreting SMART data in conjunction with file system repair efforts offers a comprehensive view of disk reliability. If SMART attributes indicate imminent hardware failure, planning for disk replacement is essential, and recovery actions should focus on preserving data quickly.

When rebuilding file systems, post-recovery procedures are equally critical. Once a partition has been repaired or recovered data has been backed up using `testdisk`, reformatting the partition and restoring data might be the most reliable option for ensuring long-term stability. Using the `mkfs` command reinforces the new file system, for example:

```
sudo mkfs.ext4 /dev/sda1
```

After creating a new file system, data recovery can proceed by copying files from the backup to the fresh partition. Administrators may also reconfigure entries in the `/etc/fstab` file to reflect updated UUIDs or device names, ensuring the system mounts the newly formatted partition correctly during boot.

Documentation of the recovery process is essential for future reference and troubleshooting. Maintaining logs of repair commands, recovered file lists, and any modifications made to the system configuration supports both operational continuity and the development of best practices. Detailed records can also be instrumental in identifying recurring disk health issues that may prompt proactive hardware maintenance or upgrades.

The process of disk and file system recovery is iterative. Administrators

384

must continually evaluate initial repair attempts, verify the integrity of recovered data, and be prepared to adopt alternative tools if the situation demands. Combining both fsck for immediate file system consistency checks and testdisk for deeper partition recovery provides a robust framework for addressing a wide range of corruption scenarios.

Periodic prevention measures complement reactive recovery techniques. Implementing regular backups, monitoring disk health through SMART diagnostics, and scheduling routine file system checks with cron can mitigate the impact of disk corruption. An example cron job entry to run fsck on an unmounted partition during scheduled maintenance may be managed by administrative scripts and integrated into system monitoring dashboards.

Understanding the nuances of each recovery tool is crucial. Fsck repairs file system-level inconsistencies by checking metadata structures like superblocks, inodes, and directory entries. In contrast, testdisk and photorec delve deeper into the disk structure, making them suitable for recovering data when file systems are too damaged for conventional repair methods. This layered approach ensures that even in cases of extensive corruption, data recovery remains viable.

The coordinated use of these utilities underscores the importance of a systematic recovery plan. As recovery efforts progress, cross-verification of repaired file systems using integrity-checking tools and file integrity monitoring utilities further enhances reliability. In the context of Debian administration, such diligence in disk recovery fosters a resilient environment where data integrity and system stability are prioritized.

A sound recovery strategy integrates the use of command-line tools, diagnostic utilities, and thorough documentation. Administrators employing these methods safeguard the system against the adverse effects of disk corruption and improve the likelihood of restoring critical data.

This systematic approach to disk and file system recovery exemplifies best practices in maintaining a robust Debian environment, where meticulous repair efforts align with strategic preventive measures.

10.5. Repairing Software Packages

Effective management of software packages is central to maintaining a stable Debian environment. When packages become broken or misconfigured, system functionality can be impaired, leading to dependency issues, incomplete installations, or runtime errors. This section details a systematic approach to identifying and repairing software package problems using the APT and dpkg utilities, building upon earlier discussions of system diagnostics and service management.

Debian employs a two-layer package management system. The lower layer, managed by dpkg, is responsible for the installation and removal of individual packages, while the higher-level APT utilities handle dependency resolution, repository management, and package upgrades. When problems arise, it is crucial to understand the interplay between these utilities and use them in a complementary manner.

A common initial step when encountering package issues is to update the local package index to ensure that the latest packages and dependency metadata are being used. The command to update the repository index is:

```
sudo apt-get update
```

This command downloads package information from configured repositories, ensuring that subsequent installations or repairs use the most current definitions.

When a broken or missing dependency is detected, the APT utility often suggests corrective measures. For instance, the -f (or --fix-broken)

386

option instructs APT to attempt to correct a system with broken dependencies. Running the following command can automatically install missing dependencies or remove partially installed packages:

```
sudo apt-get -f install
```

In many cases, this command resolves inconsistencies in the package database by ensuring that all dependencies are satisfied. Administrators should carefully review the output of this command, as it may prompt for confirmation on package removals or installations. Detailed inspection of these messages can offer insight into the underlying cause of the broken dependency.

For scenarios where a package installation has failed or left an inconsistent state, the dpkg utility provides low-level control over package configurations. A standard command is to reconfigure a package that might have been partially configured:

```
sudo dpkg --configure -a
```

This command attempts to complete the configuration of any packages that have been unpacked but not fully installed, thereby repairing any incomplete setup procedures.

Another common issue during package installation is the presence of broken or missing dependencies that dpkg alone cannot handle. Given that dpkg does not automatically resolve dependency issues, integrating APT repair commands with dpkg can yield better results. For example, after running dpkg --configure -a, it is often effective to again run the apt-get -f install command in order to address outstanding dependency problems.

Occasionally, a package may become corrupted or conflict with system libraries. In such cases, it may be advantageous to remove the problematic package entirely and then reinstall it. This procedure involves identifying the faulty package, removing it, and then reinstalling the clean version from the repositories. The following sequence illustrates this process:

```
sudo apt-get remove --purge package-name
sudo apt-get install package-name
```

Here, `package-name` must be replaced with the appropriate package identifier. The `--purge` option ensures that all configuration files associated with the package are removed, preventing potential conflicts with the reinstalled version.

In instances where package repairs remain unsuccessful, it is important to examine the package database and logs for detailed error messages. The dpkg log, located at `/var/log/dpkg.log`, can provide a history of package operations and may reveal patterns in recurring issues. Viewing the most recent entries in the log file can be accomplished with:

```
tail -n 50 /var/log/dpkg.log
```

Detailed analysis of these logs can help determine whether failures are isolated to a single package or indicative of a systemic problem within the package management system.

Another useful diagnostic command involves listing the status of installed packages with dpkg. The following command renders a list of all packages along with their installation state:

```
dpkg -l | less
```

This command outputs a list that includes columns for desired state, actual state, and package version. Abnormal statuses such as `rc` (removed but configuration files remain) or `ii` (properly installed) help administrators identify which packages might need reinstallation or removal.

APT provides additional options to search for package status and origins. The `apt-cache policy` command details the available versions of a package along with the repositories from which they originate, allowing for the identification of potential conflicts in versioning:

```
apt-cache policy package-name
```

Such information is particularly useful when troubleshooting version-related issues after a system upgrade, as inconsistencies between repository sources may result in partial upgrades or broken packages.

Configuring the package management system for stability goes beyond immediate repairs. Maintaining consistency in source lists and repository configurations is a preventive measure that reduces the likelihood of encountering broken packages. The repository configuration file, /etc/apt/sources.list, and complementary files in /etc/apt/sources.list.d/ should be periodically audited to ensure that they reference correct and trusted sources. A malformed or outdated repository entry can lead to installation failures and conflict errors during package updates.

For more granular control, the dpkg-divert utility can be employed to manage file conflicts during package upgrades, particularly when local modifications or non-standard customizations are present. The dpkg-divert command can prevent package updates from overwriting custom files by renaming or relocating them. A typical use case is illustrated below:

```
sudo dpkg-divert --local --rename --add /usr/bin/example
```

This command diverts the file /usr/bin/example so that future package upgrades do not replace the custom version. Although this utility is less commonly used in routine repairs, it offers significant value when managing locally tailored modifications that might otherwise trigger conflicts with upstream package management.

System alerts and log monitoring are also integral to diagnosing and preempting package issues. Automated monitoring tools can be configured to check the integrity of critical packages and alert administrators when discrepancies occur. Integration with tools such as `logwatch` or custom scripts scheduled via `cron` reinforces routine checks against the dpkg status database. An example cron job entry to inspect for broken packages might be:

```
0 2 * * * /usr/local/bin/check-packages.sh
```

The check-packages.sh script might incorporate commands to list package states, check for failed installations, and even trigger automated repair commands where necessary. Consistently monitoring package integrity reduces downtime and precludes the escalation of minor issues into systemic faults.

In cases where repairs fail repeatedly, reinstallation of a problematic package's configuration files may be necessary. The `dpkg-reconfigure` command forces a package to re-run its configuration scripts. This is particularly useful when configuration errors prevent a package from functioning correctly. The command is structured as follows:

```
sudo dpkg-reconfigure package-name
```

Reconfiguration helps reset the package to a stable state and prompts the administrator to re-enter any custom configurations that may have been lost or corrupted. It is advisable to consult documentation for the specific package in order to understand any specialized steps required during the reconfiguration process.

Occasionally, multiple broken packages can interact in ways that magnify the repair challenge. In such scenarios, using a combination of APT's automatic repair functions and manual intervention through dpkg is necessary. An iterative approach might involve several rounds of running `dpkg --configure -a`, followed by `apt-get -f install`, and subsequently reconfiguring individual packages reported as problematic. This methodical process ensures that interdependent package issues are progressively resolved.

Documentation of repair activities is essential for reinforcing best practices and for troubleshooting similar issues in the future. Administrators are encouraged to maintain log files or internal wikis detailing the sequence of repair commands executed, the output observed from each command, and any custom adjustments made to configuration files. Such records offer invaluable insights during subsequent package upgrades or further troubleshooting scenarios.

Integrating preventive measures into regular maintenance routines also reduces the frequency of package repairs. Regular system updates, combined with careful monitoring of repository configurations, help mitigate the emergence of broken packages. Additionally, employing tools like apt-listbugs can alert administrators to potential issues before packages are installed, thereby avoiding problematic updates that might destabilize the system.

Understanding the technical details behind APT and dpkg enhances the ability to swiftly diagnose and repair package-related issues. Whether dealing with broken dependencies, corrupted configuration files, or conflicting package versions, systematic application of the repair techniques discussed in this section helps maintain system consistency. By leveraging automated repair functions and complementing them with manual inspection and intervention, administrators can ensure that the Debian package management system remains reliable and responsive even in the face of irregularities.

The coordinated use of APT and dpkg utilities not only repairs immediate issues but also contributes to long-term system stability. As part of a comprehensive package management strategy, these tools provide the leverage needed to resolve software installation failures, manage complex dependency trees, and restore system homes to their expected operational state. Mastery of these techniques is essential for any system administrator tasked with maintaining a robust Debian environment.

10.6. Network Troubleshooting Techniques

Diagnosing network connectivity issues in Debian systems requires a systematic understanding of both the network configuration and the tools available for troubleshooting. The process begins with verifying the physical connectivity and extends to analyzing routing tables, checking firewall settings, and interpreting packet flow. Building on previous discussions of system diagnostics and service management, the following approaches combine manual inspections with automated tools to efficiently isolate and resolve network issues.

A fundamental tool for network diagnostics is ping, which tests the reachability of a host on an Internet Protocol (IP) network. By sending Internet Control Message Protocol (ICMP) echo requests to the target host, ping measures the response time and packet loss. For example, testing connectivity to a remote server involves a command such as:

```
ping -c 5 8.8.8.8
```

This command sends five packets to the destination IP address (in this case, Google's DNS server) and provides statistical feedback on packet loss and latency. Analysis of the output helps determine whether the problem is a local network misconfiguration, an intermediary routing issue, or remote host downtime.

When diagnostics require a deeper look into the network path, traceroute is an invaluable utility. Traceroute maps the path that packets take to reach the destination, listing all intermediary hops along the way. This analysis identifies potential bottlenecks or misconfigured routers. To trace the route to a particular host, an administrator can execute:

```
traceroute google.com
```

The resulting list of hops, along with round-trip time (RTT) metrics, offers insights into points of delay or packet loss. In scenarios where the network path includes multiple autonomous systems, it is critical to identify where latency begins to increase significantly. In such cases, contacting network providers or adjusting local routing may be necessary.

Beyond basic connectivity tests, utilities such as `ip` (a part of the iproute2 package) provide detailed information about network interfaces, routing tables, and socket statistics. To inspect the configuration of all network interfaces, administrators can use:

```
ip addr show
```

This command displays the IP addresses, broadcast addresses, and MAC addresses associated with each interface, allowing for verification that the correct configurations are in place. Misconfigured IP addresses or network masks can lead to connectivity issues that prevent proper routing of packets. Similarly, the command:

```
ip route show
```

lists the current routing table, ensuring that the default gateway and specific network routes are correctly defined. An error in the routing table might manifest as an inability to reach external networks, and by scrutinizing these entries, an administrator can adjust configurations either manually or via network scripts.

Another critical aspect of network troubleshooting is examining Domain Name System (DNS) configurations. Failures to resolve hostnames often point to DNS misconfigurations rather than connectivity problems. The file /etc/resolv.conf lists the configured DNS servers, and verifying its contents is a necessary step. For example, an administrator might open the file with an editor or simply display it using:

393

```
cat /etc/resolv.conf
```

Ensuring that the DNS servers are reachable and correctly entered prevents issues where services fail because hostnames cannot be resolved. In some cases, it might become necessary to bypass the local DNS settings by specifying an IP address directly in diagnostic commands.

Monitoring tools such as netstat or its modern replacement ss provide crucial insights into the network connections and socket statistics for the system. Running:

```
netstat -tulnp
```

displays a list of all active TCP and UDP connections along with the process IDs of the listening services. This information is useful when diagnosing issues where a particular service is either overloaded with connections or is not listening on the expected port. The refined interface available through ss streamlines this output further:

```
ss -tuln
```

These commands help in pinpointing services that may be misconfigured or inadvertently blocked by local firewall rules.

In addition to these standard utilities, packet capture and analysis form a core part of diagnosing advanced network problems. The tcpdump utility captures network packets in real time and allows the administrator to filter the traffic by protocol, port, or host. Capturing traffic on a specific interface for a target IP address can be done with a command such as:

```
sudo tcpdump -i eth0 host 192.168.1.1
```

By analyzing the captured packets, the administrator can detect anomalies in the packet headers, such as incorrect flags, missing acknowledgments, or unusual packet drops. Detailed examination

394

using `tcpdump` is especially valuable when troubleshooting intermittent connectivity issues or verifying that network security measures are not inadvertently interfering with normal traffic.

In many cases, problems arise due to conflicts or misconfigurations in network services. Configuration files for network interfaces (commonly found at /etc/network/interfaces or managed by NetworkManager) must be periodically reviewed to ensure correctness. A typical configuration for a static IP might appear as follows:

```
auto eth0
iface eth0 inet static
    address 192.168.1.100
    netmask 255.255.255.0
    gateway 192.168.1.1
```

Administrators must verify that these settings align with the network infrastructure. Any discrepancy in the gateway or netmask can lead to issues where the system is unable to reach the wider network despite appearing correctly configured.

Network troubleshooting also involves examining the host's firewall configuration. Debian systems may use utilities such as `iptables` or its successor `nftables`. Viewing current firewall rules is essential to identify any rules that might be blocking traffic. For instance, a command to display iptables rules is:

```
sudo iptables -L -v -n
```

This command lists all chain rules along with packet and byte counts, providing an audit trail of how packets are processed. Misconfigured firewall rules may inadvertently block legitimate traffic, leading to connection failures. Adjusting these rules requires careful consideration and an understanding of both the default policies and any manual entries made by the administrator.

Network diagnostic efforts must also take into account the behavior of local routing daemons and service managers. Tools such as systemctl can be used to verify that networking services (such as NetworkManager, ifupdown, or custom scripts) are active and operating correctly. A command such as:

```
systemctl status NetworkManager
```

provides information on the service's current state, any errors logged during startup, and recent activity. Mismanaged or failed services can disrupt the delicate balance of network configurations maintained throughout system boot and during dynamic changes.

For comprehensive network diagnostics, using monitoring tools that aggregate outputs from several commands provides a broader picture of system health. Scripting automated checks that combine ping, traceroute, and ip route show can create a baseline of connectivity metrics, which can then be used for trend analysis. An example of such a script might be:

```
#!/bin/bash

echo "Checking network connectivity..."
ping -c 4 8.8.8.8

echo "Tracing route to external server..."
traceroute 8.8.8.8

echo "Displaying current IP routing table..."
ip route show
```

This script, when scheduled to run periodically using cron, logs network performance over time. Patterns such as increased latency or frequent route changes can indicate underlying problems that require further investigation.

Advanced troubleshooting may involve the use of mtr (My Traceroute), which combines the functionalities of ping and traceroute. Running mtr continuously monitors the path to a particular host and presents real-time statistics on packet loss and delay. A simple command to run mtr is:

```
mtr google.com
```

The interactive interface of `mtr` makes it a powerful tool for ongoing network monitoring, allowing administrators to visualize where packet loss or latency issues are occurring.

Integration with logging frameworks also enhances network troubleshooting efforts. Capturing outputs of diagnostic commands and storing them in centralized logs aids in historical analysis, which can be essential when intermittent network issues are at play. Tools like `rsyslog` can be configured to log network events, while custom scripts can append network diagnostics to local log files. This proactive logging creates an audit trail that parallels other system diagnostic data, which has been discussed in previous sections.

Careful examination of network interface statistics is another elemental aspect of troubleshooting. The command:

```
ifconfig -a
```

or, in systems where `ifconfig` is deprecated, the alternative:

```
ip -s link
```

displays packet statistics for each network interface, including errors, dropped packets, and overruns. High error counts or dropped packets may indicate faulty hardware, misconfigured duplex settings, or issues with network cables and connectors. In such cases, further hardware diagnostics may be paired with the software analysis to isolate the root cause of connectivity issues.

The methodologies covered in this section demonstrate that effective network troubleshooting is the result of a multifaceted approach. By employing a combination of diagnostic utilities such as `ping`, `traceroute`, `netstat`, and `tcpdump`, and by verifying configurations through `ip` commands and firewall inspections, administrators can pinpoint where connectivity issues originate. The integration of automated scripts and continuous monitoring tools further enhances the responsiveness to network anomalies, ensuring that issues are identified and resolved in a timely manner.

10.7. Creating and Using Rescue Disks

Rescue disks are essential tools for system recovery, enabling administrators to troubleshoot and repair critical problems when the primary operating system is inaccessible. The concept of a rescue disk is predicated on the ability to boot a minimal, self-contained operating system from external media, such as a USB drive or CD/DVD, which contains diagnostic and repair utilities. This section details the process of creating a rescue disk, examines key components of rescue environments, and outlines procedures for using these disks to recover systems that are experiencing severe malfunctions.

Creating a rescue disk begins with selecting a lightweight, live operating system that includes a comprehensive suite of recovery tools. Popular choices in the Debian ecosystem include SystemRescue, Debian Live, and custom variants that integrate utilities such as `fsck`, `dd`, and network diagnostic programs. Once the appropriate rescue ISO image is selected, it must be written to bootable media. Tools such as `dd`, `etcher`, or `unetbootin` are commonly used for this purpose. An example command illustrating the use of `dd` is:

```
sudo dd if=debian-live.iso of=/dev/sdX bs=4M status=progress && sync
```

In this command, `debian-live.iso` refers to the ISO image with bundled rescue tools, and `/dev/sdX` should be replaced with the correct device identifier for the USB drive. The `bs=4M` option sets the block size to 4 megabytes, and the `sync` command ensures that all buffers are flushed before removal of the medium.

Beyond creating a bootable image, administrators might consider customizing the rescue disk to include specific drivers, scripts, or additional repair utilities tailored to the system environment. Customization often involves chrooting into a live environment and installing necessary packages prior to rebuilding the ISO. For example, if specific network drivers or proprietary firmware are needed, these can be integrated by modifying the live file system. Detailed instructions may vary depending on the customization tool, but the underlying principle is to create a rescue disk that mirrors the operational requirements of the target system.

Once a rescue disk is prepared, its usage becomes paramount in scenarios where the installed operating system fails to boot, services remain unresponsive, or the file system integrity is compromised. Booting from the rescue disk usually requires adjusting the BIOS or UEFI settings to prioritize external media over the internal hard drive. Once booted, the rescue environment provides a command-line interface and graphical tools that allow the administrator to perform tasks including, but not limited to, repairing file system damage with `fsck`, recovering lost data with `testdisk` or `photorec`, and troubleshooting network configurations using tools like `ping` and `traceroute`. By operating independently of the installed system, the rescue disk minimizes interference from corrupted system files or misconfigured services.

A practical scenario illustrating the use of a rescue disk involves a situation where the main system fails to mount critical partitions due to file system corruption. Booting into the rescue disk, an administrator can first identify the affected partitions using the `lsblk` command:

```
lsblk -f
```

After identifying the target partition, running a file system check is advisable. For example, to check and repair an ext4 file system on `/dev/sda1`,

399

the command is:

```
sudo fsck -y /dev/sda1
```

This command performs an automatic repair, addressing common file system inconsistencies without interactive prompts. If fsck encounters issues that it cannot resolve, additional tools such as testdisk may be used from within the rescue environment to attempt recovery of the partition table or extract essential data.

Rescue disks are not solely restricted to file system recovery; they also serve as platforms for additional diagnostic processes. For example, an administrator can load the environment and examine system logs from local storage even when the installed system refuses to boot. By mounting the hard drive manually, logs stored in directories such as /var/log become accessible for analysis. A command sequence may involve creating a temporary mount point and mounting the partition:

```
sudo mkdir /mnt/recovery
sudo mount /dev/sda1 /mnt/recovery
```

Once the partition is mounted, viewing relevant log files provides insight into the cause of the boot failure. Editing tools such as nano or vi are then available to modify configuration files on the mounted system. This capability is particularly useful for correcting misconfigurations in files such as /etc/fstab or restoring outdated settings that contributed to system instability.

Advanced usage of rescue disks includes network troubleshooting and remote repair. Modern rescue environments often incorporate network tools that enable the administrator to connect to external repositories to fetch updated packages, drivers, or scripts necessary for system repair. Configuring the network interface in the rescue environment is performed using commands similar to those in a standard system. For example, to configure an interface with a static IP address:

```
sudo ip addr add 192.168.1.100/24 dev eth0
```

```
sudo ip link set eth0 up
sudo ip route add default via 192.168.1.1
```

Once network connectivity is established, the rescue environment can mount remote filesystems using protocols like SSHFS or download troubleshooting packages from trusted repositories. This flexibility is particularly beneficial when local repair tools are outdated or when the rescue disk must adapt to novel hardware requirements.

Documentation of the rescue process is equally important. Administrators should maintain records of the steps taken during recovery operations, including diagnostic commands executed, repair actions performed, and configuration changes applied. Such documentation not only serves as a reference for future incidents but also contributes to a knowledge base for refining rescue disk configurations. Many rescue environments support logging to external devices or network shares, ensuring that recovery logs are preserved even if the system's internal storage is compromised.

Another critical aspect of using rescue disks is testing and validation prior to an emergency. Administrators are encouraged to periodically boot from the rescue disk on non-critical systems to verify that all tools are operating as expected and that the media is not corrupted. Regular validation helps identify issues with the rescue disk itself, such as outdated drivers or incompatible kernel modules, ensuring that it remains a reliable resource when needed.

Rescue disks also play a vital role in forensic investigations. When a system is compromised or experiences unintentional data loss due to system failures, a rescue environment can be employed to secure and analyze the data stored on the disk. By mounting partitions in a read-only mode, an administrator preserves the original data state while examining system logs, configuration files, and other evidence of the incident. For example, mounting a partition read-only is performed as follows:

```
sudo mount -o ro /dev/sda1 /mnt/recovery
```

This approach not only safeguards the integrity of the data but also allows the collection of information critical to a forensic audit.

The integration of rescue disks into routine maintenance workflows represents a proactive approach to system recovery. Instead of waiting for system failures to escalate, administrators can prepare and rehearse recovery scenarios using the rescue disk, thereby reducing system downtime and minimizing the impact of failures. In environments where reliability is paramount, such as critical servers or mission-critical applications, the investment in creating a custom rescue disk tailored to the specific configuration of the system can yield significant benefits.

Furthermore, the philosophy behind rescue disks aligns with the broader system recovery strategies discussed in previous sections of this chapter. Just as diagnosing boot failures or repairing corrupted file systems requires methodical use of command-line tools and scripts, so too does the creation and deployment of rescue disks demand careful planning and execution. By combining well-documented recovery procedures with flexible rescue media, administrators can restore system functionality even in the most challenging circumstances.

Creating and using rescue disks equips administrators with the capacity to independently troubleshoot and repair critical issues. From building bootable environments using tools like dd to deploying recovery procedures that involve file system checks, network configuration, and forensic analysis, the methodology is both rigorous and adaptable. By integrating rescue disks into their maintenance strategies, administrators ensure that they have an immediate, reliable tool at hand to preserve data integrity, restore system functionality, and minimize downtime during unforeseen failures.